The Sexual Constitution of Political Authority: The 'Trials' of Same-Sex Desire

While there is no shortage of studies addressing the state's regulation of the sexual, research into the ways in which the sexual governs the state and its attributes is still in its infancy. The *Sexual Constitution of Political Authority* argues that there are good reasons to suppose that our understandings of state power quiver with erotic undercurrents. The book maintains, more specifically, that the relationship between ideas of political authority and male same-sex desire is especially fraught. Through a series of case studies where a statesman's same-sex desire was put on trial (either literally or metaphorically) as a problem for the good exercise of public powers, the book shows the resilience and adaptability of cultural beliefs in the incompatibility between public office and male same-sex desire. Some of the case studies analysed are familiar ground for both political/constitutional history and the history of sexuality. The Sexual Constitution of Political Authority argues, however, that only by systematically reading questions of institutional politics and questions of sexuality through each other will we have access to the most interesting insights that a study of these trials can generate. Whether they involve obscure public officials or iconic rulers such as Hadrian and James I, these compelling fragments of queer history reveal that the disavowal of male same-sex desire has been, and partly remains, central to mainstream understandings of political authority.

Aleardo Zanghellini is Professor of Law and Social Theory at the University of Reading.

Social Justice

Series editors: Sarah Keenan, *Birkbeck College, University of London, UK,* Davina Cooper, *University of Kent, UK,* and Sarah Lamble, *Birkbeck College, University of London, UK*

Social Justice is a new, theoretically engaged, interdisciplinary series exploring the changing values, politics and institutional forms through which claims for equality, democracy and liberation are expressed, manifested and fought over in the contemporary world. The series addresses a range of contexts from transnational political fora, to nation-state and regional controversies, to small-scale social experiments. At its heart is a concern, and interdisciplinary engagement, with the present and future politics of power, as constituted through territory, gender, sexuality, ethnicity, economics, ecology and culture.

Foregrounding struggle, imagined alternatives and the embedding of new norms, *Social Justice* critically explores how change is wrought through law and governance, everyday social and bodily practices, dissident knowledges, and movements for citizenship, belonging and reinvented community.

The Sexual Constitution of Political Authority

The 'Trials' of Same-Sex Desire

Aleardo Zanghellini

Routledge
Taylor & Francis Group

LONDON AND NEW YORK

First published 2015
by Routledge
2 Park Square, Milton Park, Abingdon, Oxfordshire OX14 4RN

and by Routledge
711 Third Avenue, New York, NY 10017

First issued in paperback 2016

Routledge is an imprint of the Taylor & Francis Group, an informa business

British Library Cataloguing in Publication Data
A catalogue record for this book is available from the British Library

Library of Congress Cataloging in Publication Data
A catalog record has been requested for this book

ISBN 13: 978-1-138-24169-5 (pbk)
ISBN 13: 978-0-415-82740-9 (hbk)

Typeset in Galliard by
Servis Filmsetting Ltd, Stockport, Cheshire

For Giovanni Zanghellini, Adriana Mongioví and
Annamaria Zanghellini,
Who taught me to love books;
And for Hideki Kojima, who reminds me that life can live up
to them.

Contents

Acknowledgments

To say that I enjoyed every single minute of writing this book would be exaggerating, but only just. I owe a debt of gratitude to many people who contributed the time, encouragement, professional skills, intellectual stimulation and opportunities that have made this possible. Publishing the book as part of Routledge's *Social Justice* series, I had the luxury of having the series editors read and comment upon the whole book in draft form. Many thanks, therefore, to Davina Cooper and Sarah Keenan. Having looked up to Davina Cooper's work since my early days as a postgraduate student fifteen years ago, the benefit of her comments felt like a particular privilege.

I am also indebted to Chris Hilson and Grace James for reading papers extracted from or based upon the book. Many other people have become acquainted with the project or some of its aspects, in one way or another, responding constructively, suggesting lines of enquiry, providing practical advice or simply listening benevolently. Some exchanges stand out in my memory as particularly meaningful. These include those with Carl Stychin and Nicola Barker, who were the first to know about the book's concept. Carl Stychin has been a source of encouragement throughout, quite apart from his generous mentorship in all things academic. The same can be said of the brilliant Denise Meyerson, even if her acquaintance with this particular project has been solely by e-mail. Martha-Marie Kleinhans – apart from the influence of her scholarship on the project's design – was good enough to regularly solicit and enthusiastically receive detailed reports on the book's progress (with Ioannis Kokkoris, looking sharp in a suit, as a welcome witness to our exchanges). Kate Gleeson, Vijaia Nagarajan, Alpana Roy and Tawhida Ahmed have questioned me in depth about the project – whether in Bloomsbury, Izmir or Varenna. Their interest and support undoubtedly stems from their friendship; but it comes with the bonus of sharp insight. Dimitrios Kyritsis and Stephen Samuel have taken a genuine interest in some of the book's main ideas: they too have my gratitude. In telephone conversations about the book, some of the people closest to me have proved excellent listeners and rewarded me with intelligent questions: thank you to Davide Massaro, Valerio Zanghellini and Gloria Bona Nyariay. I recall with special pleasure a conversation about the book – then still in its early stages – with Mauro Miranda, Isabella

Perego and Jelena Milovanovic on a car drive 'down to' Marlow. Finally, comparing notes with Stephanie Polsky on book writing and the publication process was both fun and fruitful.

Prisca Giordani deserves my gratitude for briefing me on archival research. Ross Connell, the law librarian at the University of Reading, provided assistance in locating sources at different stages of the project. I am also grateful to other members of staff at the University of Reading library, who handled my copious requests for inter-library loans and out-of-bounds items. My gratitude also goes to staff that assisted me at the Kew National Archives, the Royal Mail Archive and the Lesbian and Gay Newsmedia Archive. The University of Reading Law School granted me a term of research leave to work on this project. This is gratefully acknowledged; so too are the University of Reading travel grants that enabled me to present aspects of the project at international conferences. I also want to thank the audiences who constructively engaged with the book's ideas at these conferences, particularly Robert Leckey and Chase Dymock. I am indebted to everyone at Routledge who helped see this project to completion, particularly Colin Perrin, Rebekah Jenkins, Richard Leatherdale, Laura Muir, Alexia Sutton and Paula Devine.

Throughout the period in which this project monopolised my thoughts, Hideki Kojima has incurred the common fate of those who have academic researchers as their life partners. He had to put up with comparative neglect, absent-mindedness and distracted or delayed responses. For his patience and generosity with this – and much else – I am forever grateful. Finally, our miniature pinscher Momotaro has been the inadvertent instrument of this book's timely completion. On several occasions, our daily walks in the Berkshire countryside helped me clarify my thoughts or come up with the right turn of phrase. He may require no thanks for this (non-human animals are morally superior to most humans in that respect), but I owe it to him at least to record the fact of his disinterested service.

Professor Aleardo Zanghellini
December 2014

Introduction

When Marie Antoinette faced the revolutionary tribunal, her effective and dignified response to the charges brought against her seemed to dampen the prospect of making of her trial the exemplary impeachment that revolutionary justice required. As the trial drew out ineffectually, Jacques René Hébert, one of the most fanatic revolutionists, was called to the witness box to bring forth what the prosecution thought was the ace up their sleeve: an allegation that the queen had committed incest with her 8-year-old son. When Hébert was done, the auditors were bewildered. Marie Antoinette deigned no reply. Hébert, realising the blunder, tried to patch it through an extemporaneous elaboration: the deposed queen had not committed incest out of sensualism; her goal was to enthral the child, which would enable her to utterly control him once he was king – as she, in her delusion, no doubt still hoped he would one day become. Marie Antoinette continued to ignore Hébert, until one of the jurors demanded an answer. Angered and hurt, she then declared that if she had been quiet, it was because, as any mother present in the courtroom could vouchsafe, Nature could not entertain the thought of answering such an allegation. Abashed, Hébert withdrew. Marie Antoinette would not escape the guillotine, but on this point she had triumphed (Zweig, 2002: 437–438).

It was the point at which Stefan Zweig's haunting biography of Marie Antoinette recounts this incident that inspired the concept for this book. The main charges brought against the queen had been exquisitely political in nature: she had been accused of plotting to destroy the republic by inviting foreign armed intervention and by attempting to stir up a civil war (Zweig, 2002: 440). Why then, this additional and incredible allegation of incest? What did it add to the prosecution's case? What made the prosecution (as it turned out, wrongly) believe that an allegation of sexual misconduct would not only assist, but constitute the very climax of, their *political* case against the queen? Zweig (2002: 437) suggests that Hébert's 'psychological-political' argument that by seducing her son the queen was hoping to acquire an irresistible influence over the future king was not premeditated; it was merely an impromptu attempt at rescuing the rhetorical force of a charge that had fallen flat. If Zweig is right, what had made the prosecution originally *assume* the relevance of the incest charge to the *political* case against the queen? Why was *sexual* misconduct automatically taken to bolster the case of Marie Antoinette's *political* treason? Isn't, after all, the habit of investing sex 'with an excess of significance' (Rubin, 1999: 151) a post-Freudian development? Could it be that political authority and the powers associated with public office have historically been sexualised in particular ways? That is, do allegations that a ruler or public official engages in certain sexual practices, or experiences certain erotic desires, or inhabits certain sexual subjectivities, undermine his or her authority – and, if so, why?

This book addresses a more focused version of the last two questions: How has political authority been constructed in ways that specifically centre or, conversely, disavow male same-sex desire? I will defend below the choice to concentrate on male same-sex desire. At this point I merely want to draw attention to the terminological implications of this choice: although I do not always use the 'male' qualifier before 'same-sex desire', virtually every time the expression 'same-sex desire' appears in the book, it will mean desire between males. This also explains my use of gendered nouns (e.g. states*man*) and pronouns throughout the book.

It quickly became apparent that interrogating the sexualisation of political authority without concentrating on a specific aspect of the sexual would have been overly ambitious, particularly as I was interested in pursuing a diachronic analysis. I was interested, in other words, in testing the hypothesis that political authority was sexualised even in a pre-Freudian world when cigars were, more frequently than they are now, just cigars; and in how this sexualisation may have shifted (or failed to shift) across time.[1] If my analysis was, therefore, to be relatively unrestricted across the dimension of time, it would be necessary to otherwise limit it: not only by narrowing the focus down to a particular aspect of the sexual (male same-sex desire), but also spatially. Thus much of this book focuses on the sexualisation of political authority in Britain. The exception to this is the first chapter. Ancient historians' notorious indictment of Roman emperors on account of their sexual practices made a consideration of the sexualisation of political authority in antiquity quite irresistible. The importance of the Graeco-Roman heritage to British culture (or at least elite culture) since the Norman conquest made such analysis not only justifiable, but virtually necessary.

In sum, then, I decided that the book would examine the shifting ways in which political authority has been culturally constructed in relation to same-sex desire in antiquity, as well as at particular points in time over the course of several centuries of British history, up until the present day. Marie Antoinette's trial also provided a model for my methodology. I would analyse a series of case studies bringing to the fore the relationship between male same-sex desire and political authority. The case studies would be incidents that involved putting a statesman's same-sex desire on trial in a way that gave away the political significance of such desire. When I use the expression 'political significance' of same-sex desire, I mean it in the specific sense of the liability of same-sex desire to be perceived as affecting the good exercise of public powers.[2] And when I speak of same-sex desire being put 'on trial', I mean it either literally (through courtroom trials like the French queen's indictment for committing incest) or metaphorically. Metaphorical trials, here, are those effected through such texts as historical accounts of a ruler's government, or newspaper articles targeting same-sex attracted public officials.

The case of Marie Antoinette and accounts of the scandalous sexual life of Roman emperors made me hypothesise that trials of rulers or public officials involving allegations of non-normative sexual conduct can tell us something important about the ways in which we construct political authority. But is the hypothesis justified – particularly when male same-sex desire is involved? This book argues that it is. The explanation starts with the idea of legitimacy. Legitimacy is central to the concept of political authority. Legitimate political authority provides the paradigm for *de facto* political authority: *de facto* political authorities, even if illegitimate, claim legitimacy for themselves (Raz, 1979: 9). The claim the book makes is that, with a few exceptions, the texts it analyses construct the legitimacy of political authority as contingent, among other things, on public officials' disavowing any experience of same-sex desire, either in itself or in some of its paradigmatic manifestations. To the extent that legitimacy is a constitutive element of the concept of political authority, and to the extent that (disavowal of) same-sex desire is one of the elements that define legitimacy, same-sex desire is then central to mainstream constructions of political authority. But exactly in what way is a statesman's same-sex desire discursively constructed as affecting the legitimacy of political authority?

Same-sex desire's effect on the legitimacy of political authority is a function of it being either assumed or argued to affect the good exercise of public powers. By 'good exercise of public powers' I mean not merely a statesman's competence in carrying out public functions, but also his ability or willingness to do so in accordance with justice. In other words, same-sex attracted statesmen have been constructed, until recently, not only as carrying out their tasks badly, but so badly as to adversely affect morally important societal interests. The inseparability of the question of the legitimacy of political authority from the question of justice in government – the fact, that is, that legitimacy is partly a function of justice[3] – explains why the trials of same-sex desire analysed in the book speak to the construction of political authority. To the extent that a statesman's same-sex desire is taken to interfere with his good exercise of public powers – and I will show that it regularly has been, from antiquity until recently – it undermines the legitimacy of political authority.[4] And because legitimacy is central to the concept of political authority, so is the disavowal of same-sex desire, either wholesale or qualified.

Thompson (2000) usefully describes political scandals in the media age as potential depleters of both reputation and trust, two sources of symbolic power, which, in turn, is understood as the power to influence processes so as to bring about desired outcomes. My point of departure is that even when it does not amount to a full-blown scandal, and even when it does not occur in the media age, putting statesmen's same-sex desire on trial has the same potential for depleting the sources of their symbolic power. This potential is grounded in, and performatively re-installs, the construction of political authority in sexual terms.

Simply put, certain sexual activities, identities, longings or attachments are taken to make someone unfit, while others are taken to recommend someone, for public office.[5]

Whether or not, as a matter of historical fact, the rulers or public officials whose cases I discuss in this book were same-sex attracted matters less to my analysis than the fact that it was alleged that they were. Evidence that they were, however, will often be relevant. First, this evidence helps clarify my subject matter and bring it to life. Secondly, such evidence is often contained in those very texts that put these statesmen's same-sex desire on trial; discussing the evidence will then be part of the process of analysing the treatment these texts afford to those statesmen. In other cases the texts discussed do not present such evidence of same-sex attraction and do not even mention a particular statesman's same-sex desire; but evidence of his same-sex desire will help make sense of these texts, to the extent that their narrative or rhetorical choices appear predicated on an awareness that the statesman was, in fact, same-sex attracted.

There are reasons for believing that the sexual has a significant effect on our understandings of the state, political authority, sovereignty and the relationship between the rulers and the ruled. There are also strong reasons for hypothesising, more specifically, that the relationship between political authority and male same-sex desire is especially discursively productive. Yet, there are only a few studies that systematically interrogate these discursive relationships, for all their political significance. I elaborate on these points below, as well as on my methodological strategy and analytical framework.

Sex, power and the state

A quarter of a century ago Sedgwick (1990: 1) famously proposed that, to be properly understood, 'virtually any aspect of modern Western culture' must be analysed in light of the fraught relationship between homosexuality and heterosexuality. There have, however, been relatively few attempts at systematically using homosexuality (or indeed sexuality) as a key analytical category in the study of the political power of the modern state, and in particular as a means of elucidating the sexual content of political authority.[6] The continuing role of state power in structuring the sexual field is fully appreciated; the ways in which the state and its authority are themselves discursively constructed in sexual terms not so much.

Most sexuality scholars accept that the discourse of sexuality inflects other discourses and the ways in which the world becomes intelligible to us (Sedgwick, 1990: 3). There is no good reason to suppose that sexuality – understood, in Foucault's (1998) terms, as a power-knowledge regime increasingly prominent over the last three centuries – does not also impinge upon those discursive domains within which such concepts as political authority and sovereignty are given content. If, however, pre-modern discourses about sex did not have the social salience of modern sexuality (Foucault, 1998: 17),[7] one could expect their influence on understandings of political authority to be correspondingly weaker; unless, perhaps, there is something about the phenomenology of sex that makes it quintessentially an experience of control and submission, power and powerlessness. If there is, then there may be, as it were, an almost trans-historical affinity between sexual discourses and other discursive domains that centre hierarchical social relationships, including ones about state authority.

That there is something about penetrative sex that makes it more or less necessarily an experience of dominance and subordination[8] is just what Dworkin (1987: 128–143) famously argued was probably (not conclusively) the case. The same year Bersani (1987) made virtually the same point from a psychoanalytic perspective. Bersani (1987: 216) argued that 'sexual pleasure and the exercise or loss of power' are inseparable because of the ways in which our bodies are built; and that human anatomy and the moves it encourages when we take sexual pleasure generate especially intense fantasies of control and subordination. Bersani (1987: 216) claimed, and I would agree, that acknowledging this is not the same as a 'prescriptive' and 'ideologically motivated' claim about the essence of sexuality.[9] More recently Bottigheimer (2004) has suggested that the association between activity and penetration on the one hand and passivity and being penetrated on the other hand is probably due less to the act of penetration itself, than the 'real-world' consequences of heterosexual penetration. In particular, 'the impregnating potential' of penile-vaginal penetration led to a 'logical' association between being penetrated and passivity (Bottigheimer, 2004: 39).

I am interested in exploring the implications of the argument that the association between penetrative sex and power/powerlessness is a fact related to our embodiment. If it is true, then it is plausible to hypothesise that there are erotic undercurrents to the ways in which political authority is apprehended, conceptualised and mobilised in many, and perhaps any, societies – whether they follow or precede the heightened concerns with sex distinctive of our most recent history. This book tests this hypothesis by interrogating political authority in the context of a plurality of political arrangements: classical Athenian democracy; the Hellenistic monarchies; the Roman principate; the late medieval and early modern English monarchy; and the late Victorian and post-war Westminster system. The hypothesis is tested, as I mentioned, in light of a definite subspecies of erotic desire: male same-sex desire.

Male same-sex desire and political authority

I take as one of my points of departure Sedgwick's (1990: 1) argument that the tensions coursing through the relationship between heterosexuality and male homosexuality are uniquely useful in interrogating and illuminating the 'major nodes of thought and knowledge' in modern Western culture. This argument provides a compelling reason for foregrounding male same-sex desire – rather than other dimensions of the sexual – in an analysis of the ways in which political authority has been constructed since the emergence of homosexuality as a category of discourse in the late nineteenth century. Sedgwick's argument, however, does not explain why my study remains focused on male same-sex desire even when the analysis moves back in time beyond the *fin-de-siècle* moment when homo/heterosexual definition became the most politically salient and epistemologically loaded dimension of the sexual. One reason accounting for this choice is that desire between males is the aspect of the sexual in which, as the book's author, I happen to have the greatest personal investment.

But there is also a theoretical reason justifying my focus on male same-sex desire. As we know, Bersani argues that the association of penetrative sex with feelings and fantasies of dominance and submission is grounded in the very ways our subjectivities are embodied.[10] Penetrative sex appears to stand, from this perspective, in a privileged discursive relation with hierarchically organised power relations (including those between the state and the citizens, or the ruler and the ruled). This explains why my focus is not on desire (such as lesbian desire) to which phallic penetration may be marginal or simply one erotic option among many. Considering, however, the different dimensions along which phallic penetrative sex can be classified (age of participants, private or public nature of its setting, etc.), what justifies my focus on the dimension of the participants' gender – that is, on sex between males? As I have noted elsewhere (Zanghellini, 2010), male same-sex penetration has been, across different societies and at different times, normatively loaded in a way that evokes – unlike its heterosexual counterpart – unjust or discreditable forms of hierarchy. In patriarchal societies, the reason for the different normative evaluation of male-to-male and male-to-female penetrative sex is readily explained. While women's subordination to men (at least if unmediated by race and class differentials) is considered both natural and normatively desirable, the subordination of men – or, rather, men that are one's social equals or superiors – is not. Thus, in patriarchal societies male same-sex desire – or some of its forms, such as same-sex desire between social equals – is capable, through its association with penetrative sex between males, of symbolically epitomising illegitimate subordination.[11] This capability strongly suggests that the gendered dimensions (male/male vis-à-vis male/female) of penetration-regarding erotic desire are especially salient to discursive constructions of political authority. This is because the concept of political *authority* necessarily references a *hierarchical,* and potentially coercive, relationship between the state and its citizenry; and normative judgements about the *legitimacy* of this relationship have been central to European reflection on political authority since antiquity. Male same-sex desire – gesturing as it does towards *illegitimate* forms of *hierarchy* – can be expected to have stood in a semantically productive discursive relationship with political authority even prior to the emergence of homo/heterosexual definition as a 'master term' (Sedgwick, 1990: 11) in the late nineteenth century.

Although it is male same-sex desire's potential for resulting in penetrative sex that bestows on this desire the power to symbolise illegitimate subordination, the book will not consider exclusively statesmen who certifiably engaged in penetrative sex. As I delved into the materials, I came across situations where a statesman's intense homoerotic attachments were clearly considered a problem for the correct exercise of public powers regardless of the nature of the acts of physical intimacy he may have engaged in with his lovers. Excluding these situations would have impoverished the study. There is also a theoretical reason why it seemed appropriate to include these situations. The political significance of penetrative sex between males generates an imperative to know whether same-sex bonds involve penetrative sex; but, as often as not, our curiosity is frustrated. It is frequently impossible to categorise a particular male same-sex relationship as either a platonic homoerotic attachment, a homoerotic attachment *cum* non-penetrative sex, or one *cum* penetrative sex – resulting in a discursive collapse of each of these categories into the next. This explains why the potential for symbolising illegitimate subordination is readily transferred from male same-sex penetrative sex to male same-sex desire itself.[12] For this reason, the book's focus is broadly on male same-sex desire, rather than specifically on penetrative sex between males.

The book's focus on male same-sex desire entails the considerable limitation that it will leave the relationship between female same-sex desire and political authority unexplored and untheorised. Although I will return briefly to this relationship in the conclusion, it awaits its own dedicated study. This might require a different methodological strategy from the trial-focused one I adopt here, if only because of the apparent paucity of trials involving female public officials' same-sex desire relative to the abundance of ones involving their male counterparts – elite males at that. This paucity is an artefact of the significance of gender and class as organising principles of inequality (Cooper, 2004: 51) governing state structures and political institutions. Infinitely fewer women than men have been holders of public office; and the invisibility of female same-sex sexuality has probably largely prevented the occurrence of lesbian political scandals. Thus, the same-sex desire foregrounded in this book would probably be largely of the male variety even if – in contrast to what I argued – there were no theoretical justifications for concentrating on same-sex attracted states*men*.

State, gender, sexuality

Having organised my study around the analytical category of male same-sex desire, I do not, for reasons of space, *systematically* follow through the implications of my analysis for women, female holders of public office or the female gender. The ways in which political authority is gendered, however, will be a subtext – sometimes a relatively conspicuous one – of my analysis of the sexualisation of political authority. The analytical relevance of gender to sexuality and vice versa is a function both of their conceptual interdependence and of how they tend to politically mediate each other.[13] With an emphasis on the political significance of the sexuality/gender nexus, Sedgwick (1990: 2–3) argues that wherever there exists a contest about gender inequality, same-sex bonds are by necessity highly regulated in ways that intersect 'virtually every issue of power and gender'.

She further argues that since the emergence of homosexuality, same-sex sexual attraction has become a privileged and intensely contradictory discursive locus in relation to gender, signifying at one time both 'gender separatism' and 'gender transitivity' (Sedgwick, 1990: 1–2). Given these imbrications, it is no wonder that, to the extent that some scholars have discussed the gendered nature of the state, they often offer reflections on its hetero- or homosexual content as well.

Those scholars who have turned their attention to the problem of the state's gender are agreed on the state's maleness. According to Mackinnon (1983: 140–141) the 'state is male in the feminist sense', in that its policies and actions embody male perspectives and promote male interests. Cooper (1993: 268–269) argues that the state, in being associated with the qualities of rationality and impartiality seen as typical of the public realm, is gendered male.[14] But not only is the modern Western state[15] metaphorically gendered male, its gendering is also sexually charged in significant ways. Consider the anthropomorphic iconography of *country*, especially in official contexts and public spaces. In its pictorial or sculptural personifications, country is usually depicted as female (e.g. Britannia, Marianne, Columbia) because country demands identification through affect.[16] Publicly commissioned art depicting personified representations of countries aims at producing just that effect. The *state*, however, acts like a traditional male: it demands subjection through the exercise of authority. Now consider the tradition of reading political communities as families and families as political communities. The authoritative maleness of the state and affective femaleness of country map onto their parental roles vis-à-vis the citizenry, so that country becomes the citizenry's 'expressive leader'/mother, and state their 'instrumental leader'/father (see Zelditch, 1955: 308–315). I will not explicitly pursue the Oedipal implications of this gendered parental model, except for pointing out that although we may *betray* our country, the object of political revolt is the authority-ridden state (cases of secession are the exception, where the very authenticity of a country's maternal identity is rejected). In fact, political revolt is often born in the name of, and out of love for, the country, to free it from the tyranny of the state.

My methodological focus on trials where a holder of public office becomes symbolically accountable to the people means that my emphasis in the book is on the sexualisation of political authority and internal sovereignty (i.e. the power relationship between the government and the people) rather than external (inter-state) sovereignty. Some of the most interesting recent work on the gendering and sexualisation of the state and its attributes, however, centres the concept of external sovereignty. Thus, Charlesworth and Chinkin (2000: 129) observe that states from the viewpoint of international law are like heterosexual male bodies: they are entitled to repel 'unwanted contact or interference' and they are self-contained in a way that 'makes forced entry the clearest possible breach of international law'.[17]

Ruskola (2010) has expanded upon Charlesworth and Chinkin's argument that the state, as constructed by international law, is both male *and* heterosexual.

He argues that, in colonial times, the rhetorical construction of European states as 'civilised' stood in a symbiotic but complex relationship with their being gendered male. Non-Western nations, on the other hand, were alternatively stereotyped either as savage and hyper-masculine – as in the case of Africa – or hyper-civilised and deficient in their masculinity – as in the case of China (Ruskola, 2010: 1495). These gendered constructions of statehood were linked to a specific sexual imagery when it came to structuring the relationships between European and non-Western states. Rape, then, became the choice metaphor for colonisation or inter-state violence, while a sexually suggestive vocabulary of 'intercourse' became commonplace to describe trade and diplomatic relationships when full-blown territorial colonisation was not an option (Ruskola, 2010: 1495–1505). Furthermore, Ruskola (2010: 1535) claims, this sexualised rhetoric continues to inflect 'the contemporary scripts of sovereignty'. Importantly, given the male gendering of statehood, in sexualising inter-state relationships, international legal rhetoric also homosexualised them. Ruskola (2010: 1497) suggests that this casting of colonial violence as homosexual violation may be integral to decolonisation processes which, at the psychosocial level, are experienced as reassertions of heterosexual masculinity, culminating in the acquisition of sovereignty as sexual inviolability.

Ruskola's (2010) characterisation of inter-state relationships as *homosexual* and Charlesworth and Chinkin's (2000) argument (which is Ruskola's starting point) referring to the logic of state sovereignty as one of *heterosexual masculinity*, however, do not quite accurately capture the dynamics that these authors so carefully describe. If states show a preoccupation with maintaining the integrity of their physical boundaries and abhor being impinged upon by their (foreign) peers, yet they either seek, or do not reject, the possibility of penetrating them, then the logic of state sovereignty cannot be one of modern heterosexual masculinity. It seems to be best accounted for, rather, by appealing to the idea of Roman masculinity. Modern heterosexual masculinity requires a rejection of same-sex desire per se – regardless of the role (insertor or insertee) one could conceivably inhabit in a same-sex sexual encounter. Roman masculinity, on the other hand, subscribed to a model where being the penetrator of one's own sex was perfectly consistent with – indeed, it might even consolidate – one's maleness (while being penetrated detracted from it). One was not supposed to violate the sexual integrity of other Roman citizens, but, crucially, *foreigners* were sexual fair game (Cantarella, 1994; Williams, 1999). It is this pre-modern model of Roman masculinity that best accounts for the international subjectivity of European states and their relationships with foreign powers during the colonial period that Ruskola describes. To my mind, this illustrates the distinctive contributions that broad historical inquiries of the kind this book conducts can make to a keener understanding of contemporary discourses and practices surrounding the sexualisation of the state and its authority. It is intriguing that it is the model of Roman masculinity, even if not invoked by Ruskola, which best explains the dynamics he describes. For Ruskola (2010: 1491) grounds both gender and sexuality, as metaphorical attributes of the state, in the hegemonic legal fiction of the state's personhood; and he credits the origin of that fiction precisely to ancient Rome.[18]

If Ruskola (2010) argues that the sexual is integral to the ways in which state sovereignty is conceived and managed in international relations, Cooper (1993) makes the same point with respect to how the state's monopoly on the use of violence is imagined and mobilised within its own borders. According to Cooper (1993: 271), because the state 'deploys erotic desire within its production of force', the state's coercive power is 'inextricably linked to a sexual imaginary or culture formulated around the eroticisation of domination'. The sexual content of state power, however, is covert, for the very qualities of rationality and impartiality that make the state male also rhetorically cast the state and its powers, at least on their surface, as asexual – sexuality being perceived as a wild force that can have no place in the public sphere (Cooper, 1993: 268–269).[19] Ruskola's characterisation of inter-state relationships as same-sex affairs contrasts with, but does not contradict, Cooper's (1993) suggestion that a male-female model better captures the dynamics of the state's internal affairs. If the state is gendered as male and its relationship with its population is one of hierarchical asymmetry, then that relationship 'is, metaphorically, a heterosexual one', where the community figures as the state's 'feminized "other"' (Cooper, 1993: 271). Cooper's point is borne out in the marriage metaphor that was often used to conceptualise the relationship between the ruler and the ruled in the early modern era (e.g. Hanley, 1989).

The political significance of the state's sexual organisation

These analyses of the sexualised qualities of both external and internal statehood assume that rhetoric and metaphor are more than just that. This is consistent with Foucault's (1998) view that the discourse of sexuality is endowed with intense regulatory power (on the assumption that the reach of such power extends, via the rhetorical personification of states, beyond interpersonal relationships to both inter-state and state-citizen relationships). Thus, Ruskola (2010: 1529) presents his analysis as rife with practical political implications, arguing that gendered and sexual rhetoric is 'a source of sovereignty'; while Cooper's (1993) investigation into the state's sexual organisation is part of a broader study directed at examining to what extent state power can be successfully utilised by sexually progressive constituencies.

Even before sexuality emerged as a modern power-knowledge regime, the sexualisation of the state appears to have been more than a purely illustrative device. Thus, in a study of the sexual content of the Athenian city-state's political life, Wohl (2002) argues that the founding myth of Athenian democracy, which credited the birth of democracy to tyrannicides and same-sex lovers Harmodius and Aristogeiton, was more than a figure of speech exploited by orators.[20] In classical Athens, erotic metaphors both expressed and produced libidinal attachments and unconscious phantasmatic investments[21] that structured and reinforced, but also potentially transformed, the community's political life and imaginary. Sanchez (2011) argues along similar lines in relation to literary representations of love in early modern England and the ways in which they articulated with conventional clichés about love being a source of political consent. By centring an idea of love proved by self-sacrifice and suffering, the literary sources Sanchez discusses provide a novel insight into the conventional idea of love-based political consent, revealing its masochistic qualities. Sanchez (2011) specifically argues that this perverse model of political submission not only complicates and blurs the distinctions between royalism and republicanism in the sixteenth and seventeenth centuries, but also informs us about the complexities of political investments in the contemporary world.

Building on these arguments, I want to suggest that in directing our attention to the erotic conventions whose transgression results (either technically or metaphorically) in disqualification from public office, the trials analysed in this book are not simply indicative of standards of acceptable sexual behaviour at a particular time. Rather, they may be an important mechanism through which certain power relationships are enacted or solidified. These trials, in other words, can be seen as 'performative' in Butler's (1990) sense of the word. What is at stake when a statesman's same-sex desire is put on trial is not so much the dignity of the public office he holds. Rather, it is potentially a whole set of institutional arrangements, policy orientations and political relationships that make the state function in particular ways. The defendant's erotic behaviour or disposition challenges the covert sexual (and gendered) assumptions on which these institutional, political and policy practices are patterned.[22] Thus, the trials staged in response to this challenge can be relatively momentous events in the life of public power.

To illustrate these points, consider the case of 'media trials' affecting same-sex attracted statesmen. In this case the sexual scandal is mobilised by a section of civil society (the press) rather than – as in the case of criminal trials instigated by the public prosecution – the government itself. But in so doing, civil society finds itself in a paradoxical position. The citizens, when engaged in the task of making a public official accountable in accordance with what I will call the ideal of 'the rule of sexual law',[23] are in the business of enforcing a heterosexual masculine subjectivity on the government. But recall that the gendered and sexual assumptions on which the modern state is patterned include precisely the state's maleness and the heterosexual nature of its relationship with the (feminised) citizenry. These sexual and gender attributes of the government are one of the very sources of the citizenry's relative powerlessness vis-à-vis the state (Cooper, 1993). Thus, a media trial in which civil society holds a public official accountable for his failure to live up to heterosexual masculinity can be seen as a key event in the citizenry's involvement in the reproduction of the conditions of its own asymmetrical relationship with the government. This perverse dynamic does not become visible until the significance of the trial is appreciated beyond the effects it may have on an individual political career or even on the reinforcement of conventional sexual morality.

Like the heterosexual nature of the relationship between the government and the citizenry, the construction of political authority around the notion that same-sex desire is a problem for good government – which is the book's main focus – has politically significant implications. The most obvious and tangible is that it can make access to public office or the carrying out of public functions unnecessarily difficult for same-sex attracted people. This is a problem for the statesmen affected, but also for a community's public life, to the extent that it may deprive it of the services of competent public officials or hinder the effective performance of their duties. Alternatively, when the trial is retrospectively enacted through historical accounts of same-sex attracted rulers, the construction of same-sex desire as a problem for good government may distort our perspective on the past.

Making the legitimacy of political authority contingent on a disavowal of same-sex desire may be bad for a society's political life in other ways too. In particular, the case studies in this book suggest that the construction of same-sex desire as a problem for good government is often (probably more than coincidentally) associated with what can be described – for want of a better term – as reactionary politics. Thus, as we will see, the construction of same-sex desire (or some of its forms) as a problem for good government has been variously bound up with a patriarchal conception of politics that required the exclusion of women from public life; with ethnocentrism, aggressive war-mongering and religious intolerance; and with political scapegoating, the rejection of trans-class solidarity and suspiciousness of political radicalism. True, the case studies also show that sometimes the construction of same-sex desire as incompatible with public office has been used in the service of progressive agendas (e.g. more participatory conceptions of government, anti-colonialism) and rule-of-law-type concerns with the equal administration of justice. However, even here, this construction is highly problematic – and not only in the obvious sense that it contributes to sexual stratification by demonising same-sex desire. As we will see, the interventions that targeted public officials' same-sex desire to attack foreign rule or breaches of the rule of law, for example, were bound up with a rhetoric that disabled the public exercise of well-considered ethical reasoning – endorsing, for example, preposterous value judgements about the gravity of homosexuality relative to murder. This suggests that the speech acts performatively constructing political authority around the disavowal of same-sex desire have a corrupting influence on public discourse. Thus, they are, in an important and concrete sense, bad for a community's political life quite regardless of the political agendas in whose service these speech acts are enlisted.

Albeit motivated by a desire to resist the normatively undesirable implications of the sexualisation of political authority, the book's analysis is, by and large, explanatory and critical in nature rather than prescriptive. In other words, it is more about directing attention to the problems associated with the construction of same-sex desire as interfering with the good exercise of public powers than about providing a blueprint for change. This is less because I share critical theorists' objections to prescriptive scholarship (Johns, 2004; Brown and Halley,

2002: 33) than on account of pragmatic considerations. Analyses of the type this book conducts can inform our practices of social transformation by supplying us with a keener insight into particular social and textual processes. But the question of what particular form our strategies for change should take is better deferred to the here and now of each political actor. This is because – like the gender and sexuality of individuals (Butler, 1990) – the gendered and sexual qualities of state power are likely to be significantly over-determined.

'Trials', legal pluralism, interpretation

The book's central thesis is that political authority, from antiquity to the present, has been constructed in ways that specifically disavow same-sex desire or some of its manifestations. The methodological strategy I employ in support of this thesis involves analysing a number of texts that bring to the fore the sexual constitution of political authority by dramatising its relationship with same-sex desire. The texts include court transcripts, judicial orations, historical accounts, political treatises, satirical work, newspaper articles, parliamentary debates and autobiographies. Recourse to literary texts is much more episodic, mainly because this genre frequently challenges and complicates, rather than merely reflects or affects, conventional morality – and the book's aim is to analyse the interplay of mainstream political moralities with mainstream sexual moralities.

The texts analysed in the book sometimes record the judicial or quasi-judicial trial a statesman endured on account of his same-sex desire. More frequently the texts themselves discursively enact such a 'trial' outside the courtroom, acting mainly as prosecutor, frequently as judge, and occasionally even putting up a mild, sometimes deliberately ineffectual, defence. The move of considering these 'discursive' or 'textual' trials alongside juridical trials is readily defensible by appealing to the framework of 'critical' legal pluralism (Kleinhans and MacDonald, 1997; Davies, 2005, 2006). Critical legal pluralism recognises the regulatory power of institutions, processes and representational systems that are conventionally classified as non-legal, and emphasises the importance such regulatory regimes have from the point of view of those who are subject to or involved in them (Kleinhans and MacDonald, 1997). The emphasis placed by critical legal pluralism on the subject's perspective on, experience of, and constitution by multiple normative orders is best explained in light of the fact that 'a pluralist approach is . . . about practical ethical positioning in the world' (Davies, 2005: 91). In particular, the pluralist's emphasis on subject-driven law expresses an ethical commitment to valuing the perspective of the other (i.e. those who are marginalised by dominant systems of knowledge), including mainstream understandings of law. It is this commitment that often animates the sort of post-modernist intellectual projects with which critical legal pluralism has an affinity.

The appeal of a pluralist methodology for my study is, however, that a pluralist vantage point enables an understanding of political authority as the product of multiple intersecting discourses and regulatory regimes, not all stemming from institutional sources. Given the nature of the question the book addresses, I am interested in law (and particularly courtroom trials) as a representational system. But law is only one representational system among many. Consideration of allied discourses is a necessary complement to a law-based analysis, not only when the law runs out, but also to assist in illuminating institutional representations themselves – not least because, as mentioned above, the sexual dimensions of political authority are often covert within official state discourses and practices (Cooper 1993: 269).

The analytical framework for the study of the texts recording or enacting the trials that I use in my case studies is based primarily on Gadamer's (1960) hermeneutics and Foucault's (1977, 1998) genealogical approach; the methods of interpretation of the texts are informed by Eco's (1990) theory of interpretation. Foucault's so-called 'genealogical' approach aims to understand certain discursive constructions (e.g. modern understandings of sexuality) in light of the history of how they came about, searching for their antecedents and origins (Dreyfus and Rabinow, 1983: 119). Foucault's genealogical approach – which he called a 'history of the present' (Foucault, 1977: 31) – can be contrasted both with the antiquarian approach interested in the past for its own sake and historical approaches tainted by presentism – the temptation to read the past in light of contemporary structures and categories (Dreyfus and Rabinow, 1983: 119).

The book's analysis follows Foucault's genealogical approach – it aims, that is, to qualify as a history of the present – to the extent that it takes an aspect of the modern domain of the sexual/erotic as an analytical *point of departure* to investigate the construction of political authority across time. In particular, I single out for study certain incidents from the past that we would today recognise as involving same-sex desire if present-day people were involved in them. I then interrogate what these incidents tell us about the construction of political authority. The reason why comparing the modern discursive relationship between same-sex desire and political authority with its historical antecedents is not like comparing oranges and apples is the capacity of same-sex activity and attraction to register across time *qua* same-sex. Throughout the historical periods the book analyses, the gender of sexual object choice was sometimes subsumed under conceptual economies that emphasised other aspects of the sexual (e.g. activity/passivity) but it never became completely irrelevant or disappeared under such alternative economies. The capacity of same-sex desire to register across time ensures, as I see it, the meaningfulness of engaging in a genealogical study of the construction of political authority in relation to same-sex desire. Such a study is genealogical in that it posits that we can meaningfully speak of historical antecedents of the contemporary discursive relationship between political authority and same-sex desire; that it considers this contemporary relationship and its antecedents commensurable;[24] and that it investigates these antecedents not only because of their intrinsic interest, but also in order to better appreciate that contemporary relationship.

If Foucault's 'history of the present' approach provides the model of investigation for the book, Gadamer's (1989) theory of interpretation provides its analytical presuppositions. Gadamer's reflections explain how it is possible for a reader or researcher to constructively and meaningfully relate to texts (Feldman, 2000: 899–900), giving texture to the idea of engaging in a history of the present. Gadamer (1989) argues that any text carries a set of values, presuppositions and a history – which he calls the text's horizon – but that we too, as readers, are burdened with our own set of beliefs, values and prejudices – the interpreter's horizon. Interpretation is usefully understood as a process in which the interpreter's horizon is challenged by (and revised in response to) the text and the text's horizon is transformed by the encounter with each new act of interpretation. Interpretation is, in this sense, ongoing and dynamic and cannot possibly aim to recoup the text's original meaning. Rather it makes the text speak to the present through the tradition in which both the text and the reader participate. Meaningful interpretation is possible thanks to both horizons being constituted within a shared tradition. This idea leads Gadamer to argue that the search for an interpretive method is misconceived as it is built on the false assumption that there is a distance between reader and text that needs to be bridged (Gadamer, 1989; Eskridge, 1990).

Established (and divergent) methods for interpreting texts are, however, a fact of twenty-first century academic life. Two broad approaches suggest themselves. One is exemplified by Eco (1990), who favours an interpretive approach which strives for congruence between interpretation and the text's intention. The other is exemplified by Derrida, who attempts to read the text against itself to allow its unconscious – its contradictions, silences, and the voices it suppresses – to come to the surface (Feldman, 2000: 907–910). Eco's (1992a, 1992b) approach requires interpreters to check the validity of their interpretation by disqualifying as unhelpful the interpretations that are not sustained by the text as a whole, in light of the stylistic and other communicative conventions that are used to produce meaning in the text. Derrida's approach, conversely, relies on the contingency and plasticity of these conventions to attempt to deconstruct the text. Generally speaking, Eco's approach is best suited to my task. My aim is not to deconstruct a text to attend to the voice of a marginalised other, but to identify and elaborate upon the ways in which dominant, mainstream social discourses sexualise political authority. These discourses rely on mainstream communicative conventions and discursive categories; as such these conventions and categories need, in a sense, to be taken at face value so that they can do the meaning-making work that the texts intend them to perform. This is why both Gadamer's (1989) hermeneutics (which stresses the common tradition within which communicative practices take shape) and Eco's (1990) theory of interpretation (which stresses the text's intention as a quasi-objective datum, ascertained through mainstream communicative conventions) provide particularly useful descriptions of the interpretive processes I employ. Nonetheless, to the extent that sometimes the text's 'unconscious' may reveal something crucial about the construction of political authority – something that may be missed by attending to the text's intention – the book's analytical mode occasionally switches to a broadly deconstructive method. In following Gadamer and Eco, the book commits itself to the proposition that not every interpretation is as good as the next and that it is possible for readers to distinguish more- from less-plausible readings of a text. For this reason, a relatively liberal use of quotes from the sources analysed is integral to my methodology, so as to let the texts, as far as possible, speak for themselves and to enable the reader to evaluate my interpretive claims and elaboration.

Centring public power

In the book I interrogate the sexualisation of political authority, understood as an attribute of governments. I take, as a point of departure, a formal and institutional understanding of the state as bearing political authority, wielding public power and carrying out the tasks of government. This does not mean, of course, that it is always, or even frequently, a good idea to reduce the state to political institutions and legal processes, let alone the kind of elite leaders whose trials the book mainly discusses. While the book foregrounds certain aspects of statehood, it does not claim that they exhaust all that there is to the state. Ultimately, the way in which such contested concepts as 'the state' are best conceptualised is, at least partly, a function of the goal of the communicative act where the conceptualisation occurs. A formal definition of the state as carrying out the task of government suits my goal of investigating the sexualisation of political authority, understood as an attribute of the state thus defined.

The focus on political authority as an attribute of states thus understood entails some limitations. The book is not about power generally; nor is it about power as exercised by powerful non-public collective actors, such as multinational corporations, media conglomerates, drug cartels, terrorist networks, organised crime, etc. It is not so much that the power exercised by non-public actors is less relevant in practice than state power, but that it is qualitatively different. Consider Weber's (1991: 78) famous definition of the state as a 'human community that (successfully) claims the monopoly of the legitimate use of physical force within a given territory'. This definition has its limitations and, as I explained above, my own point of reference will be a broader understanding of the state as the entity that carries out the tasks of government. Weber's definition does, however, point to a crucial aspect of statehood. Typically, we tend to take seriously a claim to the legitimate monopoly of coercion (over a whole community within a given territory) only if it originates from either public authorities or entities that we can picture as potential public authorities.[25] The state's claim to the legitimate monopoly of coercion is bound up with its claim to legitimate authority; and many states are organised in such a way that the out-of-hand dismissal of such claims to legitimacy is often not possible. Just as governments do not have legitimate authority merely by virtue of claiming that they do, so they obviously do not have the *legitimate* monopoly of coercion just because they say so. But the fact that we are generally disposed to take seriously public authorities' claims to legitimacy, together with the fact that governments have significant *de facto* coercive power, does make the authority of the state both symbolically and practically a crucial site of philosophical investigation.

Structure

My genealogy of the construction of political authority will necessarily be incomplete, focusing as it does on a small number of snapshots – the book's case studies – across a period of over 2,300 years. For ease of organisation, the case studies (that is, the 'trials' analysed) are grouped by historical period, following conventional historical periodisation. I group the case studies by historical period for heuristic purposes, but I make no claim to the broad historical representativeness of the trials analysed in each chapter. In fact, I specifically assume that the relationship between political authority and same-sex desire that emerges from each of the case studies does not exhaust the ways in which that relationship was constructed at that particular time – let alone during the whole historical period to which the case study is assigned. At the same time, I do make the claim that the way in which each of the trials sexualises political authority is not purely idiosyncratic. This is because I analyse each case study in light of the understandings of both same-sex desire and political authority current at the time (as identified in relevant primary sources and academic commentary); and because those understandings prove to have explanatory power when applied to the case studies.

The main question I ask in the chapters is: On what grounds has same-sex desire been constructed as affecting the good exercise of public powers? Additionally, the materials analysed in each chapter will determine the extent to which I foreground any of the following questions: Were the grounds for regarding same-sex desire as a problem for good government expressly articulated or implicit? Did these grounds resemble 'reasons' – that is, involve the use of rational arguments – or were they no more than rhetorical moves? How did the claim that same-sex desire affects the good exercise of public powers relate to the particular understandings of political authority current at the time when the claim was made? Was there a reiteration across time of the grounds on which same-sex desire was constructed as a problem for good government? Was there, in this connection, something approaching 'stock stories'? Do we have evidence of counter-discourses at any given time – ones that challenge the claim that same-sex desire is a problem for good government? How did this claim relate to the ways in which the relationship between the ruler and the ruled was sexualised or the ways in which the government itself was sexualised?

Chapter 1 considers the Graeco-Roman world. Its main focus is on historians' treatment of the rule of Alexander the Great (356 BCE–323 BCE), Hadrian (76 CE–138 CE), and Elagabalus (circa 203 CE–222 CE), as well as on Aeschines' oration *Against Timarchus* (delivered 346 BCE). The ancient texts analysed in this chapter do not always follow predictable or consistent scripts in their assessment of the relevance of same-sex desire to political authority. However, when they construct same-sex desire as a problem for good government, it is not same-sex desire generally, but some of its manifestations that Roman and Greek texts tend to find objectionable. In general, this is when same-sex desire involved a mercenary exchange, or a loss of self-control, often signalled by sexual passivity and debauchery. In these circumstances, the texts tend to construct a discourse of parallels, with public abuses mapping fairly specifically onto private sexual vices.

From chapter 2 the focus shifts to post-1066 Britain. In this chapter I consider historical accounts of the reign of Edward II (1284–1327), largely written by his contemporaries. The dominant narrative woven by these medieval sources constructs a ruler's same-sex desire as endangering well-ordered political rule on account of its special ability to make him vulnerable to the bad advice of his favourites. The favourites are seen as displacing the rightful role of the peers of the realm in assisting the king's government. They are constructed as interposing between the king and the country as well as the king and queen and acting like a second king without the legitimation derived from (God-mandated and people-endorsed) lineage.

Chapter 3, devoted to James VI (1566–1625), probes the sexualisation of political authority in the early modern age. Some of the *topoi* in the construction of political authority vis-à-vis same-sex desire emerging from the sources on Edward II are redeployed against James. Nonetheless, the emphasis is on a novel element. As revealed by historical accounts of James's rule, as well as satirical work, James's contemporaries regarded his same-sex desire as undermining his rule because they saw it as grounded in a constitutional effeminacy. They linked this effeminacy to a cowardly disposition which, they argued, had prompted James to seek religious reconciliation and a peaceful resolution to international conflict, rather than driving him to the manly aggressive foreign policies championed by his predecessor, Queen Elizabeth I.

In chapter 4 I focus on the Cleveland Street and Dublin Castle scandals of the late Victorian age. Partisan newspaper reports on these trials, as well as parliamentary debates, deploy a virulent rhetoric to portray the civil servants or politicians whose prosecution for same-sex sexual activity occasioned the scandals as prototypal of the government of the day. The ways in which same-sex desire poses a problem for the good exercise of public functions are left largely unarticulated in these interventions. Rather, the emphasis is on the abominable and horrible character of same-sex sexuality, which does the rhetorical work sufficient to establish the proposition that same-sex desire poses a problem for good government. This is in contrast to the kind of 'rational' justifications discernible in case studies from previous centuries in support of the same proposition.

The final chapter focuses on the late modern setting of post-war Britain. The trials of Lord Montagu and Ian Harvey – as recorded in newspaper reports and their own autobiographies – are contrasted to illustrate how post-war problematisations of homosexuality entailed a particular discourse about the unsuitability of homosexuals for public office. This discourse included a cold war discursive connection between homosexuality and political disloyalty, as well as vaguer appeals to the standards of public life. The final part of the chapter briefly engages with work on media representations of gay politicians in recent decades, which testify to the surprising resilience of beliefs in the incompatibility between same-sex desire and public office.

References

Baxter, H (1996) 'Bringing Foucault into Law and Law into Foucault' *Stanford Law Review*, vol 48, 449–479.

Bersani, L (1987) 'Is the Rectum a Grave?' *October*, vol 43, 197–222.

Bottigheimer, RB (2004) 'Fertility Control and the Modern European Fairy-Tale Heroine' in Haase, D (ed.), *Fairy Tales and Feminism: New Approaches* (Detroit: Wayne State University Press) 37–51.

Brown, W and Halley, J (2002) 'Introduction' in Brown, W and Halley, J (eds), *Left Legalism/Left Critique* (Durham: Duke University Press).

Butler, JP (1990) *Gender Trouble: Feminism and the Subversion of Identity* (London: Routledge).

Butler, JP (1993) *Bodies that Matter: On the Discursive Limits of 'Sex'* (London: Routledge).

Calhoun, C (1997) 'Family Outlaws' *Philosophical Studies: An International Journal for Philosophy in the Analytic Tradition*, vol 85, 181–193.

Cantarella, E (1994) *Bisexuality in the Ancient World* (New Haven: Yale University Press).

Charlesworth, H and Chinkin, C (2000) *The Boundaries of International Law: A Feminist Analysis* (Manchester: Manchester University Press).

Constable, M (1991) 'Foucault & Walzer: Sovereignty, Strategy & the State' *Polity*, vol 24, 269–293.

Cooper, D (1993) 'An Engaged State: Sexuality, Governance and the Potential for Change' *Journal of Law and Society*, vol 20, 257-275.

Cooper, D (2004) *Challenging Diversity* (Cambridge: Cambridge University Press).

Davies, M (2005) 'The Ethos of Pluralism' *Sydney Law Review*, vol 27, 87–112.

Davies, M (2006) 'Pluralism and Legal Philosophy' *Northern Ireland Legal Quarterly*, vol 57, 577–596.

Dean, M (2010) *Governmentality: Power and Rule in Modern Society* (London: Sage, 2nd edn).

Dreyfus, HL and Rabinow, P (1983) *Michel Foucault: Beyond Structuralism and Hermeneutics* (Chicago: University of Chicago Press).

Dworkin, A (1987) *Intercourse* (New York: The Free Press).

Echols, A (1989) *Daring to Be Bad: Radical Feminism in America 1967–1975* (Minneapolis: University of Minnesota Press).

Eco, U (1990) *I limiti dell'interpretazione* (Milano: Bompiani).

Eco, U (1992a) 'Overinterpreting Texts' in Collini, S (ed.), *Interpretation and Overinterpretation* (Cambridge: Cambridge University Press) 45–66.

Eco, U (1992b) 'Between Author and Text' in Collini, S (ed.), *Interpretation and Overinterpretation* (Cambridge: Cambridge University Press) 67–88.

Eisenstein, Z (1984) 'The Patriarchal Relations of the Reagan State' *Signs*, vol 10, 329–337.

Eskridge, WN, Jr (1990) 'Gadamer/Statutory Interpretation' *Columbia Law Review*, vol 90, 609–681.

Feldman, SM (2000) 'How to Be Critical' *Chicago-Kent Law Review*, vol 76, 893–912.

Findlay, EJ (1997) 'Decency and Democracy: The Politics of Prostitution in Ponce, Puerto Rico, 1890–1900' *Feminist Studies*, vol 23, 471–499.

Foucault, M (1977) *Discipline and Punish: The Birth of the Prison* (New York: Pantheon Books).

Foucault, M (1998) *The Will to Knowledge – The History of Sexuality: 1* (London: Penguin).

Gadamer, H-G (1989) *Truth and Method* (Weinsheimer, J and Marshall DG trans) (London: Continuum, rev edn).

Gose, P (2000) 'The State as a Chosen Woman: Brideservice and the Feeding of Tributaries in the Inka Empire' *American Anthropologist*, vol 102, 84–97.

Han, J and Ling, LHM (1998) 'Authoritarianism in the Hypermasculinized State: Hybridity, Patriarchy, and Capitalism in Korea' *International Studies Quarterly*, vol 42, 53–78.

Hanley, S (1989) 'Engendering the State: Family Formation and State Building in Early Modern France' *French Historical Studies*, vol 16, 4–27.

Henshall, N (2013) *The Myth of Absolutism: Change & Continuity in Early Modern European Monarchy* (London: Routledge).

Hunt, A and Wickham, G (1994) *Foucault and Law: Towards a Sociology of Law as Governance* (London: Pluto Press).

Johns, F (2004) 'On Writing Dangerously' *Sydney Law Review*, vol 26, 473–480.

King, H (1994) 'Sowing the Field: Greek and Roman Sexology' in Porter, R and Teich, M (eds), *Sexual Knowledge, Sexual Science: The History of Attitudes to Sexuality* (Cambridge: Cambridge University Press).

Kleinhans, M-M and Macdonald, RA (1997) 'What is a Critical Legal Pluralism?' *Canadian Journal of Law & Society*, vol 12, 25–46.

MacCormick, N (1999) *Questioning Sovereignty: Law, State, and Nation in the European Commonwealth* (Oxford: Oxford University Press).

Mackinnon, CA (1983) 'Feminism, Marxism, Method, and the State: Toward Feminist Jurisprudence' in Harding, S (ed.), *Feminism and Methodology* (Milton Keynes: Open University Press) 135–156.

Raz, J (1979) *The Authority of Law: Essays on Law and Morality* (Oxford: Clarendon Press).

Rubin, GS (1999) 'Thinking Sex: Notes for a Radical Theory of the Politics of Sexuality' in Parker, R and Aggleton, P (eds), *Culture, Society and Sexuality: A Reader* (London: UCL Press) 143–178.

Ruskola, T (2010) 'Raping like a State' *UCLA Law Review*, vol 57, 1477–1536.

Sanchez, ME (2011) *Erotic Subjects: The Sexuality of Politics in Early Modern English Literature* (Oxford: Oxford University Press).

Sedgwick, EK (1990) *Epistemology of the Closet* (London: University of California Press).

'state' in *Oxford Dictionaries*, retrieved 30 July 2011 http://oxforddictionaries.com/definition/state.

Thompson, JB (2000) *Political Scandal: Power and Visibility in the Media Age* (Cambridge: Polity).

Weber, M (1991) *Essays in Sociology* (London: Routledge).

Weeks, J (2003) *Sexuality* (London: Routledge, 2nd edn).

Williams, CA (1999) *Roman Homosexuality: Ideologies of Masculinity in Classical Antiquity* (Oxford: Oxford University Press).

Wohl, V (2002) *Love among the Ruins: The Erotics of Democracy in Classical Athens* (Princeton: Princeton University Press).

Zanghellini, A (2010) 'Contextualising Islam's Objections to Same-Sex Sexuality' in Habib, S (ed.), *Islam and Homosexuality* (Santa Barbara: Praeger).

Zelditch, M, Jr (1955) 'Role Differentiation in the Nuclear Family: A Comparative Study' in Parsons, T and Bales, RF (eds), *Family, Socialization, and Interaction Process* (Glencoe: The Free Press) 307–351.

Zweig, S (2002) *Marie Antoinette: The Portrait of an Average Woman* (New York: Grove Press).

Notes

1 By 'sexualisation of political authority' I mean – I repeat – the idea that certain sexual practices/desires/subjectivities prevent those who allegedly engage/experience/inhabit them from being regarded as credible, competent and fully legitimate public authorities. Conversely, other sexual practices, desires or subjectivities may lend support to a statesman's authority and recommend him, as it were, for public office. For one to meaningfully investigate *across time* the sexualisation of political authority there needs to be (a) something recognisable as political authority, as well as (b) something recognisably sexual, according to the epistemologies current during the different historical periods the book considers. The first condition is easily satisfied. As texts such as Plato's *Republic* or *Laws* and Aristotle's *Politics* demonstrate, Western thought has, since antiquity, understood the task of government as a domain of the social giving rise to distinctive concerns – including those tied up to the question of what justifies the authority of those who govern. The second condition is also satisfied, for the need to organise 'erotic life' is a trans-historical and trans-cultural one (Weeks, 2003: 28), even if the precise boundaries of the erotic and the sexual may be impossible satisfactorily to define even from a synchronic perspective (12). The idea of 'sexualisation', in this sense, does not import the complex and modern construct of 'sexuality' (with all its scientific discursive baggage) into the past. Indeed for each of the periods the book analyses, sexual constructs are investigated in accordance with what we know about the sexual epistemologies of the time.

2 As we will see, the preoccupation with good government has been prominent throughout the periods the book discusses.

3 Not all political theories regard justice in government as a prerequisite to the legitimacy of that government's political authority. The theorists of monarchical absolutism in early modern Europe denied that the legitimacy of monarchical authority could be challenged by deposing the sovereign on any ground, including their failure to rule justly. At the same time, they were generally in agreement that monarchs *should* rule justly. Failing to do so turned the monarch into a despot (Henshall, 2013: 123–126). But the proposition that monarchs should rule justly always threatens to logically collapse into the proposition that despots do not rule legitimately. Thus, even in the context of those theoretical attempts

that specifically strive to make the legitimacy of political authority independent of the justness of political rule, the latter constantly returns to haunt the former, undermining those very efforts.

4 Here I assume that the statesman's own authority is taken to either coincide or be a proxy for the state's political authority, depending on his rank and the system of government.

5 Not all curiosity about public officials' sexual life must invariably reveal a profound epistemological connection between political authority and the sexual. But it is unlikely that rumours about a public official's sexual life, let alone public discussions about or official investigations into it, will generally be neutral events with respect to our perception of their suitability for exercising the powers proper of their office. This is because of the phenomenological relationship between sexual activity and power/powerlessness, which, as I will argue, creates a potentially productive discursive overlap between sexual desire and state power.

6 This may be due to Foucault's influence on critical scholarship on sexuality. For Foucault, juridical power is the quintessential form of state power, whose modalities, he argued, are ones of interdiction and coercion (1998: 86–89). At least until his later work on 'governmentality' – a concept that encompasses both the ideas of sovereignty and discipline (Dean, 2010: 28–30) – Foucault conceived of the state as an abstraction of relatively limited significance (Constable, 1991) and argued that juridical power had been largely demoted by *disciplinary* power (Hunt and Wickam, 1994: 39–74; Baxter, 1996: 461–463). This is a form of diffused social control centred on surveillance and self-management, and working through systems of knowledge that generate social identities and attach individuals to them (Dreyfus and Rabinow, 1983). Sexuality scholars influenced by these arguments may well fail to see the point of centring political authority and state power in their studies.

7 For Foucault (1998: 103–105) it has only been since the eighteenth century that 'sexuality', understood as a condensation of discursive and power relations centred on 'sex', came into being. And it was not until the nineteenth century that the most significant component of this power-knowledge regime developed: a full-blown science of sex predicated on the idea that sex was the root cause of everything (65). Some have argued that we can speak of a science of sex as far back as Graeco-Roman times (King, 1994: 32), but clearly any such 'science' was profoundly different from the epistemological and political project of the modern science of sex.

8 This view was challenged in the 1970s by lesbian feminists in respect of lesbian sex, which they argued was about sensuality rather than sexuality, and was communicative rather than aggressive (Echols, 1989: 217–218).

9 Unlike Dworkin (1987), Bersani (1987: 222) also celebrated the dissolution of the self precipitated by sex, as he thought it conducive to political practices of non-violence; he believed that the integrity of the self, as an ethical ideal, is a 'sanction for violence'.

10 Non-penile (or at least non-phallic) penetration may more easily escape this hierarchical symbolism. Even penile penetration can signify otherwise than in accordance with Bersani's and Dworkin's account; making it so signify, however, may well require a conscious effort. Indeed, alternative accounts of penetration strike me as largely reactive. They tend to be deliberate meaning-making efforts aimed at displacing the tyranny of phallic penetration's hierarchical symbolism. I am interested in the hierarchical symbolism of phallic penetration because it accounts for the sexualisation of political authority better than any other reason I can think of. The analysis of the case studies through which that sexualisation is

illustrated in the following chapters is not dependent on Dworkin's and Bersani's (controversial) insight about phallic penetration. But for those who are convinced by it, that insight – in directing our attention to the quasi-necessary discursive affinity between power and sex – enables us to see those case studies as something more than a sequence of historical coincidences.

11 Conversely, different-sex penetration, particularly as expressed in the context of marriage, can be seen as a form of socially countenanced subordination.

12 Once the semantically productive relationship between political authority and male same-sex *desire* is acknowledged, the meanings that the relationship is capable of generating can potentially float free of the *original* reason why that relationship is semantically fertile in the first place. That is, if male same-sex *desire's* ability to symbolise illegitimate subordination (on account of its potential for resulting in *penetrative sex*) establishes a discursive link between this desire and political authority, the discursive elaborations on this link do not require a constant *conscious* return to the idea of same-sex *penetrative sex*. The idea of penetrative sex, however, may well end up haunting those discursive elaborations.

13 Butler (1990: 35) calls the mutually constitutive interrelationships between sex, gender and desire the 'heterosexual matrix'. On the one hand, gender can be understood as the social construction of bodily sex, on which, in turn, same-sex desire is conceptually dependent – although this does not mean that 'sex' itself is pure, rather than discursively mediated (Butler, 1993). Conversely, at least since the emergence of homosexuality as a discursive category, gender has been conceptually dependent on same-sex desire. Thus, in the modern West the central case of masculinity is partly defined by its disavowal of same-sex desire per se. This is illustrated, to name just two examples, in the early sexological view that homosexuals belong to a third gender or sex (Calhoun, 1997: 183–185) and in the polysemic nature of the term 'pansy', which designates both effeminate men regardless of sexual orientation and homosexual men regardless of effeminacy.

14 Eisenstein (1984: 330) argues that the gendering of public and private life as, respectively, male and female 'has been inherent in the formation of state societies'.

15 The qualification 'modern and Western' should be read into my use of the term state when I leave it implicit for ease of exposition. At other times and/or in different geo-political contexts, the state may well be gendered differently. See Gose (2000); Han and Ling (1998).

16 Political satire seems to follow less scripted patterns, with countries sometimes depicted as male – think of John Bull. It may be, however, that John Bull is often best understood as a satirical personification of Britain as a state/government rather than as a country, confirming the point that it is states that are typically gendered male.

17 It is significant, in this connection, that MacCormick's (1999: 126) metaphor of the loss of sovereignty as a loss of virginity (which he used to argue that sovereignty is not a zero-sum game) implicitly feminises states without sovereignty by rhetorically casting them as deflowered maidens.

18 The pre-modern model of Roman masculinity lying at the heart of state sovereignty also explains (whereas the one of modern heterosexual masculinity doesn't) Ruskola's (2010) argument that Europe's relationship with China was typically rationalised through the vocabulary of (consensual) intercourse rather than (sexual) conquest. While a hyper-masculine state could only be raped, China, which according to Western orientalist constructions was deficient in its masculinity, should have invited consensual penetration. Hence the European powers' frustration, which Ruskola (2010: 1501–1527) documents well, at China's impenetrability and refusal of these powers' 'right' to intercourse.

19 Cooper's (1993) argument about the ostensible asexuality of the state illuminates Findlay's (1997) account of the emergence of democratic state structures in Puerto Rico.

20 The gendered and sexualised nature of Athenian democratic citizenship entailed a gendered and erotically charged conception of public powers, for in the context of classical Athens' direct democracy each male citizen was, in a meaningful sense, a wielder of public powers.

21 Wohl (2002: 28) understands the unconscious as the discursive constitution of the self.

22 In other words, gender and sexuality here operate as what Cooper (2004: 51) calls 'organising principles of inequality'.

23 Just as the notion of trial, for the purposes of this analysis, has been expanded to include more than strictly legal trials, so the notion of the rule of law is here extended to encompass the government's subjection to regulatory orders different from state law – in particular, here, its subjection to sexuality as a regulatory practice.

24 Commensurability here does not mean that same-sex desire – let alone its discursive relationship with political authority – was understood in the past in the same way as it is now. Commensurability means only that it makes sense to *compare* the ways in which these things became intelligible across time. For example, it may be true that passivity/activity was a more salient aspect of the ways in which the Greeks organised the sexual than same/different-sex desire. But it is not as if the gender of sexual object choice did not register at all for Greek epistemologies. Thus, the Greeks were very much preoccupied with pederasty – the love of boys – and the male gender of the object of this form of love was an essential aspect of the concept of pederastic love. The fact that the gender of sexual object choice *registered* for the Greeks (as it registers for us) ensures the commensurability of our sexual epistemologies with theirs, even if same-sex desire did not *signify* for the Greeks in the same ways as it does for us. Genealogical analysis investigates these differences in signification.

25 An example of the latter may be the case of resistance to colonial rule, where certain groups with a sufficient degree of internal organisation claim to act on the grievances of a constituency that they purport to legitimately represent.

Chapter 1

Antiquity: *Eros*, lust and self-possessed government

Introduction

After a ten-year campaign that had taken him from the kingdom of Macedon through Asia Minor, Egypt, Mesopotamia, Persia and across the Indus River into the westernmost part of India, in 325 BCE Alexander the Great unwillingly halted his eastward push – forced to turn back by his own exhausted and all but mutinous army (Plutarch, 1919: 309, 401). He split the troops into three parties, each following a different route back to Babylon. Alexander reserved for his own party the hazardous route through the parched expanse of the Gedrosian desert, in present-day Balochistan. During the desert march, countless of his followers fell to famine, exhaustion and disease. When the survivors reached the safety of a royal palace, Alexander held festivities and celebratory contests (Plutarch, 1919: 411, 413). Plutarch tells us that, on this occasion, the Persian eunuch Bagoas, who had attached himself to Alexander's retinue following Alexander's defeat of the Persian king Darius and who had become one of Alexander's familiars and a favourite, won the singing and dancing contest. After processing through a thronged theatre, Bagoas took his seat next to Alexander, who at the instigation of a roaring Macedonian crowd publicly kissed him.[1]

Alexander's affections, however, were not undivided. In Pella, he had grown up in close association with a Macedonian youth of noble birth, Hephaistion, who was his closest friend (Plutarch, 1919: 361; Diodorus, 1963: 223) and was to become one of his generals. Although it is almost certain that the two were lovers sharing physical intimacy (Renault, 1973: 408), none of the sources on Alexander's life explicitly refers to them as such. In contrast, Curtius (1984: 127) expressly states that Bagoas had sexual relations with Alexander. The sources' reticence about Alexander and Hephaistion's relationship demands examination. I will suggest that this reticence can be explained in light of the distinctive ways in which a statesman's same-sex desire was constructed as a problem for good government in antiquity.

An analogy can be drawn between Homer's treatment of the relationship between Achilles and Patroclus and the way historical sources deal with Alexander and Hephaistion's bond. Homer never expressly declares the erotic nature of the relationship between Achilles and Patroclus, but the ancients were clear about it (Cantarella, 1992: 10).[2] Aeschines (1919: 133), for example, states that the Athenians believed that 'the friendship between Patroclus and Achilles . . . had its source in passion' and argues that Homer 'hides their love and avoids giving a name to their friendship, thinking that the exceeding greatness of their affection is manifest to such of his hearers as are educated men' (142). Many contemporary commentators agree about the erotic nature of Achilles and Patroclus' intense attachment (Cantarella, 1992: 9–10; Davidson, 2008: 256–260; Percy, 2006: 18–19). Ultimately, it is hard to imagine that anything other than the love of a lover could drive Achilles, following Patroclus' death, to the distraction that makes him, in a spree of vengeance and spite, drag the corpse of Patroclus' assassin, the Trojan hero Hector, behind his war cart three times around Patroclus' tomb, leaving it lying facedown in the dirt (Homer, 1998: 589).

It would have pleased Alexander, who was a devotee of Homer (Plutarch, 1919: 301; Pearson, 1960: 10), to have the historians' reticence about the erotic character of his relationship with Hephaistion compared with Homer's discreet treatment of the love between Patroclus and Achilles. According to Arrian (1884: 396), the Macedonian king had had 'an ambition to rival' Achilles 'from his boyhood'. This lends credibility to the report that – like Achilles stretching over Patroclus' corpse and yearning for unity in death with him (Cantarella, 1992: 9–10) – Alexander 'threw himself on [Hephaistion's] dead body and lay there for the greater part of that day, bewailing him and refusing to depart from him until he was forcibly carried away' (Arrian, 1884: 396). Befittingly 'for the man who was the dearest to him in this world' (Arrian, 1884: 396), Alexander arranged Hephaistion's funeral so that, according to Diodorus, '[it] not only surpassed all those previously celebrated on earth but also left no possibility for anything greater in later ages' (Diodorus, 1963: 445).

But the evidence of Alexander's love for Hephaistion is not limited to the time after his death. Consider the report that, while marrying Stateira, the eldest daughter of the defeated Persian king Darius, Alexander had Hephaistion marry one of her sisters so their children could be first cousins (Arrian, 1884: 375). Another eloquent incident is when Alexander presented himself, accompanied by Hephaistion, to Sisigambis, Darius' mother. When she prostrated herself before Hephaistion, mistaking him for the Macedonian king, Alexander told her she had made no mistake, for Hephaistion too was Alexander (Arrian, 1884: 106; Diodorus, 1963: 223).[3] Hephaistion fully reciprocated Alexander's sentiments. Diodorus (1963: 457) records that when Alexander's mother Olympia, out of jealousy, threatened Hephaistion in a missive, Hephaistion replied: 'Stop quarrelling with us and do not be angry or menacing. . . . You know that Alexander means more to us than anything.'

In the face of all this evidence, why do the sources fall short of explicitly characterising Alexander's friendship with Hephaistion using the vocabulary of erotic love – especially when they show no similar reticence with respect to Alexander's relationship with Bagoas? What does this tell us about the ways in which Greek thought sexualised political authority? To be able to address these questions, we first need to take a close look at how same-sex sexuality was constructed in the ancient world. The points made in the next section will inform my analysis of the sexualisation of political authority in ancient Greece and Rome in the rest of the chapter.

Same-sex desire in the Graeco-Roman world

There is a substantial body of scholarship on same-sex desire in the ancient world. There are important differences, but also important similarities, between Greek and Roman attitudes. Scholars disagree to some extent on questions of detail, but all except those most invested in heteronormative projects (Finnis, 1994; Thornton, 1998) agree that same-sex desire in and of itself was socially acceptable in both Rome and Greece.

In Athens, the paradigmatic case of homoeroticism involved a 'lover' (*erastes*) and a 'beloved' (*eromenos*) (Robson, 2013: 38–57). The *erastes* was an adult male citizen and the *eromenos* a boy who would one day grow up to enjoy the privileges of citizenship in the city-state. While not all *erastes/eromenos* relationships need have been grounded in a desire for sexual intimacy, the very fact that the Greeks did not consistently differentiate between love and desire (Davidson, 2008: 35) indicates that normally the two were believed to go hand in hand. This potentially sexual relationship, however, was governed by a complex ethics (Foucault, 1998: 191). The *erastes* was required to court the *eromenos* who, in turn, was supposed to resist the suit until the *erastes* proved that his love was genuine and his intentions honourable. At that point it was acceptable for the *eromenos* to give in to physical intimacy – although Foucault (1998: 209) points out that the sources fail to elaborate on what particular sexual practices the *eromenos* could honourably consent to, probably because it was a matter of common knowledge. Some scholars (Cohen, 1991: 193–198) have suggested the *eromenos* was supposed *never* to give in, but Cantarella (1992: 18–20) argues that it is highly implausible for the Greeks to have been the only society to have developed a courtship practice with no rewards for the courtier.[4] Foucault (1998: 210–211, 222) suggests that where the injunction never to give in to sexual intimacy makes its appearance, it refers to sexual practices that would put the *eromenos* in a position of subordination, or feminised him. He adds, however, that the injunction is probably best understood as warning the boy against letting himself be passively manipulated in the relationship as whole. According to Davidson (2008: 78–88), it was age that was determinative: the legal age of consent was set at 18, and because the term 'boy' (*pais*) applied to everyone up to 19, pederastic (man-boy) relationships could legitimately involve sexual activity only during the very late stages of the *eromenos*'s boyhood. In addition to protecting the *eromenos* from being stigmatised as effeminate (Winkler, 1991: 186), the etiquette of pederastic bonds was bound up with the pedagogical function of these relationships, which were seen as a means by which *eromenoi* could be inducted into adult citizenship.

This involved learning how to benefit the city in different ways, including through political participation (Percy, 2006: 15).

The *erastes* who scrupulously followed the etiquette of courtship in his pursuit of boys was idealised, at least in elite circles, as a paragon of moderation and self-restraint. Thus, not only was the pederastic relationship, in its idealised form, believed to enable the *eromenos* to flourish into a responsible citizen, but it also provided the *erastes* with fertile ground to cultivate and rehearse his personal virtues.[5] Conversely, the extent to which same-sex relationships deviated from the logic of the pederastic paradigm determined the extent of their social reprehensibility. An *eromenos* who gave in easily or was eager for sexual intimacy showed an inability to properly conduct himself, evidenced by a disregard of the requirement to put the *erastes*'s love to the test (Cantarella, 1992: 19). An *eromenos* who sought material advantages – particularly money – out of physical intimacy with adult males, turned a socially valuable relationship into a mercenary affair and his moral integrity was compromised (Ferrari, 2002: 15).

The conventional view among historians of Greek sexuality is that once an *eromenos* reached adulthood, it was normally expected that he would break off the amorous relationship, and particularly sexual activity, with the *erastes* (Cantarella, 1992: 31–32).[6] For Foucault it was at this point – when the *eromenos* reached adulthood – that the relationship might turn into *philia*. *Philia* was different from the erotic pederastic relationship that the couple had outgrown because it was a reciprocal bond between equal soulmates (Robson, 2013: 63). It is unclear to what extent the *practice* of same-sex relationships matched the theoretical expectation that former *eromenoi* and *erastai* now bonded in *philia* break off sexual relationships (Robson, 2013: 63). Once the boy reached adulthood at around 20, however, his sexual appeal – which had just peaked one or two years earlier (Davidson, 2008: 89) – was supposed to have declined. Furthermore, if it is true that sex was hierarchically organised around active and passive roles, it would have been inconsistent with the partners' equal status in the context of adult *philia* if a former *eromenos* persisted in the passive role after coming of age (Boswell, 1991: 79).[7] Finally, the former *eromenos*'s newly acquired adult age-set seemed to have required a new set of responsibilities – namely the courtship of boys in an *erastes* capacity, as well as, eventually, marriage (Cantarella, 1992: 31–32). Thus, the failure to give up sexual passivity after reaching adulthood could be seen as a failure to fully accept the rights and responsibilities of citizenship.

Davidson (2008) provides a somewhat different account. He argues that *philia* replaced the *erastes*/*eromenos* relationship not when the *eromenos* reached adulthood, but upon his acceptance of the *erastes*'s suit. *Eros* had to do with the beloved's pursuit and consisted in the force that drove the *erastes* to court him; as soon as the *eromenos* gave valid consent, *eros* ended and *philia* began (Davidson, 2008: 32–33). This, however, again leaves open the question of whether sexual activities were socially countenanced in the context of *philia* once the former *eromenos* reached adulthood. For Davidson this might be a false problem. He argues that *philia* between males in the same age-set (which the former *eromenos* and *erastes* would be, once the *eromenos* reached adulthood) was socially unremarkable: it was the age-differentiated *eros* that brought attention to itself, not *philia* between coevals (Davidson, 2008: 87–88).[8] The attention drawn by intense adult same-sex attachments between former *eromenoi* and *erastai* (Robson, 2013: 63; Boswell, 1991: 79), however, suggests that, at the very least, mainstream Greek sexual morality was not fully at ease with acknowledging the possibility of sexual intimacy between them.

Certainly, an adult male 'addicted' to sexual passivity – known as a *kinaidos* – was especially socially disreputable, for his sexual proclivities automatically marked him out as lacking in virility and moderation (Cantarella, 1992: 44–48; Skinner, 2005: 14–15; Robson, 2013: 57–59, 63–64). The problem for an *eromenos* who carried on sexual relationships with his *erastes* into adulthood was that his sexual subjectivity – particularly the older he got – apparently was not readily intelligible without recourse to the idea of the *kinaidos* (Wohl, 2002: 88).[9] Most commentators emphasise the *kinaidos*'s desire to be sexually penetrated and hence his abdication of masculinity and its privileges. Davidson (2008: 55–58), however, suggests that it was the fact that the *kinaidos* was seen as effeminate, sexually compulsive and insatiable that was crucial to his identity and the stigma attached to it. Skinner (2005: 126) argues that these two accounts are not mutually exclusive. The understanding of the *kinaidos* centred on sexual passivity was associated to a broad, 'universalising' use of the term: anyone could become a *kinaidos* if they gave in to the desire for sexual passivity (see also Winkler, 1991: 177). Conversely, the account of the *kinaidos* as sexually compulsive and insatiable relates to a more narrow, essentialist sense of the word, used to mark out certain individuals as abnormal. But, as Skinner (2005: 127–128) points out, certain ancient texts bridge the gap between the two meanings by connecting both sexual insatiability and sexual passivity to the same physical disorder, which was supposedly related to the *kinaidos*'s effeminacy (see also Robson, 2013: 58–59). As we will see, even where references to the *kinaidos* were not used in order to delegitimise a political opponent – as they predominantly were up until the early fourth century BCE (Davidson, 2008: 63) – the spectre of the *kinaidos* haunts authorial choices in certain texts that provide an account of particular political figures.

If pederastic relationships were idealised as schools of citizenship, and sexual relations between adult citizens considered problematic (particularly for sexually passive partners), being sexually active with non-citizen males (including slaves) was, in the main, socially unremarkable. That is, the kind of valuation of same-sex intimacy described above was contingent upon both participants being citizens (actual or prospective). The exception to this was, it seems logical to assume, the citizen who submitted sexually to a non-citizen. Being sexually penetrated by a non-citizen must have been even worse than for an adult citizen to sexually submit to another, for the concern with the passive citizen's lack of moderation and virility here became a matter of the collective pride of the city-state. Indeed, since the untouchability of citizens is what distinguished them from slaves (Winkler, 1991: 179), it seems likely that a citizen who sexually submitted to a non-citizen symbolically turned the whole social hierarchy on its head.

The evidence that enabled the reconstruction of this overall picture comes chiefly from Athens. We know very little about the ways in which non-Athenian Greeks problematised same-sex desire (Lear and Cantarella, 2010: 1). However, their moral valuation of same-sex desire is unlikely to have departed too much from the Athenian model (Lear and Cantarella, 2010: 3).[10] This picture of the valuation of same-sex relationships centred on the idealisation of pederasty began in pre-classical times[11] and remained largely coherent over the course of several centuries (Lear and Cantarella, 2010: 1). By the first centuries of the current era – when the main accounts of Alexander's life that have come down to us were written – this understanding of same-sex desire was still true in its main outlines. Pederasty, however – idealised in classical times as the superior form of love – underwent 'a certain doctrinal disqualification' (Foucault, 1990: 235), eventually paving the way for the emergence of a new Christian sexual morality (239). For Foucault (1990) this partial discursive shift, while being enabled by elements already present in classical Greek thought (237), can largely be attributed to the influence of Roman culture, traditionally much less permissive than its Greek counterpart in countenancing boy love with non-slave boys (189–190).

Like the Greeks – perhaps more so than them – the Romans conceived of sexuality in hierarchical terms (Parker, 1997: 53–54), and social hierarchies determined the shape of acceptable sexual relations (Skinner, 2005: 195). There was, however, no equivalent of the institution of Greek pederasty in ancient Roman society. Rather, the cardinal value was *pudicitia*, understood as the sexual integrity or inviolability of every freeborn Roman (Williams, 1999: 99). Social status determined whether or not one was a legitimate object of sexual penetration (Walters, 1997: 32). Being a social superior entailed being able to protect one's bodily inviolability and, conversely, to physically impinge upon others (Walters, 1997: 41; Langlands, 2006: 273–274). This means that traditional Roman morality objected to a man having sexual relations – essentially understood in terms of phallic penetration (Walters, 1997: 30; Parker, 1997: 48) – with freeborn Romans outside of the marriage bond, characterising these illicit relations as *stuprum*. This prohibition applied without distinction in respect of boys, girls, men and women as long as they were freeborn Romans. It did not apply, however, to prostitutes of either sex, slaves (who, male or female, were their master's sexual fair game) and foreigners (unless they had acquired Roman citizenship) (Cantarella, 1992: 97–119). According to Cantarella (1992: 106–114), an adult male who consented to the receptive role in a sexual relationship with other males may have been subject to legal sanctions. In any case, since the receptive role was considered a passive position proper of women (Parker, 1997: 50; Walters, 1997: 30), a man who was known to adopt it was socially condemned and stereotyped as a *pathicus* or *cynaedus* (the Roman equivalent of the Greek *kinaidos*).[12] As to adult males who were sexually interested in penetrating other adult males, their tastes might be seen as eccentric, as boys were generally regarded and idealised as sexually desirable in a way in which grown-up males were not (Williams, 1999: 73). In sum, according to ancient Roman sexual morality, an adult male could find legitimate sexual satisfaction outside marriage only by playing the active role with either males or females, with the further qualification that any male sexual partner had to be preferably a boy; in any case the sexual partner must not be off-limits by reason of being a freeborn (*pudicitia*-carrying) citizen (Walters, 1997: 31).

The norms just described governing Greek and Roman same-sex desire do not, of course, tell us either what people actually did in practice, or the ways in which they may have psychically engaged with these norms (Wohl, 2002: 16–17).[13] They also do not necessarily represent the norms and values that specific individuals, groups or texts may have held or expressed about sexuality. The picture drawn above does, however, constitute our best understanding of mainstream social discourses surrounding same-sex desire. As such, it is a necessary point of reference for an analysis that attempts to uncover the ways in which the relationship between sexuality and political authority was collectively constructed during antiquity.

Alexander

Having taken this detour to explore the norms governing same-sex desire in the ancient world, we are now in a position to appreciate the specific ways in which certain texts from antiquity either construct the same-sex desire of a ruler or statesman as a problem for good government, or are predicated on such a construction. The texts I will analyse include the fourth century BCE oration against the Greek statesman Timarchus, as well as historical accounts, dating from late antiquity, of the rule of the Roman emperors Hadrian and Elagabalus. The first case study in this chapter, however, is a group of historical sources whose 'discretion' in dealing with Alexander's relationship with Hephaistion requires, as I have argued, an explanation.

Self-possession and moderation in the handling of *sexual desire* is one of the leitmotifs underlying Graeco-Roman normative judgements about same-sex sexuality. But the character traits of temperance and moderation had been a key point in intellectual elaboration about the ideal king too – and that even before the Hellenistic kingdoms made reflection about the exercise of monarchical power a necessity (Eckstein, 2009: 253). We can thus safely assume that the ways in which Plutarch, Curtius and Arrian treat Alexander's same-sex desire spoke directly to his qualities as a ruler. Indeed, Plutarch in his philosophical work expressly articulated the view that moderation was crucial to good rule, that the logics of public rule and self-rule were one and the same and that only he could govern well who was capable of self-government (Foucault, 1990: 89). Thus, sexual moderation was regarded as indicative of an appropriately sober and restrained approach to the task of government. In line with this logic, as we will see, Plutarch and Arrian – interested as they are in painting a sympathetic but nuanced portrait of Alexander – depict him as sexually temperate, but they maintain a critical attitude towards his leadership qualities where they draw attention to his extravagant displays of devotion for Hephaistion. Conversely, Curtius – committed to a portrayal of Alexander as a despot – portrays the king as debauched and given to sexual excess.

Arrian's *Anabasis of Alexander*, making extensive and generally critical use of comprehensive first-hand chronicles of the Macedonian king's life (none of which has come down to us) has traditionally been considered the best surviving source on Alexander (Worthington, 2003: 6–7, 13; Hammond, 1993: 319–333; Bosworth, 1988: 13, 16). Nonetheless, Arrian's work is not value-free. By the time Arrian was writing in the second century CE, Alexander's life and personality had been used to illustrate all manners of virtue or depravity by philosophers and rhetoricians (Bosworth, 1988: 16; Pearson, 1960: 6). In this context, while we should not cynically discount Arrian's avowed aim to set the historical record straight (Hammond, 1993: 315), it is important to recognise that the *Anabasis* is uneasily divided between an aspiration to critically evaluate Alexander's conduct and the ultimately prevalent intention to celebrate the Macedonian ruler (Bosworth, 1988: 148-155). Arrian (1884: 39) made no mystery of this overriding purpose in writing the *Anabasis*: he thought Alexander's achievements had 'not been related to mankind in a manner worthy of the hero' and that no one had yet 'suitably honoured him'.

The military successes of Alexander and, before him, his father Philip II of Macedon in the fourth century BCE gave monarchy the prestige that during the Hellenistic period (323 BCE–30 BCE) enabled this form of government to be widely discussed, in the Greek world, as a serious alternative to democracy – something hardly conceivable in the democratic or aristocratic-republican city states of the classical age (Eckstein, 2009: 246). Intellectuals produced treatises – directed both at educating the ruler and the ruled – centred on the figure of the ideal king, endowed with both martial and civic virtues, who would use his great power benevolently to the benefit of all, make laws to which he voluntarily submitted and use 'self-control' in his dealings with his subjects (Eckstein, 2009: 253–255). That in the Roman period Arrian could at all contemplate writing a *celebratory* history of Alexander was due to this Hellenistic intellectual production at odds with dominant conceptions of good forms of government during the classical age.

Arrian's account does not as much as raise the possibility of a physically intimate relationship between Alexander and Hephaistion. The reason for Arrian's reserve has less to do with the nature of the *Anabasis* as a history of Alexander's campaigns (rather than a study of his character), than with Arrian's aim of celebrating Alexander. Within the discursive economy analysed in the previous section, same-sex desire was assumed to involve an insertive partner and a receptive partner. By conjuring up the spectre of kinaidic sexual passivity and incontinence, any hint of a sexual relationship between Alexander and Hephaistion would have doomed to failure Arrian's project of honouring Alexander as a hero (particularly if it were suspected that – as alluded to in Renault's (1973) fiction – the receptive partner was the king himself).

While Plutarch did not have the same celebratory intent as Arrian, he was committed to depicting Alexander in a generally positive light (Bosman, 2011: 96). From the fourth century BCE and throughout the rest of antiquity, the intention to edify readers by providing lessons in virtue and vice informs historical work (Hedrick, 2009: 428). This intention is evident in Plutarch's first-century CE *Life of Alexander*. Plutarch portrays the king's conduct, in the main, as morally exemplary, until some of Alexander's qualities are gradually spoilt by the corrupting effect of the exercise of monarchical power (Hammond, 1993: 179, 187). It is clear, however, that an allusion to the erotic nature of Alexander's relationship with Hephaistion would have disabled Plutarch's sensitive treatment of his virtues and failings. Again, any mention of Alexander's indulging in same-sex sexual activity with a social equal would have evoked the bugbear of sexual passivity and debauchery, overshadowing the kind of nuanced moral analysis Plutarch was trying to engage in.[14]

In this connection, there is some evidence that Plutarch shared the conventional dim view about male sexual passivity (Cantarella, 1992: 70–73). Indeed, he may have belonged to the camp that thought an *eromenos* could never honourably give in to the *erastes*'s entreaties for sexual intimacy. This can be inferred from Plutarch's dialogue *On Love*, which makes a case for the superiority of conjugal love over pederasty. As Foucault (1990: 193–210) notes, Plutarch develops a complex argument to the effect that the wife's consent to her husband's desire results in a reciprocal relationship in which *eros* (love) and *aphrodisia* (physical pleasure) can be joined, enabling the latter to be expressed tenderly and affectionately. Pederastic relationships, on the other hand, lack the component of properly expressed *aphrodisia*, for either the *eromenos* must reject physical intimacy to retain his honour, or, giving in, the effeminacy and disposition towards passivity evinced by his acquiescence will cast a shadow on the relationship.

If the idea of a physical relationship between Alexander and Hephaistion did not bear mentioning lest Plutarch's morally nuanced discussion were held hostage to the moral abhorrence inevitably attending an implication of either the king's or his companion's sexual passivity, a reference to the physical nature of Alexander's relationship with Bagoas held no such danger. Bagoas was, after all, a eunuch, which made him less than male to begin with.[15] It went without saying, then, that in any relationship with Bagoas, Alexander would be assumed to be the insertive partner. Furthermore, Bagoas was a foreigner and a social inferior. All the moral complexities that were involved in a citizen sexually submitting to a social equal were simply not pertinent in this case. Plutarch could then safely report that Alexander had desired Bagoas.

There are other instances in which Plutarch mentions same-sex desire and Alexander's susceptibility to it. But they are cases where, again, nothing untoward emerges from the point of view of the conventional valuation of same-sex relationships typical of ancient Greek sexual morality. For all these cases involve not adult men, but boys – a natural object of desire for grown-up males, quite regardless of Plutarch's view about the deficiencies of same-sex love compared to heterosexual unions. Furthermore, in all cases, Alexander's conduct is exemplary in two ways. First, he shows loathing of relationships that are mercenary in their nature and too distant from the pederastic paradigm. Secondly, he shows much capacity for self-restraint when presented with opportunities for sexual intimacy with these boys (Plutarch, 1919: 285–287; 1936: 419). Again, bearing in mind that Plutarch maintained that a good ruler must first be able to successfully govern himself, these reports of Alexander's capacity for self-restraint in his private affairs make a clear statement about his civil and military leadership qualities.

At the same time, one of the key passages in which Plutarch conveys the idea that Alexander has lost some of his former self-possession is where he recounts Alexander's reaction to Hephaistion's death (Hammond, 1993: 183). The same is true of Arrian, who censures Alexander's excesses in honouring the memory of his lover. He states (1884: 416) that Alexander's requiring that Hephaistion's name be engraved on all commercial contracts amounted to making 'so much ado about matters of trifling moment'; and he declares that Alexander was to blame for promising an amnesty to the provincial governor of Egyptian Alexandria provided that he built two chapels in honour of Hephaistion. Significantly, here Alexander's loss of self-control following Hephaistion's death manifests itself though misguided *public* measures and it is these that attract Arrian's censure. This creates a narrative where private self-mastery and well-considered public policy map onto each other.

Thus, it is in a nuanced way that Plutarch and Arrian make use of the moderation/excess dichotomy to link legitimate/illegitimate manifestations of same-sex desire with legitimate/illegitimate exercises of political power. Alexander is not a morally corrupt sensualist whose sexual incontinence is expressive of despotic rule. Indeed, as we have seen, Plutarch depicts Alexander as capable of restraint when it comes to physically giving way to sexual passion with boys. However, Alexander is incapable of moderation when it comes to mourning a lost object of platonic *philia* and this lapse leads him to make ill-considered policy decisions. Accordingly, if not handled with restraint, even same-sex *philia* can detrimentally affect government. To the extent that same-sex *philia* was born out of *eros*, its potential for getting out of hand is perhaps not surprising. But note that once an erotic same-sex relationship has turned into *philia*, the bar for acceptable behaviour is raised. *Eros* requires restraint in its physical expressions, but it is quite at home with – and even encourages – over-the-top, non-sexual displays of devotion (Davidson, 2008: 31, 474); *philia*, on the other hand, is the domain of reasonable (though certainly not cold-hearted) people (Davidson, 2008: 32). Thus Alexander's excessive response to Hephaistion's demise, which might have been excusable had the departed been still his *eromenos*, lays itself open to censure in the context of their *philia*. In fact, the implication seems to be that Hephaistion's death causes Alexander to inappropriately regress to a more youthful, *erotic* kind of passion for his companion.[16] Thus Arrian (1884: 416) clarifies he does not blame Alexander 'for his friendship to Hephaistion, even when dead', but he does censure Alexander's excesses in honouring his memory. Effectively, one can read Arrian as implying that the intensity of Alexander's devotion to Hephaistion was unreasonable, that it went beyond the acceptable bounds of male (adult) *philia*. Conveniently, this regression from *philia* to *eros* occurs after Hephaistion's death, which removes any risk of Alexander's conduct appearing in the sort of very bad light that both Plutarch and Arrian want to avoid. With Hephaistion dead, no sexual relations between the two are conceivable and the shadow of sexual passivity cannot taint Alexander's leadership.

Unlike Arrian and Plutarch, the Roman writer Curtius can be counted among Alexander's detractors. His *History of Alexander the Great of Macedonia*, dating from the first century CE, has traditionally been considered unreliable (Hammond, 1983: 137, 150–151, 169, 162–163). Curtius labours a literary artifice centred on the idea that the favours that the Goddess Fortune bestows upon Alexander end up corrupting the king (Bosworth, 1988: 136; Baynham, 1998: 101–131). If it is true that Curtius's treatment of Alexander conceals an attack against Caligula (Stewart, 1993: 17), this narrative strategy seems well suited to denouncing the Roman emperor's involution from sensible leader to deranged tyrant.

As we have seen, Roman and Greek mainstream sexual moralities shared a critical attitude towards male sexual passivity. One might expect, then, that Curtius would not miss the chance to discredit Alexander by recourse to sexual innuendos, notably about his relationship with Hephaistion, particularly in light of what seems to have been Caligula's own sexual extravagance. But Curtius does nothing of the kind.[17] His uncharacteristically charitable handling of the king's relationship with Hephaistion might be due to Alexander's ability to choose partners whose discretion he could trust (Renault, 1973: 408). When it is expedient to do so, however, Curtius does accuse Alexander of sexual incontinence (and, as we will see in a moment, clearly links this to Alexander's governmental excesses): no sooner does Alexander set eyes on Bagoas than, we are told, he has sexual intercourse with him, closely followed by a thirteen-night-long sexual session with Thalestris the Queen of the Amazons (Curtius, 1984: 127–128). It must, then, be something other than Hephaistion's discretion that explains why Curtius does not make much of his relationship with Alexander. I think the explanation is that, in purely chronological terms, Alexander's relationship with Hephaistion did not lend itself to illustrating Curtius' conceit of the degeneration that follows the favours of Fortune. The king and his companion had been intimate friends from the time of their boyhood in Pella. This is well before the point at which, in Curtius' narrative, Alexander's victory over Darius spells the start of his moral corruption (including the abandonment of his habits of sexual continence), which sets in motion the wheels of his eventual undoing. Furthermore, in Curtius' narrative, Alexander's sexual incontinence is presented as part and parcel of his adoption of oriental customs (Heckel, 1984: 12). Thus, Hephaistion (unlike Bagoas and Thalestris) did not have the correct ethnic credentials to qualify for the role of partner in sexual excess. In short, emphasising the erotic nature of Alexander's relationship with Hephaistion simply did not fit the artificial structure that Curtius imposed on his narrative.

In sum, Curtius' reserve in dealing with the nature of the relationship between Alexander and Hephaistion is motivated by reasons entirely different from those explaining such discretion in other sources. Plutarch and Arrian are reticent because they want to distance Alexander from the spectre of the *kinaidos*, so as not to taint his character and hence discredit his political leadership. Curtius' own reticence, on the other hand, is part of a narrative strategy to build up the suspense, as it were, in order to discredit Alexander's leadership all the more effectively when the right time comes. Thus, in a move that is almost certainly an invention for dramatic effect (Renault, 1973: 409–410), Curtius (1984: 240) makes a vindictive Bagoas exploit his sexual ascendance over Alexander so as to get the king to execute an innocent Persian noble, Orsines, against whom the eunuch bears a petty grudge. Bagoas makes the naïve Macedonian falsely believe that Orsines is responsible for the depredation of Cyrus' tomb – the legendary Persian king admired by Alexander. As Orsines walks to his fate, he sarcastically remarks that rule by eunuchs is a novelty even by the standards of Asian society – which apparently had known female rulers in the past. The last words of the falsely accused Orsines consolidate the virility of the Roman state by pitching it against the (historical) femaleness of oriental governments. At the same time, they crudely exploit Roman society's contempt for male sexual passivity,[18] held out – through its embodiment in Bagoas – as the archetype of poor government and injustice. There also surfaces an indictment of insertive males who, like Alexander, allow themselves to be seduced by passive males and become addicted to sex with them. No longer master of himself, the insertive male becomes unfit to govern others.

Mainstream Roman sexual morality, as we know, did not object to the sexual submission of a non-citizen to a citizen (particularly if the non-citizen was a boy). Alexander is, of course, not a Roman citizen, but in the narrative woven by Curtius (who was writing at a time when Roman citizenship could be, and was routinely, granted to non-Romans) the oriental foreignness of the Persians and Indians whom Alexander conquers tends to identify Alexander with Romanness. Alexander's example then speaks to the Romans, and particularly Roman political leaders, warning them of the dangers of same-sex seduction even in cases (that is, the sexual submission of a foreigner) that mainstream sexual norms did not immediately recognise as problematic. The special danger in this case seems to lie in the fact that the foreigner with whom the (insertive) ruler becomes sexually involved is a *eunuch*: Bagoas' physical constitution made him the ultimate effeminate, endowed with all the failings and even dangerousness of the *cynaedus* in magnified proportion.

Timarchus

In 346 BCE, when Alexander was a boy of ten, his father Philip II, whose interests had been clashing with those of the Athenians for a decade, agreed to what was to be a short-lived peace with them (Perlman, 1973: 1–115; Harris, 1995). Athens had sent a delegation to Philip in Pella to negotiate the peace treaty. After the treaty was ratified by the Athenians, a second Athenian delegation was charged with securing Philip's formal commitment to the peace. Demosthenes and Aeschines were members of both delegations, but Demosthenes later disassociated himself from the other envoys, accusing Aeschines in particular of having being bought by Philip and of betraying the interests and orders of the Athenians. Either Demosthenes co-opted the Athenian statesman Timarchus in his attack against Aeschines or Timarchus acted on his own accord to lodge a complaint against Aeschines (Harris, 1995: 96). In any case, Aeschines responded by instituting a counter-suit to pre-empt his accusers' moves, delivering an oration that led to Timarchus' conviction. Aeschines argued that Timarchus was unfit to prosecute him and to address the popular jury because, having prostituted himself as a youngster, he had lost his civic rights (Harris, 1995: 102).

The oration *Against Timarchus* was crucial to scholarly efforts directed at reconstructing the picture of ancient Greek attitudes towards same-sex desire. It is a particularly important piece of evidence because, as a speech addressed to a jury and appealing to their pre-existing values and beliefs, it can be considered representative of widespread societal attitudes (Dover, 1978: 13–14; Cantarella, 1992: 20). For my purposes, the oration is significant because, like the passage in Curtius' *History of Alexander* that deals with the execution of Orsines, it is a source that expressly thematises the relationship between same-sex desire and political authority. In brief, the oration provides evidence for two key propositions. First, pederastic relationships were central to the Athenian political imaginary – among other things because they were considered conducive to producing a citizen-body making a responsible use of political rights. Because pederasty enabled self-government, it was integral to the legitimacy of the democratic form of government that was distinctive of the *polis*: without the prospect of functioning well, the legitimacy of direct democracy as a form of government would have been imperilled. Secondly, and conversely, discreditable manifestations of same-sex desire were seen as destructive of good government. A history of male-to-male prostitution, in particular, unfitted one for public office, for the lack of proper self-regard manifested through prostitution signalled a lack of concern for the common good.

Aeschines (1919: 7) begins by drawing a connection between democracy and the rule of law, arguing that 'autocracies and oligarchies are administered according to the tempers of their lords, but democratic states according to established laws'. The pre-eminence given to laws in a democracy requires that its citizens must be vigilant against 'those whose words violate the laws or whose lives have defied them' (Aeschines, 1919: 7). Aeschines here characterises material violations of the law in terms of life history rather than discrete acts: this sets the stage for presenting the whole being of Timarchus, and by extension any other male prostitute who partakes in public life, as against the law. It also facilitates Aeschines' (1919: 9) next move, which is to construct a narrative where the male prostitute who partakes in public life is engaged in a flouting of the law that follows a linear progression from young to adult age and from the private out into the public sphere:

> You shall hear first a review of the laws that have been laid down to govern the orderly conduct of your children, then the laws concerning the lads, and next those concerning the other ages in succession, including not only private citizens, but the public men as well. . . . you will find that the life [Timarchus] has lived has been contrary to all the laws.

Aeschines (1919: 13) goes on to quote from the laws of Athens that were intended to protect children from being seduced by older males, namely, school regulations as well as laws punishing those Athenians who 'outrage a free-born child' or 'those who abuse the persons of slaves' (17). The punishment for this crime could be a fine, but the law allowed the child's father or guardian to require the death penalty instead. In the process of clarifying that the provision about slaves is not concerned with the well-being of slaves themselves, Aeschines (1919: 17) characterises the death penalty prescribed for those guilty of this crime not in terms of the loss of life, but in terms of a loss of citizenship: '[T]he lawgiver . . . was convinced that in a democracy that man is unfit for citizenship who outrages any person whatsoever.' This is significant, because in a direct democracy like classical Athens, citizenship rights were first and foremost rights of political participation. Thus, the concern with criminal expressions of same-sex desire was at one with a concern for protecting the integrity of the good of citizenship, which, in turn, was a preoccupation with the good government of the *polis*. This becomes even more apparent where Aeschines (1919: 11, 13) clarifies that the laws protecting free born children from seduction are there not only to permanently disqualify the abuser from citizenship by taking his life, they are also directed at preventing boys from growing up to become unfit citizens and public actors themselves:

> [T]he lawgiver believed that it is the boy who has been well brought up that will be a useful citizen when he becomes a man. But when a boy's natural disposition is subjected at the very outset to vicious training, the product of such wrong nurture will be, as he believed, a citizen like this man Timarchus.

Aeschines (1919: 20) goes on to explain that, on reaching the age when a young man is registered in the list of citizens, the former-boy-turned-man becomes the law's direct addressee. Accordingly, a citizen who prostitutes himself is, on penalty of death, disqualified from becoming one of the nine archons, from the office of priest, from acting as an advocate for the state, from holding any other office, from acting as herald or ambassador, and from addressing the assembly. For the avoidance of doubt Aeschines (1919: 20) clarifies that such a citizen therefore also loses the rights Timarchus was attempting to exercise against him – namely, to 'prosecute men who have served as ambassadors' and to 'be a hired slanderer'.

As the text of the law quoted in the oration indicates, the idea that a male prostitute is unfit for public office seems bound up with religious or superstitious beliefs about a prostitute being 'impure of body' (Aeschines, 1919: 149) and capable of defiling that which he comes into contact with: 'If any Athenian shall have prostituted his person . . . he shall not . . . be present at public sacrifices . . . and he shall not enter within the limits of the place that has been purified for the assembling of the people.' (Aeschines, 1919: 21) But there are also other ideas at play. First is the idea of decorum, and acting in accordance with it in public contexts, particularly where public powers are exercised. Here Aeschines (1919: 23) draws a contrast between those 'public men of old', who avoided uncovering even their arm when addressing the assembly, and Timarchus who 'only the other day, in an assembly of the people threw off his cloak and leaped about like a gymnast, half naked, his body so reduced and befouled through drunkenness and lewdness that right-minded men, at least, covered their eyes, being ashamed for the city, that we should let such men as he be our advisers' (25).[19]

The other rationale behind disqualifying citizens who have prostituted themselves from public office and the exercise of civic rights is that prostitution is an indicator of certain character flaws that would result, if their bearer were allowed to exercise public powers, in poor government. Aeschines (1919) is very precise here: just like a spendthrift could not properly manage the state's finances (29) and just like someone who mistreats his parents could not be trusted to treat the commonwealth well (27), so 'the man who has made traffic of the shame of his own body . . . would be ready to sell the common interests of the city also' (29). (Ironically, though perhaps not coincidentally, this is just the charge that Demosthenes had brought against Aeschines himself: that he had accepted Philip's bribes and failed to act in the interest of the *polis*.) Towards the end of the oration Aeschines (1919: 151) adds a rhetorical question to the effect that a prostitute must be conclusively presumed to be altogether lacking in moral sentiment and therefore cannot be trusted to govern: 'Whom would he pity who has had no pity on himself?'

Aeschines (1919: 30) draws the connection between private and public life in unequivocal terms: '[T]o the lawgiver it did not seem possible that the same man could be a rascal in private life, and in public life a good and useful citizen.' Further on Aeschines (1919: 87, 89) stresses that, if anything, when a citizen takes on public duties, the danger that he will behave badly – if he has given signs to do so in his private life – increases, particularly if public office removes him from the *polis*:

> If a man at Athens not only abuses other people, but even his own body, here where there are laws . . . who would expect that same man, when he had received impunity and authority and office, to have placed any limit on his license?

Ultimately, Aeschines (1919: 151) presents the necessity of enforcing the law that debars prostitutes from public office as a matter of life and death. It is crucial to the survival of a well-functioning state: 'Why then do we wonder at the futility of our public acts, when the names of such public men as this stand at the head of the people's decrees?' But it is also crucial to the survival of democracy in both the short and the long term, in terms of nurturing future generations of democracy-loving men. For the very appetites that lead some men to choose prostitution also impel them to overthrow properly constituted government:

> [T]he impetuous lusts of the body and insatiate desire – these it is that fill the robbers' bands, that send men on board the pirates' boats; these are, for each man, his Fury, urging him to slay his fellow citizens, to serve the tyrant, to help put down the democracy. For such men reck not of disgrace, nor yet of punishment to come, but are beguiled by the pleasures they expect if they succeed. Therefore, fellow citizens, remove from among us such natures, for so shall you turn the aspirations of the young toward virtue.
>
> (Aeschines, 1919: 151, 153)

In addition to making these abstract points about the reason why prostitutes should be debarred from civic rights and public responsibilities, Aeschines recounts all of the misdeeds Timarchus was allegedly guilty of in his private life. At this point Aeschines (1919: 37, 39) depicts Timarchus' prostitution to other males as one component of a broader pattern of immoderate and incontinent behaviour: Timarchus 'was a slave to the most shameful lusts, to gluttony and extravagance at table, to flute-girls and harlots, to dice, and to all those other things no one of which ought to have the mastery over a man who is well-born and free'. In fact it is Timarchus' addiction to all of these expensive things that drives him to sell himself for sex (Aeschines, 1919: 37), even to a notorious and well-off public slave (49). Aeschines (1919: 47) stresses the seriousness of Timarchus' fault by drawing a distinction between kept men – citizens who exchange sex for money with only one person – and prostitutes properly so called, who sell themselves to many men. The latter category – to which Timarchus belongs – acts even more indecently. Promiscuity, however, is not singled out, together with the mercenary nature of the relationship, as a requirement of the kind of sexual activity that legally disqualifies one from public office. It is enough for the relationship to be mercenary (Cantarella, 1992: 48–50).

Cantarella (1992: 50–51) argues that the Athenian law against prostitution that Aeschines refers to does not seem to have targeted the paying partner: the reason, she adds, is that only passive males violated the social rule whereby adult men should switch to the active sexual role after boyhood. This assumes, of course, that the kind of prostitution targeted by the law envisages the prostitute selling himself as the receptive, rather than insertive, partner in the sexual relationship. Neither Aeschines' oration nor the laws he quotes expressly mention this requirement, but it is true that the oration as a whole seems to implicitly assume that a prostitute will adopt the passive role.[20] Of course, there must have been prostitutes in Athens who were hired for the purpose of acting as insertive partners. But Aeschines' oration indicates that common societal perceptions assumed prostitutes to be passive, or at least that the rationalisations provided in support of the law that disqualified prostitutes from public office had greater rhetorical force if they assumed the prostitutes' passivity. Aeschines (1919: 147, 149) capitalises on his audience's prejudices against passive males, who are seen as making themselves into women, where he characterises Timarchus as 'a creature with the body of a man defiled with the sins of a woman'. Aeschines (1919: 107) also manages to slip in an attack against Demosthenes (who, it will be recalled, had probably convinced Timarchus to lead the case against Aeschines) 'for his effeminacy and lewdness'.

Finally, it is important to analyse the relationship between Aeschines' articulation of the Athenians' belief that prostitutes must be prevented from exercising public functions for the state's own sake and the myth of the foundation of democracy in Athens. According to Thucydides' (1900: 219–223) recounting of the myth, Athens owed its democratic system to the overthrow of the tyranny by same-sex lovers Harmodius and Aristogeiton, who responded with murder to the attempt at seducing Harmodius made by Hipparchus, the brother of Athens's tyrant Hippias. According to another version of the myth, the tyrannicide was not sparked by a desire to retaliate against the sexual hubris which Aristogeiton feared might lead to Harmodius' sexual assault, but out of love for democracy and the state (Skinner, 2005: 144). The coexistence of these two versions of the story makes Aristogeiton's love for Harmodius and his love of democracy entirely fungible. It seems no accident that it is specifically *same*-sex love which stands in for the love of democracy. A girl or a woman conceivably might have served just as well as an object of erotic interest for both virtuous Aristogeiton and hubristic Hipparchus. But, unlike Harmodius, she would not one day become one of the citizen-lovers that made up the body politic of the democratic *polis*. Thus, same-sex desire – in its morally virtuous, pederastic incarnation – was central to Athens's democratic imaginary. Indeed, soon after the overthrow of the tyranny, the tyrannicides had been publicly honoured with a famous sculptural group – the first political monument in Greece (Percy, 2006: 28) – looted during the Persian wars and later restored to Greece by Alexander.

The myth of the tyrannicides was reflected in other beliefs about the ways in which the state benefited from relationships between males. A particularly well-rehearsed one was about the near invincibility of an army made up of same-sex lovers, such as Thebes's mythical Sacred Band: soldiers would vie to outdo one another in valour in order to make their lovers proud.[21] In general terms, it has been argued that the characterisation of inter-citizen bonds in terms of *eros* was widespread in ancient Greece (Leitao, 2002: 160). Significantly, Thucydides reports that Pericles' funeral speech (following the loss of Athenian life after the first year of the Peloponnesian War with Sparta in the last quarter of the fifth century BCE) included an exhortation to the citizens that they should be Athens's *erastai* (see Monoson, 1994).[22] Thus, the myth of the tyrannicides was the centrepiece of a discourse according to which males involved in pederastic relationships had a special role in supporting political liberties and the institutions of the city-state. There is evidence, too, that although the myth originated among the aristocratic elite, by the fourth century BCE Harmodius and Aristogeiton had become popular heroes (Skinner, 2005: 118–119).

Unsurprisingly, Aeschines (1919: 113) expressly invokes the myth of the tyrannicides in the case he mounts against Timarchus, calling them 'benefactors of the state' who were 'nurtured by . . . chaste and lawful love'. Aeschines (1919: 107) also makes it clear that the fact that their 'relationship proved the salvation of the state' is not an accident, for he implicitly connects it to 'the culture of our youth'. By this, plainly, he means the pedagogical function of properly conducted relationships between *erastai* and *eromenoi* and how they prepared *eromenoi* for virtuous citizenship and the responsible exercise of political rights. Aeschines (1919: 110–126) goes to great lengths to prove that he is not attacking the institution of Greek pederasty, for which he professes his enthusiasm, and which he defends partly on the ground that it is crucial to the production of a citizen-body capable of responsibly and competently administering the state.

It is clear then that what distinguished lawful love – the one foundational to public powers – and lawless love – the one that undermined them – was not, in classical Athens, a function of the hetero- or homosexuality of desire. Both lawful and lawless love were centred on same-sex desire: it was to male homoerotic desire that the Athenians ascribed the power to make or unmake the state through the fostering of, respectively, virtuous or corrupt citizens and statesmen.[23] The distinction between the two kinds of love lay not in its object choice (in either case males) but in its chastity or lack thereof. Chaste relationships were those conducted in accordance with the etiquette of love governing pederastic relationships. Unchaste relationships were those that departed from that model. Only in extreme cases (namely, prostitution and the abuse of boys or slaves), however, was unchastity between males symbolically charged to the point of it being socially and legally considered to imperil the very survival of the state. These cases were seen to justify the physical elimination of the criminal same-sex lover from the community of citizens or his being stripped of citizenship rights.

It is worth emphasising that the ideal underlying the notion of chastity in pederastic relationships here has to do with self-restraint rather than sexual asceticism. Sexual pleasure functioned as a test: they key was to subject desire to reason and therefore make a well-considered use of pleasure, rather than abstaining from it. It was through the practice of pederasty, as regulated by the etiquette of male love, that a boy grew into a man capable of making such a use of pleasure (Skinner, 2005: 14; Foucault, 1998: 206–207). The Greeks were aware that the love that they believed enabled boys to turn into citizens and virtuous political actors sprang from physical passion. But – unlike the picture painted by some commentators (Thornton, 1998) – they did not treat the physical passion at the root of pederasty as a temptation that must be resisted at all costs. The pedagogical function of Greek pederasty – and hence its political valence (pedagogy here must be seen as citizenship training, and citizenship involved first and foremost the exercise of self-government through democratic rights) – was not centred on teaching abstinence, but moderation. Indeed, what use would such a purely negative practice as abstinence be to future citizens? It would be a seriously impoverished and ineffective political training that put refraining from any action at the centre of its teaching. The political responsibilities of citizenship, especially in a direct democracy such as Athens, demanded much more: they required a vibrant citizen-body capable of exercising judgement in action – something nurtured by teaching moderation and restraint, not avoidance and self-denial.

Hadrian

Before Arrian – a native of Asia Minor with Roman citizenship – turned to writing his sympathetic portrayal of Alexander, he had held high-profile stations in the Roman imperial service under the emperor Hadrian. Arrian and Hadrian may have met as young men studying philosophy at Epictetus's school in Nicopolis, or shortly afterwards, and maintained a life-long friendship (Bosworth, 1988: 17, 19). Hadrian visited Nicomedia, Arrian's native town in the Roman province of Bithynia, in the early 120s. It is possible that the visit gave the emperor a chance to look up his former schoolfellow, who may in fact have been his host. It seems likely, too, that during his stay in Bithynia, Hadrian visited the city of Bithynium, whose territory was the birthplace and home of Antinous, whom the emperor may have first met here as a boy on this occasion (Birley, 1997: 157–158, 180).

Although Hadrian and Antinous' relationship is one of the most celebrated affairs in the history of same-sex love, we do not know much about it up to the point of Antinous' untimely death by drowning in the Nile. But the emperor's reaction to the young man's death is evidence of a love whose intensity rivalled Alexander's feelings for Hephaistion. Not only did Hadrian have a city (Antinoopolis) built near the site of the youth's death, as well as a sanctuary (the *Antinoeion*) erected in the grounds of his luxurious country villa in Tivoli to honour the youth's memory, but also, like Alexander, he gave instructions for the deification of his lover. The cult of Antinous took hold in a way in which that of Hephaistion never did, partly because Hadrian saw to its systematic spread, including by having countless marble likenesses of the deceased young man carved and sent throughout the empire. The success of Antinous's cult perhaps was also due, as some have argued, to the fact that it gave religious legitimacy to the practice of pederasty in the more heavily Hellenised parts of the empire (Skinner, 2005: 271; Birley, 1997: 253).

The main sources on Hadrian's reign are not noted for their reliability. Of Dio Cassius (writing in the early third century CE), who was born only a few years after Hadrian's death, it has been said that, in keeping with the historiographical style of his time, rhetorical effect sometimes got in the way of strict adherence to facts in his *Roman History* (Cary, 1914: xiii–xv). As to the later *Historia Augusta*, some see it as an exercise in 'deliberate mystification' (Browning, 1982: 43).

Others assert that, plagued though the *Historia* may be by mistakes and incon-sistencies, it tends to be accurate more often than not, at least for the segment on Hadrian's life (Benario, 1980: 13–14). In any case, both the *Roman History* and the *Historia Augusta* are useful in illustrating the perspective of Roman families of senatorial rank – the aristocratic repository of traditional values (Cary, 1914: xvi; Mennen, 2011: 15).

Unlike its Athenian counterpart, Roman citizenship did not require active political participation. Those leaders (generally of the patrician class) who had become the mainstays of Rome's political mythology were idealised precisely because of their supererogatory, so to speak, all-consuming devotion to the public good, which in time came to be demanded of Rome's political leadership (Saxonhouse, 1985: 94–96, 101, 103). The sustained attention paid by Roman historians to their emperors' private affairs has perhaps its origin in the higher standard to which their conduct was held as a consequence of this – a standard that, in fact, ideally required an absence, or a bare minimum, of private life. Additionally, it has been argued that the seeming stability of the empire made it look pointless to formally interrogate the current political system in light of pos-sible alternatives. Rather, coupled with the theoretically unlimited powers of the emperor and the idea that he inevitably provided an example to his subjects, this stability encouraged ethical reflection on the emperor's character, including his private virtues and weaknesses (Norena, 2009: 266–268, 277).

Skinner (2005: 241, 255) points out that imputing excesses on its leaders was, for the Romans, a particularly effective way of explaining any disaster that might befall Roman society. They believed that Rome's political supremacy was granted to it by the gods and could be revoked if its leaders proved unworthy. This also explains why allegations of a statesman's private excess were particularly powerful tools for delegitimising political rivals. Indeed, during the principate, struggles between the senate (Rome's longest-lived political organ, made up of representa-tives of the original Roman nobility) and the emperor often resulted in the latter being accused of all manner of private misconduct (Skinner, 2005, 240–241). The belief that the gods might change Rome's fortunes if its rulers proved unworthy, however, does not in itself explain why the excesses that emperors were accused of were so frequently of a sexual nature. It is the hierarchical conception of sexual rela-tionships outlined earlier in this chapter that provides the key to this puzzle. Such a conception lent itself especially well to being deployed for political purposes – for if sexual hierarchies mirrored the asymmetries of the Roman social and political organisation, imputing sexual misconduct to a political rival more or less automati-cally functioned as a charge of subversion of the political order. We can, therefore, expect historians dealing with the reign of 'bad' rulers to make much of these lead-ers' sexual misconduct. At the same time, as we will see, historians allow themselves a degree of latitude in their treatment of 'good' rulers, in some cases mention-ing their questionable sexual practices without drawing adverse implications with regard to their public life. Historical accounts of Hadrian's reign illustrate this range of approaches to his sexuality and its relationship to his political leadership.

As a Greek from Asia Minor who became a Roman senator and administrator, the value judgements underlying the work of Dio Cassius are difficult to pin down in light of either the Greek or Roman models of mainstream sexual morality. The fact that he wrote his *Roman History* in Greek suggests that his assumed audience was Greek, yet some of his sexual value judgements seem to betray a Roman sensibility. Dio (1925: 446) maintains that Hadrian's reason for building Antinoopolis was not, as the emperor professed, his love for the youth. Rather, it was Hadrian's desire to repay Antinous for voluntarily sacrificing his life so that some wish of the emperor's could come to fruition (as foreseen in some oracular message revealed to Hadrian). Dio's argument about Hadrian's reasons for the foundation of Antinoopolis seems to suggest a refusal to accept that a Roman leader of distinction could love so passionately as *erastai* did their *eromenoi*. Elsewhere, Dio (1925: 447) states that the emperor incurred some ridicule for apparently believing that a new star had appeared in the heavens out of Antinous' soul. So Dio's narrative seems to oscillate between being in denial about Hadrian's uncontainable love and an urge to censor the emperor for it. It is true that passionate and romantic love *á la grecque* was not in keeping with traditional ideals of Roman masculinity – much as the poets from the Augustan period had started singing its praises (Cantarella, 1992: 120–141). But since Dio was Greek, one would expect him to be more tolerant of romantic and passionate feelings for boys. I think that Dio's treatment of Hadrian's love for Antinous can be explained by the fact that temperance – alongside justice, courage, benevolence and piety – was regarded as one of the primary virtues of emperors according to thinking at the time (Norena, 2009: 273–276). As in Alexander's case, then, Hadrian's displays of excessive devotion to his dead lover mattered because they reflected negatively on the quality of his political leadership.

The treatment of Antinous' death by the writer of the *Historia Augusta* (1921: 44) reveals a similar concern with a ruler's self-control. Antinous' status as Hadrian's favourite is declared without the slightest hint of unease – the author uses the expression '*Antinous suus*': his dear Antinous. Unlike Dio, the *Historia* (1921: 44) does not take a position between different reports concerning Antinous' death; it simply indicates that some claimed it was Antinous' willing sacrifice, while others asserted '*quod et forma eius ostentat et nimia voluptas Hadriani*' – which translates to 'that which both his beauty and Hadrian's excessive lust make apparent'. It is actually unclear what Antinous' beauty and Hadrian's lust would make apparent in relation to the youth's death – perhaps that, while cruising the Nile, Antinous was pushed overboard by a rival for the emperor's attentions? In any case, the passage naturalises a man's desire for a beautiful young male at the same time as decrying a lack of moderation in handling it. This is matched by a criticism of Hadrian's lack of moderation in responding to Antinous' death, which shows a temporary relinquishment of manliness on the emperor's part, Hadrian having 'wept like a woman' (*Historia Augusta*, 1921: 45). As in Dio, the concern seems with Hadrian's loss of control engendered by a susceptibility to excessive amorous passion, rather than a concern with same-sex desire per se.

There are, however, certain forms of same-sex desire that are indeed objectionable for the writer of the *Historia Augusta*. The *Historia* (1921: 36–37) reports that among Hadrian's greatest faults was his passion for adult males, which he lists alongside his affairs with married women and his habit of having his friends spied upon. It may be surprising that Hadrian's penchant for adult males is listed as a serious fault. After all, the preference for smooth boys as objects of desire in Rome (Williams, 1999: 72–76) did not necessarily carry with it the implication that desiring (non-citizen) adult males was reproachable or illicit – unless, of course, one desired to be penetrated by them. We can infer, therefore, that what is being objected to here is Hadrian's (real or imputed) sexual passivity. One might expect that innuendos about Hadrian's sexual passivity would be either avoided by commentators committed to a positive portrait of the emperor, or deliberately used by his detractors to impeach his authority (*auctoritas*) and his ability effectively to exercise political power (*imperium*). The *Historia*, however, makes the allegations while at the same time appearing to treat them as pointing towards private vices rather than matters of public concern.

A possible explanation for this can be found in Cantarella's (1992: 156–164) argument that during the first centuries of the empire we observe some contradictory tendencies. Many commentators became more vocal about male sexual passivity (of which many high-profile public figures were accused) but there was some relaxation of social attitudes towards males adopting a passive role in same-sex relationships. Cantarella (1992: 156–164) argues that these two processes were connected, for the outcry about the sexual behaviour of certain public figures actually had the function of legitimising and normalising sexual passivity. Julius Caesar's virility, for example, could not be seriously questioned despite his sexual submission to other males. The apparently idiosyncratic treatment of Hadrian's sexuality in the *Historia* can perhaps be explained in light of these cultural shifts.

The *Historia Augusta*'s treatment of Hadrian's adoptive son Lucius Aelius (whom the *Historia* calls Aelius Verus) provides further support for the view that at this time some commentators looked with indulgence at statesmen's non-normative sexual practices – as long as, on the whole, they had not proved themselves bad leaders. While the *Historia* does not say that Lucius was sexually passive, its account of the statesman falls just short of a caricature of the effeminate, languid man who submits sexually to other males. Thus, after stating that it was Lucius' beauty that endeared him to Hadrian, the *Historia* (1921: 93) informs us that Lucius had a special bed filled with rose petals where, 'anointed with perfumes from Persia', he buried himself under a blanket of lilies with his lovers (*concubinis*). *Concubinis* here is traditionally translated as 'mistresses' (*Historia*, 1921: 93) but the atmosphere of effeminate decadence conjured up by the imagery in this passage – particularly the reference to perfumes (compare Panoussi, 2010: 282–283) – suggests that 'male lovers' is a more likely interpretation. Interestingly, however, the *Historia* (1921: 92) expressly denies that these aspects of Lucius Aelius' private life made him useless in public life (*'in re publica etiam non inutilis'*). Thus, the *Historia* (1921: 93) draws a distinction between pursuits that are blameworthy and ones that are simply eccentric: his 'pleasures . . . were not indeed discreditable but somewhat luxurious' and 'in his private life, though there was little to be commended, yet there was little to be blamed'. Furthermore, in informing us that, in addition to lying with his lovers in a bed bedecked with flowers, he 'made couches and tables of roses and lilies',[24] the *Historia* (1921: 93) – ironically, but significantly – expressly refers to this as 'a practice, which, if not creditable, at least did not make for the destruction of the state'. Finally, the *Historia* (1921: 93–95) treats us to some seriously camp imagery, while also reassuring us of the social and political unimportance of such behaviour:

> Still more trivial was his custom of fastening wings on many of his messengers after the fashion of Cupids, and often giving them the names of the winds, calling one Boreas, another Notus, others Aquilo, or Circius, or some other like name, and forcing them to bear messages without respite or mercy.

In a context where political attacks almost invariably included allegations of inappropriate sexual conduct, the levity with which the *Historia* treats Lucius explicitly demystifies the assumed nexus between statesmen's sexual character and their fitness for public life.

Sextus Aurelius Victor's approach in his fourth-century CE account of Hadrian strikes a more strident note. In *De Caesaribus* Aurelius Victor (1966: 92–93) reports that Hadrian left the government of Rome in Lucius' hands and retired to his Tivoli villa as soon as he had managed to pacify the empire. Aurelius Victor (1966: 93) then declares that Hadrian gave himself over to a highly hedonistic lifestyle: rumours abounded about his violating the chastity of adult males as well as of his burning passion for Antinous due to the infamous services (*'famoso ministerio'*) that the Bithynian rendered him. The author of *De Caesaribus* then refers to two familiar alternative explanations of why Hadrian built Antinoopolis and had many statues of the youth erected: it was either out of his excessive passion for the young man, or out of gratitude for Antinous' willing sacrifice. Aurelius Victor (1966: 93) professes an unwillingness to decide the matter, save for adding that in a man of loose morals such as Hadrian, the friendship of somebody much younger must be considered suspicious.

It is possible to make sense of Aurelius Victor's censorious tone purely on the basis of the traditional code of Roman sexual morality, on the assumption that the emperor's male sexual partners were citizens (and hence should have been off-limits), and that Antinous was just past the age when Hadrian should have found him attractive. But this seems artificial. Taken as whole, the passage quivers with an ill-conceived antipathy for same-sex desire per se, anticipating the kind of sexual morality that would become dominant with the ascendancy of Christianity over the pagan worldview. After all, Aurelius Victor was writing at a time (the fourth century BCE) where a sentiment progressively more inimical to same-sex desire had started taking hold (Cantarella, 1992: 173–191).

In any case, the relationship between same-sex desire and public life as it emerges from Aurelius Victor's narrative of Hadrian's years as an emperor constructs an either/or scenario: either one is engaged in the task of managing a political community or one retires to private pursuits and a life of leisure. The latter can easily degenerate into a life of sexual excess in which same-sex desire will figure prominently if the right conditions obtain – these being an undisciplined nature in conjunction with attractive males close at hand. There is also some indication that Aurelius Victor might have regarded same-sex attracted men as especially likely to give up the responsibilities of public life for the sake of pursuing a hedonistic lifestyle. The argument is not directly made, but the trajectory of Aurelius Victor's (1966: 92–93) narrative subtly suggests it. It begins by introducing Hadrian as something less than a paragon of Roman manliness and martial virtues, describing him as having more aptitude for civil affairs than military ones; it then goes on to characterise him as a confirmed Hellenophile concerned with promoting the arts, gymnasia and Greek religious rituals; then it proceeds to inform us of his seclusion in the luxury of Villa Adriana and his relinquishment of public duties; and finally it reveals the detail that makes the whole narrative come together: a burning passion for males.

Contrast Aurelius Victor's fourth-century CE judgemental approach to Hadrian's penchant for beautiful youths with the indifferent treatment afforded by authors of the first centuries BCE and CE to same-sex desire vis-à-vis different-sex desire in the context of a serious scandal involving the statesman Lucius Quinctius Flamininus. The scandal resulted in his expulsion from the senate at the instigation of Cato the Elder in the second century BCE. As Livy (1936: 355–356) recounts the incident, while proconsul in northern Italy, Lucius had taken with him his younger same-sex lover – a Carthaginian boy-prostitute – who declared that out of love for Lucius he had missed the gladiatorial contests in Rome. Under the influence of wine, Lucius replied that if his lover was curious to see someone die, his desire could be easily satisfied and he proceeded to kill, before the boy's very eyes, a defecting Gaul who just then was seeking an audience with Lucius. There are a few variants of this story: Livy reports that according to Valerius Antias it was a female courtesan who elicited the bloodshed and the victim was a prisoner who had been condemned to death (Livy, 1936: 355–358). According to Cicero's (1923: 53) philosophical work *De Senectute*, in which he purports to have Cato himself deliver the punch lines, the lover was a male prostitute but the man killed had been sentenced to death. Plutarch (1914: 351–353; 1921: 373–375) confirms Cicero's version is the one given by most writers and adds that Lucius had the prisoner killed by a bodyguard rather than slaying him himself. In all of these accounts sex and desire are presented as elements compounding the moral reprehensibility of Lucius' crime – not because the Romans thought sex sinful, of course, but because Lucius' murderous act, given its sexualised context, is suggestive of extreme sexual sadism. However, male and female lovers are treated as entirely fungible: the gender of the lover is a matter of complete indifference. Thus Livy (1936: 356) says that Valerius Antias's account (in which the prostitute is female and the victim is a prisoner sentenced to death) is 'similar . . . in its lust and cruelty' to his own version (where the prostitute is male and the victim a deserter):

> This deed, whether it was performed in the manner for which the censor rebuked him, or as Valerius reports it, was savage and cruel: in the midst of drinking and feasting, where it is the custom to pour libations to the gods and to pray for blessings, as a spectacle for a shameless harlot, reclining in the bosom of a consul, a human victim sacrificed and bespattering the table with his blood!
>
> (358)

Plutarch, who, unlike Livy, leans towards the version of events according to which the victim was a condemned prisoner, draws more subtle distinctions. He thinks the account that Livy believes in, and that Livy ascribes to Cato himself (according to which Lucius killed with his own hands a deserter, accompanied by his family, who was seeking Lucius's protection), 'was probably introduced by Cato to strengthen the force of his denunciation' against Lucius (Plutarch, 1921: 375). In other words, for Plutarch, some versions of the events are more morally reprehensible than others; but the gender of Lucius' lover is clearly not counted among the elements that make a moral difference – on this Plutarch and Livy appear to be in perfect agreement.

Cicero's (1923: 53) Cato confirms that the reason why the crime disqualified Lucius from public service was that 'to his crime against an individual he had added dishonour to the state'. The dishonour accruing to the state as a result of Lucius' crime is obviously a function of the crime's heinousness, and this in turn partly rests on its sexual overtones (a murder undertaken to satisfy a sadistic whim in a context of sexual titillation). Yet same-sex desire is not a necessary ingredient of the crime: the bloodthirsty boy-prostitute and his female counterpart are interchangeable. Nor is same-sex desire an aggravating circumstance. After all, if Lucius' lover was male, he was also a prostitute, a foreigner and a boy (*puer*) – which made him, from the point of view of traditional Roman sexual morality, just about the least problematic sexual partner for a Roman male, whether a private citizen or a public man.

The sources analysed in this section reveal a varied attitude to same-sex desire and its relationship to public powers. Writers from the first century BCE to the first century CE condemned the crime of Lucius Quinctius Flamininus, which brought dishonour to the state, without drawing a specific connection between this dishonour and same-sex desire. This is consistent with what we should expect to see, as the statesman's same-sex desire does not feature, in this case, in one of the problematic incarnations that would have troubled traditional Roman sexual morality (Lucius Quinctius was not a *cynaedus*, nor did he compromise the *pudicitia* of freeborn Romans). For Dio Cassius – writing in the third century CE – Hadrian's desire for Antinous is problematic because of its lack of moderation (which implies a critique of Hadrian's rule as well), rather than because of its same-sex nature. Once again this conforms to what one would expect to find: Antinous' foreignness and youth made him sexual fair game from the point of view of conventional Roman sexual morality. In sharp contrast with these sources, in Aurelius Victor's treatment of Hadrian – dating to the fourth century CE – we start to detect an attitude of antipathy, or at least ambivalence, towards same-sex desire per se. Furthermore, Aurelius Victor indirectly links same-sex desire to Hadrian's failings as a political leader, via the idea that such desire tends to incline one away from devotion to public duty. Finally, the *Historia Augusta* is surprisingly indulgent towards Hadrian and Lucius Aelius: where one might have expected to see both Hadrian's implied sexual passivity and Lucius's unmanly sexual subjectivity deployed against their political *personae*, the *Historia* treats them as 'private vices'.

Elagabalus

The *Historia Augusta* reserves an entirely different treatment for the young Syrian emperor Marcus Aurelius Antoninus, better known as Elagabalus, as he was posthumously named after the deity of whom he was a priest. The *Historia* (1924: 105) is explicit in regarding Elagabalus as an unworthy ruler: 'The life of Elagabalus Antoninus . . . I should never have put in writing.' The *Historia* (1924: 115) comes close to expressly declaring that it was Elagabalus' sexuality that disqualified him from being a good ruler, asking '[W]ho could tolerate an emperor who indulged in unnatural lusts of every kind?' Even without this explicit statement, the account of Elagabalus' brutal murder – following as it does a detailed rehearsal of a three-year career of outrageous excesses, mainly of the sexual kind and notably of the same-sex variety – is eloquent enough in conveying how his sexuality unfitted him for the role of supreme leader.[25]

Elagabalus was killed by his own soldiers when still in his late teens: 'Next they fell upon Elagabalus himself and slew him in a latrine . . . And he was the only one of all the emperors whose body was dragged through the streets, thrust into a sewer, and hurled into the Tiber.' (*Historia Augusta*, 1924: 139, 141)[26] His death was apparently the result of strictly political incidents – the praetorian guard's response to his second attempt at murdering his designated successor. But the trajectory of the narrative in both the *Historia* and Dio Cassius makes it look like this act of treason was simply the last straw or even a convenient pretext for orchestrating his demise, given his unsuitability to rule due to his scandalous sexuality and gender presentation. The *Historia* (1924: 173) is clear that deliverance of Rome from 'such a scourge' was long overdue and its belatedness was simply due to a 'lack at that time in the state of any who could remove him from the government of Rome's majesty'. Dio Cassius (1927: 465) states that the soldiers' displeasure with the emperor on account of the man Elagabalus loved as a husband 'was one of the things that was destined to lead to his destruction'. Herodian (1961: 150) too – whose account of the emperor's reign is not marred by the sensationalism and embroidery of the *Historia* and Dio – gives a clue about the real causes for complaint against the emperor:

> With everything that formerly had been held sacred being done in a frenzy of arrogance and madness, all the Romans, especially the praetorians, were angered and disgusted. They were annoyed when they saw the emperor, his face painted more elaborately than that of any modest woman, dancing in luxurious robes and effeminately adorned with gold necklaces.

The grievances voiced in the *Historia* and by Dio Cassius against the teenage emperor can be usefully classified into five categories: his gender/sexual subjectivity and his sexual activities; crimes of a religious nature; acts of betrayal; his 'proto-feminism'; and acts of bad rule. As I will show, the complaints that fall within the last four categories are linked (often expressly) to complaints about Elagabalus' sexuality (the first category). Furthermore, virtually all the grievances ultimately go to the core issues of Elagabalus' unworthiness as a ruler, and thus constitute, directly or indirectly, evidence of his bad rule (fifth category).

The *Historia*'s and Dio Cassius's treatment of Elagabalus' sexuality reveals the entwinement, within mainstream ancient Roman epistemologies, of male sexual passivity with a deviant gender subjectivity, and the inextricability of both from excessive or immoderate sexual appetites. This is encapsulated in Dio Cassius' (1927: 451) statement that Elagabalus 'appeared both as man and as woman, and in both relations conducted himself in the most licentious fashion'. Dio (1927: 457), furthermore, portrays Elagabalus as such an extreme specimen of the effeminate male that his sexual relationships with women are explained away as instrumental to his same-sex desire. Thus, Dio (1927: 463) declares that he 'simply . . . wanted to imitate [these women's] actions when he should lie with his [male] lovers'.

Elagabalus' effeminacy, if we are to believe Dio Cassius (1927), prompted the emperor to make up his face, wear women's garb, pluck his beard and work with wool; to give himself in marriage to other males, having himself called 'wife, mistress, and queen'; to contemplate castration (456) and ask 'the physicians to contrive a woman's vagina in his body' (471); and to show feminine 'affectations in his actions and in the quality of his voice' on all occasions except 'when trying someone in court' (465). It seems that standing as judge in a trial was a public function that, even for this emperor partial to gender-bending and sexual passivity, called for the dignity of conventional, sexually active, masculinity.

If Dio Cassius enlarges upon Elagabalus' effeminacy, the *Historia Augusta* mainly stresses his desire for sexually active males. Thus, while the *Historia* (1924) reports such transgressive gender practices as bathing with women (169), as well as consorting with prostitutes (159),[27] it mostly treats us to descriptions of a vast array of same-sex erotic activities. According to the *Historia* (1924: 115) 'at Rome he did nothing but send out agents to search for those who had particularly large organs and bring them to the palace in order that he might enjoy their vigour'; he made up his face and depilated his body because 'the chief enjoyment of his life [was] to appear fit and worthy to arouse the lusts of the greatest number'; he opened one bath to the general public so 'that by this means he might get a supply of men with unusually large organs' (123); he had the city and docks combed in search of men 'who seemed particularly lusty' (125); and 'such was his passion for Hierocles that he kissed him in a place which it is indecent even to mention' (117).

Dio Cassius (1927) too reports that Elagabalus had a penchant for well-hung men (469); that he prostituted himself to other males both in brothels and in a room of the royal palace (463); and that 'he wished to have the reputation of committing adultery, so that in this respect, too, he might imitate the most lewd women' and incur the ire of his 'husband', whom he worshipped all the more for his violent reactions (465). This passage provides an insightful clue into Roman beliefs about male sexual passivity: because sexual passivity was considered proper of women rather than adult males, a male willingly choosing to renounce his manliness and the social privileges attaching to it must do so only if his drive towards sexual passivity with males was so intense as to be irresistible. But such an irresistible drive would make of this male not just a woman, but a woman of the worst kind – the woman who gave in with free abandon to her insatiable sexual appetites: a prostitute or an adulteress. This conceptual economy is very similar to mainstream sexual discourses operating in ancient Greece with respect to the *kinaidos*, which, as we have seen, left little room for contemplating either sexual passivity in adult males clearly divorced from sexual excess and gender inversion, or sexually active male prostitutes.

In accusing Elagabalus of impiety (the second category of Elagabalus' crimes), the sources do not renounce the sexual imagery. So, Dio (1927), among other religious crimes, takes care to spell out that the emperor had himself circumcised – an act foreboding his contemplated castration and sex change (457); that he used charms involving 'shutting up alive in the god's temple a lion, a monkey, and a snake, and throwing in among them human genitals' (461) – reminding us of the youth's fetish for large penises, and that – in one of his characteristic acts of sexual wantonness – he defiled the Vestal Virgin Aquilia Severa (459). Likewise, where the sources describe Elagabalus' acts of betrayal (the third category of his crimes) against those closest to him – his guardian Gannys and his adopted son and first cousin Alexander – sexual motives or sexual implications are never far behind. Thus, the killing of Gannys is in retaliation for being forced 'to live temperately and prudently' (Dio Cassius, 1927: 452), and the failed assassination of Alexander leads the praetorian guard to compel Elagabalus to 'surrender such of his companions in lewdness as the soldiers demanded' (477) and 'return to a decent mode of living' (*Historia Augusta*, 1924: 137).

The fourth category of the emperor's crimes is what I called his 'proto-feminism'. Elagabalus, the *Historia* (1924) claims, was altogether under the influence of his mother Symiamira; he required her consent for carrying out any public business (107) and he let her – as well as his grandmother (131) – enter the senate chamber and there perform public functions 'just as though she belonged to the senatorial order' – the only Roman emperor ever to allow a woman to do so (113). It should not be supposed that Rome denied any role to women in its political mythology. Thus, the feature that immediately stands out in the founding myth of the Roman republic (compared to its Athenian democratic equivalent) is its heterosexuality. As Livy recounts it, before committing suicide after being ravished by the son of the last king of Rome, Lucretia entreated her husband and his male friends to seek revenge, prompting them to overthrow the tyrannical monarchy. Yet, as Saxonhouse (1985: 108–109) points out, this is a case of female 'private virtue' providing the impetus for male 'public virtue', where women do not enter political life as public actors in their own right. Thus, although Rome did make a place for women in its political mythology, it did so in a way that is fully consistent with the historians' outrage at Elagabalus' 'proto-feminism'.

In the process of condemning Elagabalus' endorsement of Symiamira's involvement in the management of public affairs, the *Historia* (1924: 107) sexualises Symiamira's formal entry into political life by stating that she assumed public functions 'although she lived like a harlot and practised all manner of lewdness'. Likewise, immediately prior to duly informing us that the first public act after the emperor's death was to enact a measure prohibiting anyone upon penalty of death from allowing women access to the senate, the *Historia* (1924: 143) immediately reminds us that with Elagabalus died his mother Symiamira, 'a most depraved woman and one worthy of such a son'. The sexual perversity of both mother and son (which is of one and the same kind – the insatiable sexuality of the prostitute/adulteress lusting after sexually active males) is here presented as dangerous to the state, public powers and social and political hierarchies. Elagabalus and Symiamira are sexually unruly subjects who defy the properly constituted social and political order. An impious and treacherous male who turns himself into a woman to satisfy his sexual lust can be expected to surrender all too easily the civic responsibilities, public privileges and political authority proper of elite men to those least qualified to exercise them – disreputable women.

For Roman historians, Elagabalus' opening up of state organs to women is only one instance of a broader pattern of bad rule. Once again, the sources make this category of Elagabalus' misdeeds (the abuse, misuse and reckless exercise of public functions) largely a function of his sexuality. Thus, we are told that he elevated his sexual partners to positions of power and influence (Dio Cassius, 1927: 465), including the athlete Zoticus (*Historia Augusta*, 1924: 127)[28] and the ex-slave Hierocles, whom Elagabalus had apparently married and would have liked to appoint as his successor (Dio Cassius, 1927: 463, 465). In commenting on Elagabalus' relationship with Zoticus, the *Historia* (1924: 127) is especially clear in spelling out one of the dangers that a ruler's same-sex desire may pose to well-ordered political rule:

> Zoticus, furthermore, was the kind to abuse such a degree of intimacy ... [M]en of this kind ... once admitted to too close an intimacy with a ruler, ... sell information concerning his intentions, ... and so, through the stupidity or the innocence of an emperor who does not detect their intrigues, batten on the shameless hawking of rumours.

Elagabalus is also reported, in the *Historia* (1924: 117), to have sold positions of power, including appointments to the senate, to high military and civil positions, as well as posts in the royal palace; or to have filled them with common men he found attractive, or men 'whose sole recommendation was the enormous size of their privates' (131). The sources do not draw an express connection between corruption (the sale of political posts) and Elagabalus' sexuality, but it seems likely that the same ideas articulated in Aeschines' oration are at play here: someone who sells his own body for gain can be depended upon to put a price on everything else.

Even Elagabalus' mismanagement of public money is imputed by the sources to his sexual inclinations. The reason why he travelled with a suite of 600 vehicles, according to the *Historia* (1924: 169), was to carry his retinue of 'procurers and bawds, harlots, catamites and lusty partners in depravity'. And he squandered Rome's grain reserves, carefully amassed by Trajan, on 'harlots, procurers, and catamites' (*Historia Augusta*, 1924: 161). Finally, it goes without saying that such a confirmed and self-centred sensualist would neglect public duty by devoting himself ceaselessly to private and trivial occupations such as perfumery, confection, cooking and pimping (*Historia Augusta*, 1924: 165). Likewise, such a ruler would have no regard for those public forms that it is his duty to preserve in the interest of social and political stability, showing 'contempt for the senate, calling them slaves in togas' and treating 'the equestrian order as nothing at all' (*Historia Augusta*, 1924: 145).

Conclusions

Foucault (1990: 50) notes that because sexual pleasure in classical Greece was seen as a force that always had the potential for excess, it became crucial to think of the ways in which this force could be appropriately restrained. He goes on to say that it was men's relationship with boys that, requiring the 'most subtle forms of austerity', became the object of the most elaborate forms of reflection (Foucault, 1990: 253). When it came to husband-wife relationships, given the wife's lack of meaningful agency, the problem of subjecting pleasure to reason was conceived of in unilateral terms, in the same way as moderation in the consumption of food. In the case of pederasty, on the other hand, there was a dialectic relationship between the man's need to control his passions and the boy's own (Foucault, 1990: 202–203).

The dialectical logic of same-sex *eros* explains why the relationship between *eromenos* and *erastes* could successfully function as a metaphor for intersubjective public relationships in the direct democracy of the city-state. In an important sense, Athens's direct democracy made no formal distinction between the ruler and the ruled. Each (male) citizen carried out public functions of a legislative and judiciary nature and each had formally equal entitlement to access public offices – a state of affairs that Athenian political mythology justified by constructing the image of a homogenous body politic made up of men born and bred into excellence (Sissa, 2009: 106–108). Heterosexual marriage, given its rigidly asymmetrical nature, may have been a natural candidate (as we will see in chapter 3) for metaphorically describing the relationship between the ruler and the ruled in early modern monarchies, but it could clearly not be the metaphor of choice for the political life of classical Athens. Convenely, where Pericles in his funeral oration invites the citizen to become *erastai* (rather than husbands) to the *polis*, the metaphor does the work it is supposed to. For he can then be seen to be appealing to each citizen/*erastes* (but particularly the political leaders selected for public office) to make a reasonable and responsible exercise of public functions in his relationship to the rest of the democratically active citizen-body.[29] In turn, the citizenry, as a virtuous *eromenos*, must remain in control of its destiny, retain the power to say no, and refrain from giving in to the seduction of being manipulated.[30]

If the Athenians of the classical age charged same-sex desire with positive political significance in the context of properly conducted pederastic relationships, they burdened this desire with inescapably negative political connotations when it took unchaste forms – particularly the sexual assault of a boy or a mercenary exchange. This is powerfully illustrated in Aeschines' oration against Timarchus. Indeed, the clearest evidence of the necessary connection between same-sex desire and public power in Athens's collective imagination is the very fact that the unlawfulness of male prostitution was not a matter of criminal prohibition, but of imposing disabilities in terms of the prostitute's political participation.

Mainstream social norms about same-sex desire in ancient Greece appear to have made little room for openly acknowledging the possibility of non-disreputable adult same-sex sexual relationships. By the time Arrian and Plutarch were writing, the *kinaidos* had virtually become an 'obsession' (Davidson, 2008: 55). Thus, references to the physically intimate nature of Alexander and Hephaistion's *philia* are conspicuous by their absence in Plutarch's first-century CE and Arrian's second-century CE sympathetic accounts of the king. An intimation of same-sex physical intimacy between Alexander and Hephaistion would have risked conjuring up ideas of incontinence, casting a dark shadow on Alexander's credibility and legitimacy as a political ruler. Conversely, that neither Alexander nor Hephaistion could be *kinaidoi* was proven by their valour, manliness and leadership qualities.[31] Plutarch and Arrian, nevertheless, do provide a critique of Alexander's lack of self-control in his response (including through ill-advised public measures) to Hephaistion's death. The implication is that even a ruler's same-sex adult platonic attachments need to be handled with care lest they prove a problem for the wise exercise of public powers.

Curtius' first-century CE hostile account of Alexander's rule does not draw attention to the erotic qualities of the king's relationship with Hephaistion for different reasons – namely, doing so did not fit the account's artificial narrative structure. Curtius, however, makes sure to fully exploit the idea that an insatiable same-sex desire detracts from the ruler's capacity for temperance. In particular, where Curtius portrays the eunuch Bagoas as manipulating Alexander into punishing the innocent Orsines, he depicts sexually passive kinaidic males and their seduction of insertive males incapable of self-control as seriously imperilling the just exercise of public powers.

Because in Rome manliness was the citizen's cardinal virtue (Cantarella, 1992: 158), a political figure's effeminacy and sexual passivity were obvious targets for those seeking to undermine his political leadership. Conversely, effective and dominant political leadership could be used to restore one's sexual reputation as aggressively virile and sexually active (Cantarella, 1992: 159). Nonetheless, Roman discourses about political authority and same-sex desire during the first centuries of the current era seem characterised by a high degree of complexity and plasticity. This is illustrated by the disparities in the treatment afforded in the *Historia Augusta* to Hadrian on the one hand and Elagabalus on the other, as well as those in the treatment afforded to Hadrian by Aurelius Victor's *De Caesaribus* on the one hand and the slightly later *Historia Augusta* on the other.

Between the third and fourth centuries CE, same-sex desire could clearly be presented as a problem for political rule. Same-sex desire could be constructed as a problem for good government either – albeit perhaps infrequently – merely by virtue of its same-sex quality (as in Aurelius Victor's treatment of Hadrian) or when it was expressed in one of its traditionally problematic embodiments. These are those forms of same-sex desire involving sexual passivity or unmanly and insatiable sexual subjectivities, as in the accounts of Elagabalus' reign provided by both Dio Cassius and the *Historia Augusta*.

It does not necessarily follow, however, that in Rome there was a privileged discursive connection between the problematic manifestations of same-sex desire and ineffective or incompetent political leadership. After all, Roman emperors were frequently accused of sexual misconduct that was not of the same-sex variety. Apart from Aurelius Victor's treatment of Hadrian, which objects to same-sex desire in itself, the reason why certain manifestations of same-sex desire are morally problematic, and the reason why, consequently, they present a problem for the exercise of public powers, was ultimately the disposition to passivity that they evinced. But the man who sought to be penetrated was not the only sexual subjectivity marked by such a disposition: there is some evidence that the sexual practice of cunnilingus may have been even more suspect in terms of revealing an abdication of the male prerogative to be in control (Parker, 1997: 56–58). It is conceivable, then, that if taken seriously, charges of being a *cunnilinctor* could be at least as damaging to a political career as those of being a *cynaedus*.

The writers of the late Roman period could also choose to de-emphasise (as in the *Historia Augusta*'s account of Hadrian's life) or even openly contest (as in the *Historia*'s treatment of Lucius Verus) the proposition that same-sex desire, even in its traditionally most problematic manifestations, doomed political leadership to incompetence or mediocrity. In opting either to treat same-sex desire as a problem for the exercise of public powers or as indifferent to it, the author of the *Historia* was probably responding to a contingent set of circumstances. These may have included the recalcitrant quality of his material, which, as in the case of Hadrian, simply did not lend itself to being successfully reworked to make him into a bad leader.

In sum, in classical Athens same-sex desire was at the heart of the political imagination of the *polis*, rhetorically invested with the power to make or unmake the state and its institutions. On the contrary, in Rome, during the early centuries of our era, the set of meanings around same-sex desire and political authority was more fluid. Those Roman historical texts invested in discrediting a same-sex attracted statesman, however, could capitalise not only on an emergent discourse suspicious of same-sex desire per se, but also on the well-established negative evaluation of some forms of same-sex desire. Prime among these was the cliché of the gender-nonconforming, passive male's sexual insatiability, which bore directly on discourses emphasising temperance as central to virtuous political rule.

References

Aeschines (1919) 'The Speech against Timarchus' in *The Speeches of Aeschines* (Adams, CD, trans) (London: William Heinemann) 1–156.
Arrian (1884) *The Anabasis of Alexander* (Chinnock, EJ, trans) (London: Hodder and Stoughton).
Athenaeus (1845) *The Deipnosophists: Or Banquet of the Learned*, vol iii (Yonge, CD, trans) (London: Henry G Bohn).
Aurelius Victor, Sextus (1966) *De Caesaribus* (Leipzig: BG Teubner).
Badian, E (2012) *Collected Papers on Alexander the Great* (London: Routledge).
Baynham, E (1998) *Alexander the Great: The Unique History of Quintus Curtius* (Ann Arbor: University of Michigan Press).
Benario, HW (1980) *A Commentary on the* Vita Hadriani *in the* Historia Augusta (Ann Arbor: Scholars Press).
Birley, AR (1997) *Hadrian: The Restless Emperor* (London: Routledge).
Bosman, P (2011) 'Signs and Narrative Design in Plutarch's Alexander' *Aktroterion: Journal for the Classics in South Africa*, vol 56, 91–106.
Boswell, J (1991) *Same-Sex Unions in Premodern Europe* (New York: Villiard Books).

Bosworth, AB (1988) *From Arrian to Alexander: Studies in Historical Interpretation* (Oxford: Clarendon Press).

Browning, R (1982) 'Biography' in Kenney, EJ and Clausen WV (eds), *The Cambridge History of Classical Literature: The Later Principate* (Cambridge: Cambridge University Press) 41–49.

Cantarella, E (1992) *Bisexuality in the Ancient World* (New Haven: Yale University Press).

Cary, E (1914) 'Introduction' in Cassius Dio, *Roman History*, vol i (Cary, E, trans) (London: William Heinemann) vii–xxiv.

Cassius Dio (1925) *Roman History*, vol viii (Cary, E, trans) (London: William Heinemann).

Cassius Dio (1927) *Roman History*, vol ix (Cary, E, trans) (London: William Heinemann).

Cicero (1923) *De Senectute* (Falconer, WA, trans) (London: William Heinemann).

Cohen, D (1991) *Law, Sexuality and Society: The Enforcement of Morals in Classical Athens* (Cambridge: Cambridge University Press).

Curtius Rufus, Q (1984) *The History of Alexander* (London: Penguin).

Davidson, JN (2008) *The Greeks and Greek Love: A Radical Reappraisal of Homosexuality in Ancient Greece* (London: Phoenix).

deSilva, DA (2000) *Honor, Patronage, Kinship & Purity: Unlocking New Testament Culture* (Downers Grove: Intervarsity Press).

Diodorus Siculus (1963) *The Library of History*, vol viii (Bradford Welles, C, trans) (London: William Heinemann).

Dover, K (1978) *Greek Homosexuality* (London: Duckworth).

Eckstein, MA (2009) 'Hellenistic Monarchy in Theory and Practice' in Balot, RK (ed.), *A Companion to Greek and Roman Political Thought* (Chichester: Blackwell) 246–265.

Edwards, C (1997) 'Unspeakable Professions: Public Performance and Prostitution in Ancient Rome' in Hallett, JP and Skinner, MB (eds), *Roman Sexualities* (Princeton: Princeton University Press) 66–95.

Ferrari, G (2002) *Figures of Speech: Men and Maidens in Ancient Greece* (Chicago: University of Chicago Press).

Finnis, JM (1994) 'Law, Morality, and "Sexual Orientation"' *Notre Dame Law Review*, vol 69, 1049–1076.

Foucault, M (1990) *The History of Sexuality, vol III: The Care of Self* (London: Penguin).

Foucault, M (1998) *The History of Sexuality, vol II: The Use of Pleasure* (London: Penguin).

Hammond, NGL (1983) *Three Historians of Alexander the Great: The So-Called Vulgate Authors, Diodorus, Justin and Curtius* (Cambridge: Cambridge University Press).

Hammond, NGL (1993) *Sources for Alexander the Great: An Analysis of Plutarch's Life and Arrian's* Anabasis Alexandrou (Cambridge: Cambridge University Press).

Harris, EM (1995) *Aeschines and Athenian Politics* (Oxford: Oxford University Press).

Heckel, W (1984) 'Introduction' in Quintus Curtius Rufus, *The History of Alexander* (London: Penguin) 1–16.

Hedrick, CW, Jr (2009) 'Imitating Virtue and Avoiding Vice: Ethical Functions of Biography, History, and Philosophy' in Balot, RK (ed.), *A Companion to Greek and Roman Political Thought* (Chichester: Blackwell) 422–439.
Herodian of Antioch (1961) *History of the Roman Empire* (Echols, EC, trans) (Berkeley: University of California Press).
Historia Augusta (1921) vol i (Magie, D, trans) (London: William Heinemann).
Historia Augusta (1924) vol ii (Magie, D, trans) (London: William Heinemann).
Homer (1998) *Iliad* (Fagles, R, trans) (London: Penguin).
Hope, VM (2007) *Death in Ancient Rome: A Sourcebook* (London: Routledge).
Keuls, EC (1993) *The Reign of the Phallus: Sexual Politics in Ancient Athens* (Berkeley: University of California Press).
Langlands, R (2006) *Sexual Morality in Ancient Rome* (Cambridge: Cambridge University Press).
Lear, A and Cantarella, E (2010) *Images of Ancient Greek Pederasty: Boys Were Their Gods* (London: Routledge).
Leitao, D (2002) 'The Legend of the Sacred Band' in Nussbaum, MC and Sihvola, J (eds), *The Sleep of Reason: Erotic Experience and Sexual Ethics in Ancient Greece and Rome* (Chicago: University of Chicago Press).
Livy (1936) [*Ad Urbem Conditam*], vol xi (Sage, ET, trans) (London: William Heinemann).
Ludwig, PW (2009) 'Anger, Eros and Other Political Passions in Ancient Greek Thought' in Balot, RK (ed.), *A Companion to Greek and Roman Political Thought* (Chichester: Blackwell) 294–307.
Mennen, I (2011) *Power and Status in the Roman Empire, AD 193–284* (Leiden: Koninklijke Brill).
Monoson, SS (1994) 'Citizen as *Erastes*: Erotic Imagery and the Idea of Reciprocity in the Periclean Funeral Oration' *Political Theory*, vol 22, 253–276.
Newell, W (2000) *Ruling Passion: The Erotics of Statecraft in Platonic Political Philosophy* (Lanham: Rowman & Littlefield).
Norena, CF (2009) 'The Ethics of Autocracy in the Roman World' in Balot, RK (ed.), *A Companion to Greek and Roman Political Thought* (Chichester: Blackwell) 266–279.
Panoussi, V (2010) 'Sexuality and Ritual: Catullus' Wedding Poems' in Skinner, MB (ed.), *A Companion to Catullus* (Chichester: Wiley-Blackwell) 276–292.
Parker, H (1997) 'The Tetratogenic Grid' in Hallett, JP and Skinner, MB (eds), *Roman Sexualities* (Princeton: Princeton University Press) 47–65.
Pearson, L (1960) *The Lost Histories of Alexander the Great* (London: American Philological Association).
Percy, WA, III (2006) 'Reconsiderations about Greek Homosexualities' in Verstraete, BC and Provencal, VL (eds), *Same-Sex Desire and Love in Greco-Roman Antiquity and in the Classical Tradition of the West* (London: Routledge) 13–61.
Perlman, S (1973) *Philip and Athens* (Cambridge: Heffer).
Plutarch (1914) *Parallel Lives*, vol ii (Perrin, B, trans) (London: William Heinemann).
Plutarch (1919) *Parallel Lives*, vol vii (Perrin, B, trans) (London: William Heinemann).
Plutarch (1921) *Parallel Lives*, vol x (Perrin, B, trans) (London: William Heinemann).
Plutarch (1936) *Moralia*, vol iv (Babbitt, FC, trans) (London: William Heinemann).

Reames-Zimmermann, J (1999) 'An Atypical Affair? Alexander the Great, Hephaistion, and the Nature of Their Relationship' *The Ancient History Bulletin*, vol 13, 81–96.

Renault, M (1973) *The Persian Boy* (London: Book Club Associates).

Rhodes, PJ (2009) 'Civic Ideology and Citizenship' in Balot, RK (ed.), *A Companion to Greek and Roman Political Thought* (Chichester: Blackwell) 57–69.

Ringrose, KM (2003) *The Perfect Servant: Eunuchs and the Social Construction of Gender in Byzantium* (Chicago: University of Chicago Press).

Robson, J (2013) *Sex and Sexuality in Classical Athens* (Edinburgh: Edinburgh University Press).

Saxonhouse, AW (1985) *Women in the History of Political Thought: Ancient Greece to Machiavelli* (New York: Praeger).

Scanlon, TF (2006) 'The Dispersion of Pederasty and the Athletic Revolution in Sixth-Century BCE Greece' in Verstraete, BC and Provencal, VL (eds), *Same-Sex Desire and Love in Greco-Roman Antiquity and in the Classical Tradition of the West* (London: Routledge) 13–61.

Sissa, G (2009) 'Gendered Politics, or the Self-Praise of *Andres Agathoi*' in Balot, RK (ed.), *A Companion to Greek and Roman Political Thought* (Chichester: Blackwell) 100–117.

Skinner, MB (2005) *Sexuality in Greek and Roman Culture* (Oxford: Blackwell).

Spencer, D (2002) *The Roman Alexander: Reading a Cultural Myth* (Exeter: University of Exeter Press).

Stewart, AF (1993) *Faces of Power: Alexander's Image and Hellenistic Politics* (Berkeley: University of California Press).

Thornton, BS (1998) *Eros: The Myth of Ancient Greek Sexuality* (Boulder: Westview Press).

Thucydides (1900) [*The History of the Peloponnesian War*], vol ii (2nd edn; Jowett, B, trans) (Oxford: Clarendon Press).

Walters, J (1997) 'Invading the Roman Body' in Hallett, JP and Skinner, MB (eds), *Roman Sexualities* (Princeton: Princeton University Press) 29–43.

Williams, CA (1999) *Roman Homosexuality: Ideologies of Masculinity in Classical Antiquity* (Oxford: Oxford University Press).

Winkler, JJ (1991) 'Laying Down the Law: The Oversight of Men's Sexual Behaviour in Classical Athens' in Halperin, DM, Winkler, JJ and Zeitlin, FI (eds), *Before Sexuality: The Construction of Erotic Experience in the Ancient Greek World*, (Princeton: Princeton University Press)171–210.

Wohl, V (2002) *Love among the Ruins: the Erotics of Democracy in Classical Athens* (Princeton: Princeton University Press).

Worthington, I (ed.) (2003) *Alexander the Great: A Reader* (London: Routledge).

Notes

1 See also Athenaeus (1845: 962). On the likely authenticity of this incident, see Badian (2012: 26–31).
2 The ancients disagreed, however, about Achilles' and Patroclus' roles in the relationship (Robson, 2013: 39). As we will see, the paradigmatic case of erotic relationships between males in ancient Greece was role-differentiated.

3 The sources paint the picture of a relationship involving complete intimacy and absolute trust. Plutarch (1936: 417), for example, reports that when Alexander was perusing a confidential letter from his mother Olympia, Hephaistion, sitting next to him, was also appraising himself of its contents. Upon realising this, Alexander simply turned towards him and pressed the signet ring he was wearing on his companion's lips.

4 The argument that Athenian sexual morality required boys never to give in is unconvincing for other reasons too. Among other things, Cohen (1991) hypothesises that Athenian laws included an offence of statutory rape (115) – whereby sex with a boy under a certain age would have always been illegal. If such laws existed, however, they may well have left boys of 18 and 19 in pederastic relationships free to consent to sexual intimacy, for it appears that the age of consent (set at 18) was lower than the age when a boy reached adulthood (20) (Davidson, 2008: 78–88).

5 The two functions were linked, for, as Skinner (2005: 116) reminds us, the justification of pederasty as a social institution was contingent on the *erastes* setting an example of virtue for the *eromenos*.

6 While Foucault (1998: 199–201) says that the appearance of a beard was often taken to mark the time when this should happen, he points out that departures from this guiding principle were permissible on a number of grounds. The Greeks apparently reached puberty much later than we do: a shaveable beard did not appear until a boy was about 20 (Davidson, 2008: 80–81).

7 Boswell (1991: 79) argues that in any case this would be a problem less for the partners themselves – whose erotic and emotional interactions no doubt often escaped the strictures of established discursive conventions about sex – than for the public image, so to speak, of the relationship.

8 Additionally, while Davidson (1998: 50–52) apparently does not disagree with the view that the passive role in sexual relationships was conventionally assigned to (former) *eromenoi*, he does appear to challenge the widely accepted notion that dishonour attached to sexual passivity per se.

9 However, the undeniable condemnation meted out to the *kinaidos* in different discursive contexts may have run parallel to a social reality in which, in elite environments, same-sex relationships carried on into adulthood were tolerated (Skinner, 2005: 129; Foucault, 1998: 194–195).

10 In general, we have some evidence suggesting that, far from being socially unacceptable, both in and outside Athens pederasty was integrated into initiatory/pedagogical practices that give some credibility to the controversial (Scanlon, 2006: 63–85), hypothesis that Greek pederasty was rooted in ancestral forms of ritualised homosexuality (Cantarella, 1992: 3–16, 28–32). Keuls (1993: 276) has argued that initiation rites involve subjecting the initiated to something painful as a way of making them accept their place in a social structure; that Greek pederasty, as an initiation ritual, involved just that; and that adult same-sex sexual activities between social equals were met with disapproval precisely because they undermined the idea that sex functioned as the foundation of 'a power structure'.

11 The classical age covers the years between 479 and 323 BCE.

12 The terms *pathicus* and *cynaedus* may not have been exactly equivalent (Parker, 1997: 56–58), but both indexed male sexual passivity. As with the *kinaidos*, there is no evidence that the subjectivities these terms describe existed other than as literary ideal-types (Skinner, 2005: 251–252).

13 The ambivalence of classical Athenians' psychic engagements with the 'official' protocols of same-sex desire is illustrated particularly powerfully in

Wohl's (2002: 124–170) analysis of their relationship with Alcibiades' political leadership.

14 This explanation also accounts for the way in which Alexander and Hephaistion's relationship was dealt with by Diodorus. That Diodorus (1963) was sympathetic to Alexander and thus, like Arrian and Plutarch, would not have risked tainting his memory with allusions to his – or indeed Hephaistion's – sexual passivity is clear from the ways in which he introduces Alexander in Book XVII of his *Library of History*.

15 For Aristotle, for example, eunuchs were constitutionally very much like women (Cohen, 1991, 188–189). Both women and eunuchs could be seen as imperfect males and for the same physiological reasons – like women, eunuchs were incapable of producing sperm – a condition associated with their 'coolness' (lack of 'heat'), which in turn made them passive (Ringrose, 2003: 53).

16 Note, however, that Arrian and Plutarch do not say that the relationship was grounded in a former (pre-adult) erotic relationship. The rule-breaking quality of the relationship might be the reason: if Hephaistion and Alexander's pre-adult relationship fell outside the pederastic paradigm by reason of their being contemporaries, who could guarantee that it had appropriately evolved into a *philia* that excluded physical intimacy?

17 When Roman authors impute a lack of self-restraint to Alexander, the passions concerned are generally not of the sexual variety. This is at odds with the Roman tradition of making imputations of sexual wantonness part of their political attacks. It is doubly surprising because Alexander's conquest of the Orient – for the Romans a land of moral decadence – provided a perfect opportunity to exploit the theme of sexual degeneration. The atypical treatment of Alexander's affairs by Roman authors may be due to a belief in Alexander's sexual continence taking hold early on (Spencer, 2002: 117, 193).

18 Curtius (1984: 240) here speaks of Bagoas' 'self-degradation' and implicitly endorses Orsines' indictment of males who let other men sexually use them as women.

19 The social forms that become established as decorum in a society may or may not be originally rooted in more ancient beliefs of cleanliness and uncleanliness, purity and defilement. Even if they are, the concept of decorum is not centred on a need to act in certain ways *in order to avoid pollution*. Unlike purity and defilement, decorum indexes a concern with *conventional* social codes. Conducting oneself in a decorous manner and avoiding shame de-emphasises the deep, ultimate reasons for behaving in particular ways and draws attention to surface conformity with conventionally accepted social rules about propriety. Precisely for this reason, the idea of sexual decorum is potentially more insidious as a basis for allocating social advantages and disabilities than ideas about purity/defilement: for the latter have a tendency to become obsolete in a way in which the notion of decorum does not. For example, ancient religious taboos about purity and defilement are difficult to relate to for contemporary observers (see deSilva, 2000: 241–242). The idea of decorum or seemliness, on the other hand, is still widely popular. Thus, most people who do not regard the loss of virginity as defilement still buy into social codes that make it indecorous to walk around naked in public.

20 For example, the rhetoric used by Aeschines (1919: 149) to describe male prostitutes is very much the same as that which we commonly find in discussions of the *kinaidos*. And elsewhere, when Aeschines (1919: 111) is trying to distinguish prostitution from legitimate same-sex love, he compares the prostitute with the *eromenos* – the passive partner in legitimate pederastic relationships – and the man who hires the prostitute with the active pederast.

21 It appears that the Sacred Band of Thebes was an invention of Athenian narratives that conceptualised same-sex love as foundational to the state. It has been argued that in ancient Greece same-sex love acquired this exalted status in relation to political organisation not out of philosophical necessity, but as a matter of histori-cal contingency. Such traditions as that of Spartan soldiers sacrificing to Eros prior to battle in order to promote soldierly solidarity established a cultural association between, on the one hand, same-sex love and, on the other hand, military valour and the institutions of the city-state for which the citizen-soldiers fought (Leitao, 2002: 160).

22 Aristophanes' *Knights* satirically reworks this exhortation, portraying the citizenry as the aged *eromenos* of political leaders and each prostituting themselves to the other. For a discussion see Wohl (2002: 73–123).

23 This is reflected in some of Plato's dialogues, which construct *eros* as the drive potentially most conducive to, but also most destructive of, civic virtues, making same-sex desire figure centrally in their account of the erotics of politics (Newell, 2000).

24 Lovemaking during banquets was the order of the day among the elites in impe-rial Rome.

25 This is in contrast with the measured account provided by Herodian (1961). Like Dio Cassius, Herodian was a contemporary of Elagabalus', but unlike Dio he portrays Elagabalus less as a paragon of perversity than 'in every respect, an empty-headed young idiot' (149).

26 The deliberate denial of the right to be buried was thought to condemn the soul of the deceased to restlessness (Hope, 2007: 109).

27 Prostitutes in ancient Rome were 'symbols of the shameful' (Edwards, 1997: 66).

28 According to Dio Cassius (1927: 469, 471), Zoticus actually never successfully entered into Elagabalus' graces because a jealous Hierocles secretly administered him a concoction that prevented him from reaching an erection on the occasion of the athlete's first sexual encounter with the emperor.

29 While the *polis* is often metaphorically personified, in the *Politics* Aristotle defined it simply as a 'body of citizens' (Rhodes, 2009: 57).

30 However, in Thucydides' account, the outcome of the Athenians' rivalry in 'making love' to the *polis* turns out to imperil democracy precisely because the city's most excellent *erastes* – Alcibiades – is poised to become its tyrant (Ludwig, 2009: 297–298).

31 Reames-Zimmermann (1999: 85–86) has argued that there is some evidence that the Athenian pederastic model may have been less rigid elsewhere, par-ticularly in Sparta and Macedonia, where *eromenos/erastes* (in Sparta they were called *eispnelos/aitas*) relationships may have legitimately persisted into adulthood without anyone disavowing their sexual elements. Davidson (2008: 379) simi-larly argues that there was an 'infinite variety' of socially acceptable Macedonian same-sex relationships. If this was the case at the time Arrian and Plutarch were writing, the intended readership of their work was nonetheless not limited to (and probably not primarily identified with) audiences in those localities where adult same-sex relationships involving sexual intimacy were completely accept-able. Avoiding references to any erotic elements in Hephaistion and Alexander's relationship enabled these writers to convey their positive accounts of Alexander to a much broader audience.

Chapter 2

The Middle Ages: Edward II's favourites – One throne, two kings

Introduction

There is evidence of considerable interest in texts from Graeco-Roman antiquity in medieval England since the mid-twelfth century. By the early fourteenth century – namely, the time of the reign of Edward II, whose rule historians routinely characterise as disastrous (e.g. Phillips, 2006: 1)[1] – educated people were well-acquainted with the stories recounted in these texts and others were often somewhat familiar with them (Childs, 2005: xxviii). In the *Vita Edwardi Secundi* – a contemporary and, according to historians, reliable account of Edward's reign (Childs, 2005: xxiii–xxv, xxxi) – the anonymous author makes express references both to the myth of Achilles and Patroclus and to events in the life of Alexander the Great. The author of the *Vita* (2005: 29) does not use Alexander's love for Hephaistion to draw a parallel with Edward II's relationship with his favourite Piers Gaveston, but he does compare Piers and Edward's bond to the friendship between Achilles and Patroclus. If in classical Athens, however, there were no doubts about the erotic nature of Achilles' attachment to Patroclus, the matter was not as straightforward for the author of the *Vita* and his contemporaries. By the fourteenth century the Christian world view had become predominant: Homer's failure to expressly characterise in sexual terms the heroes' love for each other could then be used to disavow the erotic nature of their relationship. Accordingly, it is to provide a contrast, rather than an analogy, that the *Vita* compares Achilles and Patroclus' friendship with Edward and Piers's intimacy. Thus, the *Vita* (2005: 29) declares that Edward's love for Piers was immoderate and unprecedented, exceeding the 'usual' sentiments that Achilles had for Patroclus or David for Jonathan; and that Piers was thought to have (literally) cast a spell on the king.

Despite contrasting Edward's love with the 'usualness' of Achilles' feelings, the *Vita* does not spell out that Edward and Piers had sex with each other. This sort of discreet treatment of their relationship is fairly characteristic of fourteenth century sources. This is, at first sight, surprising. Because many of these sources are unsympathetic to the king and his rule, one might expect accusations of sodomy to be much more frequent than they are. True, sodomy was the 'unnameable' vice for a reason – dwelling on it, some medieval theologians believed, was futile, because the enormity of the crime defied rational and ethical investigation, and inadvisable, as it might put ideas into people's heads (Jordan, 1997: 30–31; see also Karras, 2005: 137–138). Yet the same chronicles that tell us of Edward's reign often record the trials against the Templars which were taking place at the same time; in doing so the sources report in graphic detail the sinful acts that the members of the order supposedly committed (e.g. *Annales Londonienses*, 1882: 180–198).[2]

Perhaps the reserve displayed by the sources in their treatment of Edward has to do with the patron/favourite structure of Edward and Piers's bond. It was common for members of the aristocracy to have 'favourites' at the time of Edward II and these patronage relationships no doubt were sometimes of a sexual nature. However, the conventions of public discourse – as distinct, say, from servants' prattle or courtiers' backtalk – may have required that same-sex relationships of patronage be treated as presumptively chaste in all but the most egregious cases. Furthermore, in the case of the Templars, the sources were reporting from accusations of sodomy independently made and formally certified; in the case of Edward the sources themselves would have to be the accusers.

While the *Vita* does not say that Edward and Piers had sex, there is more than meets the eye to the contrast it draws between Edward's excessive love for his favourite and the purportedly 'usual' sentiments of Achilles for Patroclus. Drawing on the old Graeco-Roman discourse on moderation, the *Vita* emphasises the quantitative rather than qualitative difference between the two relationships: unlike the Homeric hero, Edward loved his bosom friend *too much*. The statement is surprising, for we know that Achilles' attachment to Patroclus is depicted as extraordinarily intense in the *Iliad*. Edward's love for Piers could hardly outdo Achilles' love for Patroclus in intensity. To the literate readers of the *Vita*, it must have been obvious that the author was writing euphemistically: stating that Edward loved Piers too much compared to Achilles' love for Patroclus really meant that the king loved his favourite in the 'wrong' way – namely, erotically. It is possible too that in the Middle Ages erotic and non-erotic same-sex love were not thought of as two qualitatively distinct types, but continuous with each other: same-sex desire kicked in when you escalated love for your same-sex friend to the next (namely, the immoderate) level.[3] This is consistent with treating sodomy as the vice that does not bear mentioning lest people fall prey to its seductions, which portrays same-sex desire in universalising terms.

There is some independent ground for believing that the excessive fondness of Edward for Piers to which the *Vita* draws the reader's attention was a coded way of implying same-sex desire. For St Thomas Aquinas at least, same-sex sexual activity was the sin against nature *par excellence* (because it ran counter to the natural law of male/female 'commingling'); but the sin against nature was in turn a sub-species of the vice of *luxuria* – the essence of *luxuria* was precisely an *excess* of sexual pleasure (Jordan, 1997: 25–28). This understanding makes the idea of excess central to same-sex sexual activity. At the same time, if the *Vita*'s reference to *too much love* implies *too much sexual pleasure*, it does not follow that the pleasure – however much it may have been desired – was consummated. For according to medieval medical knowledge – re-elaborating Graeco-Roman sources, often through the mediation of Arab writing – the best cure for a man suffering from too much love ('lovesickness') was, at least in the heterosexual context, intercourse with the object of his desire (Bullough, 1994: 38–39). Because Edward's immoderate infatuation with Piers showed no signs of abating throughout the lifetime of the latter, it might have been taken by some of his contemporary observers as conclusive proof that the king's desire was not consummated. This too may explain the relative infrequency of sodomy accusations against the king in fourteenth-century sources.

An erotic bond

Some commentators have pointed out that the intensity of Piers and Edward's bond – rather than whether or not they had sex with each other – is the most significant fact from the point of view of a historical inquiry directed at understanding the motives that actuated the king and the reasons for his downfall (Haines, 2006: 43). Nonetheless, the impetus to demonstrate that the two were not 'homosexual' has bedevilled mainstream scholarship up to the present day. Twenty years ago Chaplais (1994) concluded an otherwise reasonably persuasive case that Piers and Edward may have sealed a 'brotherhood' pact involving mutual loyalty with the argument that they were very unlikely to be lovers.[4] Chaplais's (1994: 113–114) case for Edward's heterosexuality ultimately rests on the question-begging assumption that other famous same-sex attachments (that of Achilles and Patroclus, or David and Jonathan) had no erotic element and on the fact that contemporary sources do not specifically mention that Edward and Piers were lovers. Recent scholarly analyses coming to analogous conclusions are no more convincing, treating as they do the question of Edward's same-sex desire in the same way as a proof of guilt in a criminal trial: they inexplicably presume Edward to be heterosexual until proven otherwise, and they require that the evidence of same-sex desire or intimacy be proven beyond reasonable doubt, if not beyond any doubt at all. They then proceed to forensically explain away every piece of evidence, instead of treating the matter holistically. Burgtorf (2008) is a case in point, concluding his study with the statement that 'the evidence does not bear the interpretation that there was sexual intimacy' between Edward and Piers (Burgtorf, 2008: 50). The truth, however, is that even if there is no incontrovertible evidence of sexual intimacy, the evidence is perfectly capable of *bearing the interpretation* that such intimacy existed – and in fact common sense invites just that interpretation. To be sure, the categories of male friendship and sodomy were not necessarily assumed to coincide in the Middle Ages (Karras, 2005: 129). But in the case of Edward II, the fourteenth-century sources – both early and later ones – could not get much more specific in conveying just what these commentators, oddly, deny that they do: namely that Piers and Edward were lovers. It is important to settle this preliminary point, for reducing the two men's relationship to a non-erotic bond disables an appreciation of the specific ways in which the sources construct same-sex desire as a problem for the good exercise of public powers.

While accusations of sodomy against Edward are infrequent in the fourteenth-century sources, virtually all of them are clear in their characterisation of Edward and Piers's relationship in erotic or near erotic terms. As in the *Vita*, in the *Flores Historiarum* (1890: 146) – whose segment on Edward II dates from the king's lifetime – we read of the 'intensity' of the king's 'immoderate love' for Piers. A chronicle composed around the time of Edward's deposition depicts his first meeting with the slightly older Piers (Phillips, 2010: 97) as a case of love at first sight: 'The king's son gazing at Piers immediately aroused so much passion in him, that he sealed a pact of loyalty with him' and they bound themselves in an 'everlasting bond of love' (Haskins, 1939: 75, my translation). Another contemporary source, the *Chronicle of Walter of Guisborough* (1957: 382, my translation), tells of Edward's predilection for Piers in these terms:

> During his father's life, when he was Prince of Wales, the king was extremely close to a certain soldier from Gascony, whom he elevated from almost nothing and enriched as much as possible owing to the greatness of the love with which he favoured him.

Elsewhere we are informed that when Piers returned from the exile imposed on him by Edward's father, Edward 'renewed in his thrilled soul the flame of his habitual love' (Haskins, 1939: 75). The *Annales Londonienses* (1882: 154–155), another contemporary account, describe Piers as Edward's 'comrade' (*consors*) during his adolescence and declares that the king 'loved him exclusively' after Piers's return from his first exile.

The *Polychronicon* (1871), whose earliest version was completed around the time of Edward's recorded death, refers to Piers as *amasium suum* (his lover or beloved) (296), and that on his account 'he neglected his queen Isabella' (300). The expression *amasium suum* is also used in Thomas de Burton's *Meaux chronicle* (1867: 279), dating from several decades after Edward's reign. The *Annales Paulini*, whose first part is contemporaneous with Edward's reign, also come close to declaring that the king and Piers were lovers. This source begins by telling us that Edward's father had banished Piers because his son loved him beyond measure (*ultra modum*) (*Annales Paulini*, 1882: 255, my translation). The *Annales Paulini* (1882: 258) go on to report that, when Edward went to France to marry the daughter of king Philip the Fair, he had the ring and other wedding gifts he received from his father-in-law sent to Piers, in whose care Edward had left the kingdom (Trokelowe, 1866: 65). This could have been merely for safe keeping and carry no particular symbolic significance, except that later we read that at Edward's coronation banquet the queen's uncles were outraged that Edward engaged more with Piers's couch than that of the queen herself; accordingly, the rumour spread that the king loved him more than his 'most beautiful' bride (*Annales Paulini*, 1882: 262, my translation). The *Annales Paulini* (1882: 259) also report that the people were wont to call Piers 'the king's idol'. The later *Chronicle of Lanercost* (1913: 196) – a composite work taking its final form no later than two decades after Edward's death – similarly states that the king of France 'cordially detested' Piers because Edward loved his daughter 'indifferently because of the aforesaid Piers'. This insistence on the exceptional and even exclusive love Edward had for Piers, when coupled with the sources' comparing it with Edward's love for Isabella, makes it implausible to disavow the erotic elements to the king/favourite relationship. In treating the king's love for his favourite as commensurable with love between heterosexual spouses, the sources fall just short of explicitly portraying Edward's attraction for Piers in terms of same-sex desire.

Consider also how fourteenth-century sources characterise the king's relationship with his favourite when using it to account for Piers's first exile at the hands of Edward's father. Murimuth's *Continuatio Chronicarum* (1889: 9, my translation) – whose part devoted to Edward II was written during the decade following the king's deposition – tells us that Piers's first exile was ordered by Edward's father on account of the bad advice he had given the prince, who loved Piers with an 'irregular affection' (*inordinata affectione*). Recounting the same episode, the *Chronicle of Lanercost* (1913: 184) reports that Piers had been exiled because of the 'improper familiarity that my Lord Edward the younger entertained with him'. According to the *Flores Historiarum* (1890: 139, my translation) Piers's 'infamous sins' were the cause of his first exile. The very fact that the details of the sins are glossed over leaves little doubt about their nature, particularly when read in conjunction with a concurrent mention of Edward's exclusive love and predilection for Piers (*Flores Historiarum*, 1890: 139) and a later reference to Edward's 'illicit and sinful sexual intercourse' (229, my translation). Similarly, the *Scalacronica* (2005) – a work written three decades after Edward's death – reports that Edward I had banished Piers because, on account of his 'various crimes and vices', he considered him bad company for his son (55), who 'had lavished great affection on Piers' (71). These 'crimes and vices' are not described as being of the homoerotic variety, but the conclusion that they were is made almost irresistible by the very vagueness with which they are alluded to, coupled with the statement, later, that Edward 'loved too much a certain person in particular' (*Scalacronica*, 2005: 95).[5]

As in the *Vita*, the emphasis in the *Scalacronica* is apparently not on the misdirection of Edward's desire (its object being male) but on its excessive intensity. Yet, it is intriguing that in another passage of the *Scalacronica* (2005: 91) we read of Gascony being a bone of contention between England and France, and of Edward spending 'a great fortune' in this connection, 'as though for the land and nation which he loved most'. Here we are clearly dealing with a case of misdirected love – Gascony benefits from the love that the king should reserve to his own country. But Gascony was precisely Piers's homeland, so that the remark about Gascony featuring too highly in the king's affections can be read as an implicit criticism of his misdirected love for Piers. The passage implicitly draws a connection between the private and the public, implying that when the king's love is oriented towards the wrong object in his personal life, his allegiances in the affairs of state are likely to shift accordingly in the wrong direction.

In sum, the degree of Edward's attachment for Piers was on all accounts out of the ordinary even for a patron-favourite relationship, standing head and shoulders above any attachment the king may have had to anyone else. As Johannis de Trokelowe's *Annales* (1866: 64, my translation) – written at some point during the reign of Edward II's son – state, neither the command of Edward II's father nor the advice of the kingdom's magnates 'could separate [Edward and Piers] from each other until death – in their heart at least'. Fourteenth-century sources make it clear that Edward's contemporaries regarded his relationship with Piers as highly unusual because of the exceptional intensity of Edward's love. To picture the relationship as devoid of erotic content defies credibility and does violence to what the sources themselves convey. This is, I think, what Hamilton (1988: 109) means where he declares that it is indisputable that Edward and Piers were lovers.[6]

Yet some have remained intent on denying this proposition. In one of the most high-profile recent studies of Edward II, Phillips (2010: 96–103, 481, 610), elaborating on Chaplais's underwhelming arguments, has concluded that it is likely that Edward regarded Piers as his 'brother by blood', which would rule out any sexual intimacy between the two (Phillips, 2010: 103). I am less concerned with the argument's naiveté about the messiness of individual erotic investments, than the urge, in whose service the argument is marshalled, to implausibly erase same-sex desire out of Edward II's history. Admittedly, we do not know if the relationship was ever physically consummated[7] – but where does one draw the line of physical consummation? Penetration surely sets the bar too high. Feminists have pointed out the male-centredness of a perspective that makes 'real' sex hinge on penetration (de Lauretis, 1987: 14–15; Mackinnon, 1987: 87) but that perspective is distortive even when used to make sense of male – indeed, male-to-male – sexuality. Is fondling each other's bodily parts consummation – and do all bodily parts count or only some make the cut? How about the reflexive production of sexual arousal as a result of hugging and kissing – activities that belonged to the common repertoire of exchanges between same-sex 'brothers', but could also signify sodomy (Mills, 2007: 29; Kuefler, 2003: 153–154)? There is no non-arbitrary reason for regarding the occurrence of sexual activity as a prerequisite to identifying Piers and Edward's relationship as a case of same-sex desire (see also Karras, 2005: 148–149). Acknowledging the erotic (desire-driven) quality of the bond between Edward and Piers, and the fact that it signified as such to Edward's contemporaries, enables a fuller understanding of what was at stake in what historians and constitutionalists regularly treat as the most significant aspect of Edward's reign. This is the conflict between the king and the barons over the mode of the country's governance, leading to the ordinances of 1311, civil war in 1321 and Edward's eventual deposition in 1326.

A second king

There is no doubt about the centrality of Edward's same-sex bonds to the sources' understanding of the troubles that beset his rule. These bonds are constructed as interfering with the good exercise of public powers because they make the king particularly vulnerable to his favourite's bad counsel, and because they effectively, but illegitimately, elevate the favourite to the status of second king.

The sources more or less concede that the difficulties England faced on the external front (disputes with France in relation to Gascony and independentist struggles in Scotland) were not of the king's own making – much as they criticise the way the king responded to them. When it comes to the troubles affecting England's internal affairs, however, and particularly the wars between the king and the barons, not only do the sources impeach the king's handling of these affairs, but they also identify the origin of the troubles in Edward's own myopic political choices. In either case – whether it is a matter of preventing discontent from brewing, or responding to it in the most appropriate manner – the king's failings are portrayed as a direct result of his relationship first with Piers Gaveston and later with Hugh Despenser the Younger.

This much is evident from the very structure of the narrative that the sources weave. Almost invariably, accounts of Edward's reign start with his act of recalling Piers from the exile that Edward's father had imposed on him. Piers had been Edward's chamber officer while the latter was still a boy, but the prince's father, King Edward I, had taken exception to his son's excessive attachment to Piers and consequently had banished him from England. Upon the death of Edward I, however, Edward II immediately revoked Piers's exile. Thereafter, the partiality Edward showed Piers – resulting in considerable material advantages[8] – combined with Piers's own presumptuousness, resulted in bitter resentment on the barons' part. Opposing a largely united front against the king, they had Piers banished twice more, although in both cases the king managed to recall him. They also got Edward to accept the appointment of twelve ordainers, charged with settling some important matters of policy that the barons felt could not be left to the king, who, they thought, was proving unequal to the task of government. After Piers returned for the third time from exile, he was captured and assassinated, although Edward eventually saw that his death would be avenged.

There is less uniformity among the sources in the extent to which they foreground the figure of Hugh Despenser the Younger in the course of events that follow Piers's death. External affairs (the wars with Scotland, the disputes with France) tend to be prominent in the second part of the accounts of Edward's reign, and, as we have just seen, the seeds for the baronial wars had already been sown during Piers's life. Nonetheless, several sources present the king's new bias towards the ruthless and self-aggrandising Young Despenser as a renewed source of considerable tension between the king and the barons. They also identify the king's adherence to Hugh's advice (as well as that of his father, Hugh Despenser the Elder) as the main reason for the civil war that ensued. The Despensers were exiled, but, like Gaveston, they returned. Eventually, Queen Isabella, Edward's French wife, became the leader of the cause against the king. The Despensers were hunted down and killed, while the king was deposed.

Even the bare structure of this narrative constructs Edward's relationships with his male favourites as fatal to the success of his rule and ultimately responsible for spelling his political and physical demise. A closer analysis of how the chronicles treat particular people and incidents confirms not only the uncommonly close relationships between the king and his two favourites, but also how the sources (and the king's antagonists) linked these relationships to Edward's failings as a ruler. The *Polychronicon* (1871: 300) does so early in its account of Edward's reign, stating in the same breath that on Piers's account Edward neglected Queen Isabella and insulted the lords of the realm. The *Annales Paulini* (1882: 255, my translation) too draw the connection between Edward's love for Piers and his troubled rule at the outset, reporting that Edward I had Piers banished because he conjectured that his son's inordinate love for the man might result in the kingdom incurring 'much inconvenience'. This passage naturalises the relationship between same-sex desire and poor leadership by making the latter a likely forecast consequence of the former. In other words, Edward's poor leadership is not simply retrospectively ascertained to have occurred as a matter of contingent fact happening to be linked, in his specific case, to certain circumstances, which included his attraction for his favourites. Rather, it is prospectively assumed that his same-sex desire does not bode well and will likely be a source of trouble for the kingdom.

Later the *Annales Paulini* (1882) elaborate on the sense in which same-sex desire is a source of trouble for good government. Explaining that Edward was too ready to confer with Piers about matters that 'as a matter of royal prerogative, were incumbent on him [the king] alone and no-one else' and to solicit and act on the advice given by Piers, the *Annales* (1882: 259, my translation) declare that 'all the people were outraged that two kings were ruling in a single kingdom'. The same theme is apparently echoed in a political song dating from the last few months of Piers's life, which recites that 'no king may be prosperous in land . . . unless he can counsel himself' and imputes the land's lack of 'strength' to the fact that 'one is two' – presumably an allusion to Edward's 'sharing' the throne with Piers (Wright, 1839: 255).[9] Some sources go so far as to declare that Edward entirely delegated governmental functions to Piers. According to Walsingham's *Historia Anglicana* (1863: 122) (whose segment on Edward II is derived from a source building on previous chronicles and dating from the last quarter of the fifteenth century), the great men of the realm were outraged that 'the entire organisation of the kingdom was done at [Piers's] will'.

Significantly, the emphasis in the *Annales Paulini* is not on the poorness of Piers's advice: the objection is not to the quality of the advice but to the fact of it. The underlying idea seems to be that the king's natural prerogative to rule is also the best guarantee of the goodness of his rule. This, in turn, seems to hinge on the particular version of the divine right of kings as articulated in medieval sources. For example, in the twelfth century John of Salisbury (Ioannis Saresberiensis, 1909: 298) had argued that kings are chosen by God to rule their commonwealth, either through providence, through the choice of His ministers, or the votes of the population as a whole. To the extent that the king renounced the prerogative to rule – as Edward did because of his love for his favourites – then, the country's good government was compromised no less than it would have been if the king abused his God-given position and ruled badly.

We can observe in other medieval sources the same idea of a 'natural' convergence of (a) the God-endorsed, lineage-based prerogative to rule, (b) the popular will that will rightly support that prerogative and (c) actual good rule. Consider, for example, the account of events leading to King Arthur's coronation in Sir Thomas Malory's fifteenth-century *Le Morte d'Arthur*. The young Arthur, fostered in ignorance of his identity as the rightful heir to the throne of England, is asked by his foster brother Kay to fetch his sword, which Kay, due to take part in a tournament, has forgotten at his lodgings. Arthur finds the lodgings locked but soon chances upon a sword thrust into an anvil sitting on a rock in a churchyard. He pulls the sword out of the anvil and brings it to Kay – without realising that this is the sword that bears a gold engraving declaring that whoever pulls the sword out of the anvil is rightfully 'king born of all England' (Malory, 1996: 6). Eventually, the commons exult and declare that they want Arthur as king because it is obviously God's will that he should be; and Arthur swears to be 'a true king' standing 'with true justice' (Malory, 1996: 9–10). Thus, the people support God's will by endorsing the right to rule of those who have it by virtue of their lineage, and this lineage is the best guarantee of the goodness of their rule. The crown does not go to those power-thirsty knights who unsuccessfully tried to remove the sword from the rock; but to a boy who, ignorant of his own blood-based claims to royalty, takes the sword in all humility thinking not of his aggrandisement, but only of rendering a service to his brother.

Thus, same-sex desire is dangerous to well-ordered rule because a king in love with another man may treat him, or allow him to act, as a co-ruler even if the latter lacks the prerogative – and hence the natural capacity – to rule in the best possible way. After all, if it is true that, as John of Salisbury put it, a rightful ruler may be placed at the head of the commonwealth through divine providence, it seems hardly likely that God would choose a king's same-sex desire as a conduit for his providence. In fact, John of Salisbury (Ioannis Saresberiensis, 1909: 247–248) was clear too that the prince had an obligation to be chaste, that is, avoid sexual activities and relationships not sanctioned by monogamous marriage. From this perspective, Edward, in sharing governmental functions with his lover (let alone wholly delegating them to him) was thwarting God's plan that he should rule, and rule well.

In the *Flores Historiarum* (1890: 140, my translation) we are told that Piers 'fully resolved to exceed royal greatness' and in the *Vita* (2005: 1) that the barons hated Piers because Edward favoured him exclusively and he behaved like a second king, treating the lords like his subordinates. This source goes on to declare that Edward's love and tenderness seemed to increase as he realised that the barons were attempting to sever his bond with Piers (*Vita*, 2005: 1). The words used to describe the king's feelings – 'love' (*amor*) and 'tenderness' (*affectio*) – in conjunction with the characterisation of Piers as a 'second king' conjure up an imagery of same-sex marital companionship that implicitly displaces the legitimate king and queen pair. At the same time as conveying the nature of Piers and Edward's bond as something that surpasses ordinary friendship between males, the passage draws attention to the political repercussions of this relationship. Monarchical *de facto* authority spills over from the king to his favourite, but in practice the net effect is one of concentration of political power rather than its diffusion, as the exclusive object of the king's favour means that the political role of aristocratic elites becomes marginalised.

Paradoxically, perhaps, at the same time as being seen as a threat to the balance of power between the king and the lords, the relationship between Edward and Piers was the object of the lords' envy. The chronicles mention the magnates' resentment at not being accorded the favours reserved for Piers. For instance, Trokelowe (1866: 65, my translation) points out that when the nobility came to pay their respects upon Edward's return from France with his new wife, the king singled out Piers for special treatment ('bestowing kisses and redoubling his embraces, he paid him homage with a singular degree of familiarity'), sparking the jealousy of the magnates. Same-sex desire here appears to be perceived as a conduit for an increase in the political power of those who are fortunate enough to be the king's objects of affection. Thus, while the lords objected to the king's relationship with Piers because they saw it as diminishing their political clout, the chronicles imply that their objections were not based on a desire to maintain an equitable distribution of power: for at the prospect of increasing *their* own power to the detriment of everyone else they would have gladly made love to the king. Sedgwick (1985) argues that contexts about political power often play out according to the logic of love triangles, where two rivals vie for an object of desire. Sedgwick (1985) – interested in the tensions between homosocial and homosexual power relationships in male-dominate societies – argues that a productive feature of the erotic triangle as a lens of analysis is its ability to illustrate that relationships between (male) rivals are as meaningful as those between each contestant and his (typically female) object of desire (21–27). The erotic triangle between Edward, Piers and the barons, however, goes beyond this: it wears its homosociality on its sleeve, so to speak, as all three corners of the triangle are male. Furthermore, the tensions between homosociality and homosexuality in the triangle are particularly unstable and fraught, because, as I have argued, the erotic nature of the king's attachment for Piers was at one time the object of the barons' censure as well as of their jealousy.

At the 1308 London Parliament, the king agreed to Piers's second exile. The writ of banishment was followed by a sentence of excommunication in case of return, in which Piers is identified as the source of discord in the kingdom (*Annales Londonienses*, 1882: 154–155). The king, however, made sure to safeguard at the same time his beloved's comfort and authority by appointing him royal lieutenant in Ireland, and saw that he would not lose face by personally accompanying Piers to the port of departure (*Vita*, 2005: 13). Ironically, this defiant gesture could be read as the ultimate triumph of the rule of law – the king showing his respect for an outcome of the legitimate political process while at the same time making clear his personal disapproval of it. In practice, however, the sources tend to present the different actions through which the king manifested his staunchness to Piers as acts through which he undermined the good government of the country and his own authority.

In accounting for Piers's exile, the *Vita* (2005: 13) suggests that the barons had economic considerations – the expense of Piers's upkeep – in mind. They were also actuated by a political concern with limiting his influence and with defusing the quarrel arisen between the king and the lords (*Vita*, 2005: 9, 11). However, the *Vita* (2005: 13) also argues that these political preoccupations were bound up with the feeling that Piers and Edward should not 'remain intimate' – an expression that subtly captures the inseparability between a perceived need, felt by the lords, to limit Piers's ascendant on the king (as ruler and as a source of policy), and their taking exception to the personal bond between the two.[10]

Severing the bond

The king's relationship with Piers became so potent a symbol of unwelcome interference with the good exercise of governmental functions as to justify the suspension of ordinary political and institutional processes, leading to a restriction of Edward's powers. When the king summoned Parliament in 1310, the lords refused to congregate unarmed in Westminster palace unless Piers (who had returned from Ireland exploiting the divisions arisen among the formerly compact front against the king)[11] was removed from his chamber nearby (*Vita*, 2005: 17-19). Edward was sent away to a safe place, but formal political processes were restored only to precipitate a constitutional crisis of sorts, where the lords expressed an unequivocal motion of no confidence in the king. At the Parliament, after much deliberation, the lords took the extraordinary step of asking for the election of a body of reputable men, later known as the lord ordainers, endowed with the power to issue ordinances that would relieve the kingdom of any burden and redress any deficiency (*Vita*, 2005: 19).[12] Evidence of the exceptional quality of this step is the lords' confirming in a formal letter that neither they nor their successors would treat the king's assent to the appointment of the ordainers as a precedent, or invoke it other than on the basis of the king's free will and courtesy; and that the ordainers' power would cease upon the expiration of their term of office (*Annales Londonienses*, 1882: 171).[13]

When the ordainers finished their work, they sought approval from the king and the barons for the ordinances they had drafted (*Vita*, 2005: 31). One commentator, writing only a few years after the ordinances were passed, states that the rationale for the ordinances was to ensure that Edward 'would live more wisely' and that the people would be protected from oppression (Haskins, 1939: 77). The connection drawn in this statement between the king's private life and his administration of the commonwealth is noteworthy. As I will argue below, the idea of a continuum between the king's private life and his public conduct (coupled with the belief that Edward's being under the sway of same-sex desire posed a problem for both) is a recurrent motif in the sources.

Many of the measures adopted in the ordinances addressed royal abuses that Edward's father had been guilty of and were supported by magnates who during the reign of Edward I had been staunch royalists (Prestwich, 2003: 75). Edward II's relationship with Piers was key to this volte-face. Indeed, in addition to imposing significant curtailments of royal power (e.g. through constraints on fiscal and defence policy), the ordinances also provided that Piers should be exiled for a third time. According to the *Vita* (2005: 33) this provision was the main obstacle as far as the king's approval of the ordinances was concerned. Once again the relationship between the king and his favourite risked precipitating a breakdown of formal political processes. The barons threatened to resort to armed rebellion if the king insisted on denying his approval of Piers's banishment. Eventually Edward was forced to execute the ordinances, including the provision for Piers's exile, as well as a declaration that they would be observed forever (*Vita*, 2005: 33).

Significantly, of all the clauses in the ordinances, the *Vita* chooses to quote precisely the one providing for Piers's exile: controlling the king's erotic life here becomes a proxy for securing the country's good government. Indeed, it is clear from the text of the provision that the main concern was with the way in which Piers's relationship with the king resulted in misadministration. The first set of charges is that Piers advised Edward badly, misled him and tricked him into doing wrong. In addition to allegedly appropriating the king's treasure, leading the king into war, and obtaining the king's pardon for criminals at his service, Piers is charged with assuming royal functions, interfering with the legitimate functions of government officers, and replacing legitimate and competent office-holders with foreigners and others who had no regard for law and justice (*Vita*, 2005: 35). The Anglo-Norman version of the ordinances recorded on the parliamentary rolls expressly states that Piers had usurped 'royal power and royal dignity' ('Ordinances of 1311', 1961: 15). Thus the king's relationship with his favourite was seen to have upset the balance of properly constituted government. A more intangible offence listed in the clause providing for Piers's exile is his responsibility for the king's becoming disaffected from his 'liege men' (*Vita*, 2005: 35). The explicit inclusion of this charge seems significant, as it provides a link between the king's poor choices as a ruler and the particular nature of his bond with Piers, making apparent the distinctive nature of the threat posed by Piers's presence to the country's good government. In other words, it is by acquiring his prominent and exclusive place in Edward's affections that Piers had been able to steer the king away from the good advice of others (directed to promoting the good of the kingdom) and towards Piers's own, self-interested, counsel.

The *Vita* (2005: 69) declares that Edward had all of the makings of an excellent king: he had lineage, wealth, connections with other European royal families and the potential for excelling at the use of arms, for he was tall, strong and handsome. His predilection for Piers and his advice, however, meant that he had proved an utter failure as a ruler. That his relationship with Piers should be deemed to incapacitate Edward from the task of governing, however, was too much for the king. Thus, the *Vita* (2005: 39) reports that when the earls took further measures to the effect that Piers's supporters should remove themselves from the king's court, Edward, incensed that all his affairs were ordered by others as if he were an 'idiot', defied them by recalling Piers. When Piers returned, Walsingham (1863: 126) states, the king, oblivious to all promises and agreements, welcomed him like a 'gift from the Heavens'.[14]

But the lords, according to Trokelowe (1866: 69, my translation), were convinced that 'while that same Piers was alive, there could be no peace in the kingdom, the king could not enjoy a copious treasury, he could not treat his queen with due love, nor could he respect, as is appropriate, his magnates'. This sequence of impossibilities creates a continuity between the king's personal affairs (his treatment of the queen) and matters of state (public order, public finances, the lords' political participation), at the same time as implicitly representing same-sex desire as disruptive of both. The idea that same-sex desire poses a threat to the marriage-based family as well as the state is reinforced a few pages later in this same source. In a section entitled 'Of the king's flight with Piers', we read that the king tried to elude the earls by sailing to Scarborough with Piers, 'failing to be moved by the tears of the queen, who was then pregnant, and who had asked him in grief to stay with her' (Trokelowe, 1866: 75, my translation). At this point, the Earl of Lancaster, who was championing the lords' *political* cause in the name of the interests of the *state*, is also presented as the custodian of *family* values: he is said to have consoled the queen promising that he would not cease pursuing the pair 'until he would completely remove Piers from his intimacy with the king' (Trokelowe, 1866: 76, my translation). In the *Flores Historiarum* (1890: 148), on the other hand, it is the queen herself that, as representative of the *heterosexual* order threatened by Edward's love for Piers, takes on the role of restorer of the *political* order, by attempting to persuade the king to give up Piers's advice. The relevant passage, rather than mentioning Piers by name, calls him 'Aman': in the Old Testament, Haman is the royal adviser whose attempt at persuading the king of Persia to slay the Jews is thwarted by his wife, Queen Esther.

Despite Piers and Edward's flight, the earls soon managed to capture the king's favourite and beheaded him in 1312, leaving the king 'distressed beyond belief' (Trokelowe, 1866: 77, my translation).[15] Even with Piers dead, however, his bond with the king was capable of disrupting ordinary political processes: when the king summoned the next Parliament, the lords appeared in arms fearing that the king would seek to avenge the death of his favourite (*Vita*, 2005: 57). After hearing the petitions of the earls, Edward reconfirmed the validity of the ordinances, but did not budge from his refusal to declare Piers a traitor (*Vita*, 2005: 65).

Seducing the king and kingdom

Eventually, Piers's ghost got some respite from the task of haunting the affairs of state by souring the relations of the king with the barons and earls. By 1320 that had become the chief prerogative of the king's new favourite, recently appointed to the office of Chamberlain (*Vita*, 2005: 183).[16] This was Hugh Despenser the Younger, who is described in the *Chronicon* of Geoffrey Le Baker (1889) as 'handsomest in body, proudest in spirit and most shameful in deed' (7, my translation).[17] Once again the chronicles construct same-sex desire as interfering with good government through its tendency to make same-sex attracted kings receptive to their favourites' bad counsel. Significantly, they do so by recourse to an erotic imagery that verges on the overtly sexual.

Le Baker (1889: 6), as well as the *Vita et Mors Edwardi Secundi Regis Angliae* (1883: 299) – both notable for their sympathetic portrayal of Edward – state that Hugh was installed in the inner royal circle by prelates and others who knew he was hateful to Edward.[18] Not long afterwards, however, Hugh had managed 'through good sense and deference' to win the king's heart (*Vita et Mors*, 1883: 299, my translation). The relationship would then give rise to the barons' quarrel, which would prove 'the ruin of the barons, the kingdom's tragedy and the near overthrow of the royal bloodline' (*Vita et Mors*, 1883: 301). According to the *Vita et Mors* (1883: 301, my translation), the cause of the troubles was the barons' jealousy of Hugh, of whom some declared that he was 'a second, or even the sole, king; and that he had bewitched the king's soul, not unlike Piers Gaveston once did'.

The *Annales Paulini* (1882: 292, my translation) report that prior to the Parliament of 1321, great discord arose between the king and the earls and barons because Edward 'cherished very much' the Younger Despenser, allowing him to dismiss 'at whim' the royal officials and install his own men in the royal palace, without asking for the consent of the kingdom's magnates. This complaint rehearses the grievances of the barons with respect to Edward's relationship with Piers. As John of Salisbury (Ioannis Saresberiensis, 1909) had declared two centuries before, a ruler had a duty to 'embrace the population as a whole within the arms of his good deeds' (299, my translation). If the king's diffused concern for his subjects were replaced by a passion for a single man, a dangerous power imbalance would ensue, as the aristocratic elite would experience a loss of political authority. The erotic dimensions of the kind of love that, if the ruler abandoned himself to it, was considered likely to lead to this concentration of political power were not lost on fourteenth-century commentators. At one point the *Annales*

Paulini (1882: 295, my translation) refer to Hugh and his father as 'seducers of the king and kingdom'. The later *Chronicon Henrici Knighton* (1889: 421) (dating from the last quarter of the fourteenth century) uses a similar expression – 'seducers of the king'. A military history of the campaigns of Edward's successor plays on the similarity between the Latin verbs 'to lead' (*duco*) and 'to seduce' (*seduco*) to describe Edward II as '*ductus, quin verius seductus*' ('led, or in fact, more accurately, seduced') by the Younger Despenser (Robertus de Avesbury, 1889: 280).[19] The vocabulary of seduction evokes the favourite's manipulation of the ruler with a view to his own self-interest; but, crucially, it is through their erotic appeal that seducers do (and, apparently, Hugh was deemed to have done) the manipulating.

The *Scalacronica* (2005: 91) tells us that at this point opposition to the king by the magnates of the land continued because, among other things, of the 'dissolute life which he led, and because of Hugh, whom at the time he loved and trusted completely'. It adds that, while under Hugh's influence, Edward 'gave himself completely to that which debarred him from chivalry, delighting himself in avarice and the delights of the flesh' (*Scalacronica*, 2005: 91). Whatever else they may cover (such as gluttonous pleasures), there is little doubt that the 'delights of the flesh' alluded to here include those of the lustful variety. We are not told that the king and his chamberlain indulged lustful 'delights' with each other, but it is notable that, within a Christian conceptual economy, same-sex sexual activity could only be understood in terms of lust (there being no legitimate, sinless way in which it could be expressed). At any rate, the passage constructs the picture of a leader who, under the sway of his beloved, is indiscriminately given to a number of cardinal sins, pointing towards the corrupt quality of his rule.

Hugh proved ruthless in asserting and pursuing his self-interest (*Vita*, 2005: 195), undermining in the process whatever was left of Edward's authority to such an extent that the earls were eloquent like never before in articulating how the king's legitimacy, and the whole political order, hung in the balance. If the king refused to dismiss Hugh or try him, they would disown him as king and take justice in their own hands by seeking revenge on Hugh; these extreme, unlawful measures were justified because, being without a king, they also lacked a judge and justice (*Vita*, 2005: 187). The barons were as good as their word, appropriating Hugh's goods and estates; and at the Parliament Edward summoned in 1321 to put a temporary end to their attacks (*Vita*, 2005: 191), they are said to have appeared in arms (Trokelowe, 1866: 109; *Anonimalle Chronicle*, 1991: 93), reiterating the threat to renounce their homage and replace the king if he failed to provide satisfaction (*Vita*, 2005: 193).

The official charges against Hugh mirror those that had been levelled at Piers, rehearsing the familiar theme of how the favourite's influence on the king undermined good government through bad counsel. According to the *Vita* (2005: 193–195), it was claimed that Hugh was bad company for the king owing to his greed, that he provided him with bad advice, and that he was an enemy of both king and kingdom. The *Gesta* (1883) contains what purports to be a transcript of the proceedings against the Despensers, where they are called 'false and terrible royal advisers, disinheritors of the Crown and destructors of the people' (69, my translation).[20]

The parliamentary rolls record, among others, the grievance that the Despensers had appropriated 'royal power over the king, his ministers, and the government of his kingdom' ('Charges against the Despensers', 1961: 30, my translation).[21] They go on to set out a theory of government to the effect that homage and the oath of allegiance were due less to the person of the king than to the office of the crown, and that those who were bound by this oath had the responsibility to take action to correct the king's ways and redress injustice if the king happened to rule against reason. This action included the use of force (as a resort to law would prove fruitless in the absence of a judge above the king himself) in accordance with the principle that the king 'is bound by his oath to govern the people and those required to render feudal service, and the latter are bound to govern in his aid and in case of his absence/incapacity' ('Charges against the Despensers', 1961: 30, my translation).[22] Such a clear articulation of principles of government is evidence not only of the abuse of the king's favour on the part of Hugh, but also of how threatening to good government the king's relationship with his male favourite was perceived to be. In the absence of anyone defending the Despensers (Hugh's father also was on trial), judgement was passed against them and they were forced into exile (*Vita*, 2005: 195, 197).[23]

The heterosexuality of the political order

When Queen Isabella and her lover Roger Mortimer led a rebellion against the king and his supporters,[24] Edward unsuccessfully attempted to sail with Hugh (who by then had returned to England) to Lundy (*Scalacronica*, 2005: 93), an island off the coast of Devon.[25] The attempt was unsuccessful, however, and both Hugh and Edward were apprehended. Hugh was put to death, without the chance of responding to the charges against him (Murimuth, 1889: 50).[26] The sentence against him is specific in relating all his misdeeds since the time of his exile. Significantly, much of the sentence is devoted to recounting his alleged crimes against Queen Isabella. In addition to putting her life in danger on several occasions, dispossessing her, persuading the king to remove himself from her and conspiring against her, Hugh is charged with always 'exciting discord between the same and her lord the king' (*Gesta*, 1883: 89, my translation).[27]

An obvious parallel immediately suggests itself between Hugh's interfering with the marital union of king and queen and his interposing his persona between the king and his kingdom, particularly the barons. Murimuth (1889: 31, my translation), for example, explains how Hugh 'guided the king at will and didn't allow anyone other than himself to be useful to him, and did not permit any nobleman of the kingdom to obtain an audience with the king except rarely, Hugh himself listening to their words and providing an answer at his own discretion'. Furthermore, as we have seen, Hugh's usurpation of governmental functions was a prominent charge in the proceedings that led to his exile. These complaints about Hugh's interference with both the private and public affairs of the king have the effect of establishing a functional equivalence between the queen and the kingdom. This equivalence, coupled with the fact that the interference in either case was deemed to have been possible because of Edward's erotic pull towards Hugh, heterosexualises the relationship between king and country, while posing same-sex desire as a threat to the well-ordered functioning of this relationship.

A similar idea emerges where the *Scalacronica* (2005: 95) reports that, after Edward's capture, the king wrote a message to the queen to the effect that he desired to remedy 'the wrongs he had done to her, and to all his men, by good governance'. The original Anglo-Norman of this passage does not specify 'men', using the possessive pronoun '*soens*' (his), so that perhaps a more accurate translation might be 'the wrongs he had done to her, and to all his *subjects*'. The passage is particularly interesting because of the connection it draws, once again, between the public and the private. Wronging the queen becomes interchangeable with wronging the subjects/country: in both cases, the wrong was committed by virtue of Edward's allegiance first with Piers and later with Hugh; and in either case – whether the wrong is private or public – 'good government' is offered as the remedy. The passage is predicated on the assumption of a heterosexualised relationship between the male ruler and his feminised country. If this is reflective of broader societal discourses heterosexualising political rule in the fourteenth century, it would seem that a same-sex attracted ruler could not fail to be perceived as a problem for good government.

Alternative discourses: deviance, moral corruption and God's disfavour

In its closing lines, the *Gesta* (1883) provides an analysis of Edward's character. In terms of his qualities as a ruler, it declares that Edward trusted more the counsel of others than his own. These others are, of course, Edward's favourites and the *Gesta* ends up by connecting the king's inappropriately self-effacing style of government, which led to his political undoing, with his erotic life. Edward was 'ardently attached to one of his associates, whom he supported to the highest degree, enriched, preferred, from whom he could not stand being apart, and honoured before all others; from this derived disgrace to the lover, opposition and ruin for the beloved, the downfall of the people and damage to the reign' *Gesta* (1883: 91, my translation).[28] This is in line with the account emerging in virtually all the sources discussed, which makes the king's vulnerability to his favourites' bad counsel the centrepiece of the construction of same-sex desire as a problem for the good exercise of public powers.

At times, however, we catch glimpses of different discourses, offering alternative rationales for the proposition that same-sex desire is a problem for good government. In particular, some sources vaguely suggest that Edward's same-sex desire is grounded in a deviant subjectivity, which in turn accounts for his weakness as a ruler. Others imply that it is related to a state of general moral corruption. Still others invoke God's disfavour for those who practice sodomy.

Consider the *Gesta*'s (1883: 91, my translation) own remark that Edward was 'handsome in body, of surpassing physical strength, but, as is commonly said, very different in his habits'. His habits needn't have been 'different' because of particular character traits invariably associated with same-sex desire – they needn't be seen as grounded in a deviant subjectivity. Yet, for a present-day reader, that interpretation may seem almost irresistible when the *Gesta* goes on to state that Edward had a ready tongue, a taste for lavish entertainment and that he ignored the company of noblemen while consorting with the likes of actors, singers, grooms and sailors.[29] A twenty-first century reader might be excused for thinking this apparently random collection of facts about Edward to be designed, if not absolutely to disprove protestations about Edward's heterosexuality, at least to strain their credibility.[30]

A subtly different account surfaces in the section of the *Flores Historiarum* authored by Robert of Reading. Robert paints Edward as a despot devoted 'to insane tyranny, the persecution of the people and the church, and other iniquitous deeds contrary to God and truth' (*Flores Historiarum*, 1890: 214, my translation). Edward's cruelty, falsity, stupidity and greed are variously decried, culminating, in the last few pages, in an invocation against the folly of a king who courted 'his own infamy', removed from his side the 'sweet conjugal embraces' of his 'generous spouse' and prized 'illicit and sinful sexual intercourse' (*Flores Historiarum*, 1890: 229, my translation). In this passage Robert of Reading seems to portray same-sex desire as an indicator not so much of a deviant subjectivity, as of a broadly corrupt nature. The imagery of sin seems to emphasise a deliberate decision to embrace evil. From this perspective, same-sex desire is the all-too-obvious private counterpart of public evildoing, which in a political leader expresses itself through tyrannical rule.

Like Robert of Reading, Thomas de Burton's *Meaux chronicle* (1867: 95) explicitly imputes sinful sexual conduct – specifically, sodomy – to Edward.[31] Unlike Robert of Reading, however, it is not mainly by invoking the idea of a corrupt nature that this chronicle (dating either from the late fourteenth century or from the turn of the fifteenth century) links Edward's same-sex desire to the weakness of his rule. Rather, having explained that, despite the request that he be sanctified, there was no proof that Edward was a saint, Burton (1867: 355) states that Edward 'delighted in the vice of Sodom very much' and that his whole reign was characterised by a lack of fortune and divine grace. The chronicle goes on to list the several losses and misfortunes experienced during his government (Burton, 1867: 355). This passage appears to argue that Edward II's government necessarily turned out to be a failure, owing to the fact that God does not extend His favour to sinners. This echoes an idea already encountered, in the context of ancient Rome. In Burton's *Meaux chronicle*, however, the idea of a lack of divine favour for Edward's reign is probably modelled on the biblical myth of God's displeasure with, and punishment of, Sodom.

The *Meaux chronicle*'s singling out same-sex sexual intercourse[32] in support of its argument that Edward was a sinner and hence would not enjoy a successful rule is an uncharacteristic way of problematising the relationship between political authority and same-sex desire in the fourteenth-century sources' treatment of Edward's reign. As we have seen, other fourteenth-century texts do not mention sodomy at all. This appears to conform to broader patterns of restraint in the deployment of sodomy charges in England at the time. It is true that a heightened concern with sodomy can be detected in Europe starting from the thirteenth century. At this time the legal preoccupation with sodomy (and sexual behaviour more generally: Karras, 2005: 21) increased. This may have been out of fear that divine punishment might be visited upon societies that harboured such sinners (Brundage, 1987: 472); or in connection with the social ascendancy of asceticism (Richards, 1990: 137), which in the thirteenth century spread from the cloister out into the world as a result of the deliberate efforts of friar orders (McNeil, 1936: 23). It is at this time too that theologians refined their theories of sodomy; in canon law, sodomy became a crime that brought with it infamy, entailing the loss of office for clerics and of civil and political rights for laymen (Goodich, 1979: 71). In continental Europe, secular penalties became harsher, the association between sodomy and heresy was consolidated, accusations of sodomy became commonplace in the context of political attacks and prosecutions became more widespread (Brundage, 1987: 472–473; Goodich, 1979: 7, 10). These developments, however, were not mirrored in England. Undeniably, under the reign of Edward's father, legal compilations of the common law appeared which prescribed burning or burying alive for sodomites (Mills, 2007: 27, 40) and noted that secular courts had the power to try those accused of sodomy alongside the established jurisdiction of ecclesiastical courts (Goodich, 1979: 77). But it looks as if these laws may not have been enforced (Mills, 2007: 40) and sodomy prosecutions for political purposes were uncommon (Karras, 2005: 142–143).[33] Edward, with his high-profile male favourites was, of course, an easy target for sodomy accusations; but for those who made same-sex desire central to their political critique of his reign, making a specific imputation of sodomy was the exception rather than the rule.

Conclusions

The principal story told by most fourteenth-century sources about the relationship between good government and same-sex desire is both simpler and subtler than the discourses examined in the last section. According to this story, Edward's same-sex desire made him vulnerable to the bad and self-interested advice of his favourites. This ran counter to understandings of the common good as the goal of government for much medieval political thought, for the common good required one to put aside private interests and subordinate kinship and friendship ties to the interest of the polity (Black, 1992: 25).

The special danger that same-sex desire poses for good government, then, is not that it is indicative of a broader state of moral corruption, nor of a deviant subjectivity, nor even that it attracts God's displeasure and his curse. Rather, for most of the sources examined, same-sex desire creates the conditions that facilitate the cultivation of bad habits in a leader. Thus, when the king was deposed, the main charge against him was that he was incompetent to rule, that he was led by poor advisers and that he willingly failed to distinguish between what was in the common interest from what ran counter to the common good, as well as to comply with the magnates' requests to remedy the wrongs done ('Charges against Edward II', 1961: 37). The second charge was that he was unwilling to listen to and believe in good advice, and to occupy himself with the task of government, preferring undignified pastimes.[34]

Thus, exclusive and intense, let alone erotic, bonds between males divert the ruler's attention from the common good and interfere with his God-given and people-endorsed role as ruler. This role, decreed by God and sanctioned by the people, is ordinarily the best guarantee of right rule or good government – government that rises above sectional interests (Black 1992: 136–137). Similarly, a lover-favourite, in seducing the king and monopolising his trust, displaces the key role that, according to medieval political thought (Black, 1992: 156–157, 159, 163), the many (barons and parliaments) rightfully had in feeding their views to the king through processes of consultation. In a context in which women's participation in the managing of public affairs was de-emphasised,[35] the potential that male same-sex desire had for disrupting these 'physiological' political processes perhaps appeared greater than in the case of different-sex relationships. The affinity of elite males with the public world of politics meant that male favourites could be assumed to be more effective in craftily exploiting their ascendant on the king, thus misleading him all the more successfully in his public functions.

Not surprisingly, perhaps, two sources that attempt to rescue the king's reputation – the *Vita et Mors* and Le Baker – conclude their small hagiography of Edward II by heterosexualising the king, who, while in captivity, is described as inconsolable over his separation from Queen Isabella 'whom he could not help loving' (*Vita et Mors*, 1883: 315, my translation). The *Vita et Mors* and Le Baker are also two of the sources for the story, probably apocryphal, of Edward's murder while in captivity. We read that Edward was incarcerated in a cell above a vault where corpses were stored, but proved immune to death from the pestilential vapours; thus, a candescent rod was inserted in his anus through a hollow horn or tube, fatally wounding him in his innards and leaving no outward sign of an orchestrated murder (*Vita et Mors*, 1883: 318; Le Baker, 1889: 33; see also Walsingham, 1863: 189; Burton, 1867: 355; *Chronicon Henrici Knighton*, 1889: 46). Historians believe that this particular account of Edward's death may be manufactured and even that, against the authority of all the chronicles, Edward might not have died in captivity (Mortimer, 2003; Moore, 1887). Be that as it may, this account of Edward's death through anal penetration is commonly regarded as a testament to the (later) belief that he engaged in passive sodomy and was punished for it.

The charges against Edward II that were used to justify his deposition do not mention sodomy as one of his crimes. Apart from the already discussed passage in Burton's *Meaux chronicle*, however, there is at least one more fourteenth-century source ascribing the crime of sodomy to the king. A text from 1334 reports that in 1326, Adam Orleton, a churchman supporting Queen Isabella, publicly denounced Edward as *tyrannus et sodomita* – tyrant and sodomite (*Register of John de Grandisson*, 1899: 1540, 1542). In this expression, the connection between poor government and same-sex desire hinges entirely on the copula '*et*', and on the fact that these two very charges – sodomy and tyranny – were singled out as representative of all that was bad about Edward II.

Mortimer (2006: 48–57) has made a strong case for the political nature and motivation of Orleton's sodomy charge. He argues the churchman was the originator of the sodomy rumour, subsequently taken up by chroniclers like Burton, and that he probably conceived the idea of making the charge following a series of visits to Avignon (at the time seat of the Papal Court) between 1307 and 1317. In Avignon, Orleton realised the potential that sodomy imputations had for spelling the undoing of powerful political actors in the context of the Templars' trials. Accordingly, he proceeded to accuse the king of sodomy in his sermons.

Omrod (2006: 28–40) has built on this account to explain why Edward's contemporaries did not impute sodomy to him. First, in the Middle Ages sodomy was not necessarily thought of as coinciding with same-sex sexual activity. Secondly, same-sex attachments, like those between Edward and his favourites, were not necessarily believed to entail same-sex sexual activity. However, once Orleton, relatively belatedly, came up with a sodomy charge against Edward II, it all gradually started to register: Edward's same-sex attachment did entail same-sex sexual activity and the category of sodomy could be used to characterise this activity. The later fourteenth-century sources thus started constructing a narrative of Edward as guilty of sodomy.

The weakness in this argument is its tendency to sidle from the idea that people in the fourteenth century did not necessarily read same-sex attachments in erotic terms towards the idea that they necessarily didn't, unless certain conditions obtained. It seems incredible that Edward's contemporaries should need Orleton to make an independent and generic sodomy accusation against the king before the notion dawned upon them that he might have had sex with his male favourites. Likewise, it seems implausible that they would need Orleton to remind them of the fact that same-sex sexual activities fell within the ambit of sodomy. The failure, on the part of the king's contemporary opponents and early detractors, to capitalise on an accusation of sodomy cannot stem from all of them being blind to the fact that Edward, with his intense attachment to Piers and his unflinching loyalty to Hugh, was a relatively obvious target for the accusation.

Zeikowitz (2003: 113–118) has downplayed the distinction between the sources that expressly make the sodomy accusations and those that do not. He has argued that even if the latter do not expressly impute sodomy to Edward, they make use of 'discursive sodomy' – that is, they sexualise the relationship between Edward and his favourites in a way that leaves the possibility of sodomy as a distinct implication. In doing so, the sources depict in a negative light certain 'homosocial and homoerotic' relationships and interactions that contemporary discourse would have otherwise 'tolerated' or even 'celebrated' as a cornerstone of 'courtly culture' (Zeikowitz, 2003: 129). The sources do so because they express the political concerns of the magnates of the realm, whose role Edward had marginalised (Zeikowitz, 2003: 114–116). This, however, assumes that those who wrote these texts, and/or the magnates whose views they reflect, appreciated the politically damaging potential of making Edward the object of sodomy rumours. If they did, however, why not make the imputation more openly, as some of the later sources did?

I have already suggested some possible reasons for the absence of express sodomy accusations in the early sources. I hypothesised the existence of discursive conventions requiring the public desexualisation of relationships of patronage. I also argued that the very fact that Edward's love appeared to be unflagging might have generated an assumption that it was not consummated. I now want to make a further suggestion, which speaks directly to the question of the specific ways in which same-sex desire was considered a problem for the good exercise of public powers in Edward's times. I want to argue that the reason why most of Edward's contemporary opponents and early fourteenth-century detractors did not charge him with sodomy was their failure to see that the imputation could add much to their case for the weakness of the king's rule.

For most of Edward's opponents the case for the weakness of the king's rule did not hinge on the degree of physical intimacy to which the king and his favourites pushed their relationship. Rather, as I have argued, it essentially hinged on the fact that the king's irresistible erotic pull towards those favourites made him vulnerable to their bad counsel and alienated him from the kingdom's magnates and his subjects. From this perspective, the king's attraction to his favourites was the cause of his poor government, by making him susceptible to their influence and willing to let them rule alongside him contrary to God's will. The king's attraction to his favourites may well have been the cause, too, of sinful physical intimacy between them. But this sexual activity was not in itself a cause of poor government. Pressed to articulate their hunch, perhaps, those who held this view would have said that a king practising sodomy was not necessarily an incompetent ruler, as long as he – unlike Edward – managed to avoid becoming hopelessly infatuated with his partners in sin. Indeed, if physical intercourse was a cure for lovesickness, the physical consummation of Edward's desire might have made him less, rather than more, sensitive to his favourites' damaging influence. So there was no particular need for many of the opponents and detractors of

Edward to openly insist specifically on the sodomy charge. The idea that there might be a causal connection between sodomitical sex and poor rule – or that Edward's poor rule was made worse by sodomitical sex – may simply have failed to register for most of them.

If Mortimer is correct, however, something like that idea did register for Orleton following his travels to France, where he became aware of successful politically motivated deployments of sodomy accusations. Thus, in Orleton's charge – as well as Robert of Reading's chronicle – a parallel and less prevalent discourse emerges about the relationship between political authority and same-sex desire. This discourse echoes, albeit in modified form, some equivalent discourses circulating in late antiquity. It also portends what appears to have been, as we will see, the prevalent way in which same-sex desire was constructed as a problem for the correct exercise of public powers in the late Victorian age. This discourse does not make a ruler's same-sex desire a potential problem for good government on account of its tendency to expose the ruler to his lovers' bad advice. Rather, it links sexual 'vice' and poor government through a more amorphous idea of moral corruption, presenting same-sex desire as the all-too-obvious private counterpart of oppressive political rule.

References

Annales Londonienses (1882) in Stubbs, W (ed.), *Chronicles of the Reigns of Edward I and Edward II*, vol i (London: Longman).

Annales Paulini (1882) in Stubbs, W (ed.), *Chronicles of the Reigns of Edward I and Edward II*, vol i (London: Longman).

Anonimalle Chronicle (1991) Childs, WR and Taylor, J (eds) (Leeds: Yorkshire Archaeological Society).

Black, A (1992) *Political Thought in Europe 1250–1450* (Cambridge: Cambridge University Press).

Boswell, J (1980) *Christianity, Social Tolerance and Homosexuality* (Chicago: University of Chicago Press).

Boswell, J (1991) *Same Sex Unions in Premodern Europe* (New York: Villiard Books).

Bruce, H (1918) *Notes Ascribed to Geoffrey le Baker, of Swinbrook* (Cardiff: William Lewis).

Brundage, JA (1987) *Law, Sex and Christian Society in Medieval Europe* (Chicago: University of Chicago Press).

Bullough, VL (1994) 'On Being a Male in the Middle Ages' in Lees, CA (ed.), *Medieval Masculinities: Regarding Men in the Middle Ages* (Minneapolis: University of Minnesota Press) 31–45.

Burgtorf, J (2008) 'With my life, his joyes began and ended': Piers Gaveston and Edward II of England Revisited' in Saul, N (ed.), *Fourteenth Century England*, vol v (Woodbridge: Boydell Press) 31–51.

Burton, T de (1867) *Chronica Monasterii de Melsa*, Bond, EA (ed.) (London: Longman).

Chaplais, P (1994) *Piers Gaveston: Edward II's Adoptive Brother* (Oxford: Oxford University Press).

'Charges against the Despensers' (1961) in Chrimes, SB and Brown, AL (eds), *Select Documents of English Constitutional History 1307–1485* (London: Adam & Charles Black) 29.

'Charges against Edward II' (1961) in Chrimes, SB and Brown, AL (eds), *Select Documents of English Constitutional History 1307–1485* (London: Adam & Charles Black) 37.

Childs, WR (2005) 'Introduction' in *Vita Edwardi Secundi* (Oxford: Oxford University Press) xv–lix.

Chronicon Henrici Knighton (1889) vol i, Lumby, JR (ed.) (London: Eyre and Spottiswide).

Chronographia Regum Francorum (1891) vol I, Moranville, H (ed.) (Paris: Libraire Renouard).

de Lauretis, T (1987) *Technologies of Gender: Essays on Theory, Film and Fiction* (Bloomington: Indiana University Press).

Dodd, G (2006) 'Parliament and Political Legitimacy in the Reign of Edward II' in Dodd, G and Musson, A (eds), *The Reign of Edward II: New Perspectives* (York Medieval Press) 165–189.

Flores Historiarum (1890) vol iii, Luard, HR (ed.) (London: Eyre and Spottiswide).

Gesta Edwardi de Carnarvan (1883) in Stubbs, W (ed.), *Chronicles of the Reigns of Edward I and Edward II*, vol ii (London: Longman).

Goodich, M (1979) *The Unmentionable Vice: Homosexuality in the Later Medieval Period* (Santa Barbara: ABC-Clio).

Haines, RM (2006) *King Edward II: His Life, His Reign, and its Aftermath, 1284–1330* (Montreal: McGill-Queen's University Press).

Hamilton, JS (1988) *Piers Gaveston, Earl of Cornwall, 1307–1312: Politics and Patronage in the Reign of Edward II* (Detroit: Wayne State University Press).

Haskins, GL (1939) 'A Chronicle of the Civil Wars of Edward II' *Speculum*, vol 14, 73–81.

Holmes, GA (1955) 'Judgement on the Younger Despenser, 1326' *English Historical Review*, vol 70, 261–270.

Ioannis Saresberiensis (1909) *Policratici*, vol i (Oxford: Clarendon Press).

Jordan, MD (1997) 'Homosexuality, *Luxuria*, and Textual Abuse' in Lochrie, K, and McCraken, P and Schultz, JA (eds), *Constructing Medieval Sexuality* (Minneapolis: University of Minnesota Press) 24–39.

Karras, RM (2005) *Sexuality in Medieval Europe: Doing Unto Others* (London: Routledge).

Kuefler, MS (2003) 'Male Friendship and the Suspicion of Sodomy in Twelfth-Century France' in Farmer, SA and Pasternack, CB (eds), *Gender Difference in The Middle Ages* (Minneapolis: University of Minnesota Press) 145–180.

Lanercost, Chronicle of (1913) Maxell, H (ed.) (Glasgow: James Maclehose).

Le Baker, G (1889) *Chronicon Galfridi le Baker de Swinebroke*, Thompson, EM (ed.), (Oxford: Clarendon Press).

Mackinnon, CA (1987) *Feminism Unmodified: Discourses on Life and Law* (Cambridge: Harvard University Press).

McNeil, JT (1936) 'Asceticism versus Militarism in the Middle Ages' *Church History*, vol 5, 3–28.

Malory, T (1996) *Le Morte d'Arthur* (Ware: Wordsworth).

Mills, R (2007) 'Male-Male Love and Sex in the Middle Ages, 1000–1500' in M Cook *et al.*, *A Gay History of Britain: Love and Sex between Men since the Middle Ages* (Oxford: Greenwood) 1–43.

Moore, SA (ed.) (1887) 'Documents Relating to the Death and Burial of King Edward II' *Archaeologia*, vol 50, 215–226.

Mortimer, I (2003) 'A Red-Hot Poker? It was just a Red Herring' *Times Higher Education Supplement*, 11 April.

Mortimer, I (2006) 'A Reconsideration of Edward II's Sodomitical Reputation' in Dodd, G and Musson, A (eds), *The Reign of Edward II: New Perspectives* (Woodbridge: York Medieval Press) 48–57.

Murimuth, A (1889) *Continuatio Chronicarum*, Thompson, EM (ed.) (London: Eyre and Spottiswide).

Musson, A (2006) 'Edward II: The Public and Private Faces of the Law' in Dodd, G and Musson, A (eds), *The Reign of Edward II: New Perspectives* (Woodbridge: York Medieval Press) 140–164.

Omrod, WM (2006) 'The Sexualities of Edward II' in Dodd, G and Musson, A (eds), *The Reign of Edward II: New Perspectives* (Woodbridge: York Medieval Press) 22–47.

'Ordinances of 1311' (1961) in Chrimes, SB and Brown, AL (eds), *Select Documents of English Constitutional History 1307–1485* (London: Adam & Charles Black) 11.

Phillips, JRS (2006) 'Introduction' in Dodd, G and Musson, A (eds), *The Reign of Edward II: New Perspectives* (Woodbridge: York Medieval Press) 1–3.

Phillips, S (2010) *Edward II* (New Haven: Yale University Press).

Polychronicon Ranulphi Higden (1871) vol iii, Lumby, JR (ed.) (London: Longman).

Prestwich, M (2003) *The Three Edwards: War and State in England, 1272–1377* (London: Routledge, 2nd edn).

Prose Brut to 1332 (2011) Pagan, H (ed.) (Manchester: Anglo-Norman Text Society).

Rajsic, J (2013) 'Prose Brut to 1332' *French Studies*, vol 63, 396–397.

Register of John de Grandisson (1899) Hingeston-Randolp, FC (ed.) (London: George Bell).

Richards, J (1990) *Sex, Dissidence and Damnation: Minority Groups in the Middle Ages* (London: Routledge).

Robertus de Avesbury (1889) *De Gestis Mirabilibus Regis Edwardi Tertii*, Thompson, EM (ed.) (London: Eyre and Spottiswide).

Scalacronica (2005) King, A (ed.) (Woodbridge: Boydell Press).

Sedgwick, EK (1985) *Love between Men: English Literature and Male Homosocial Desire* (New York: Columbia University Press).

Sponsler, C (2001) 'The King's Boyfriend' in Burger, G and Kruger, SF (eds), *Queering the Middle Ages* (Minneapolis: University of Minnesota Press) 143–167.

Trokelowe, J de (1866) *Annales* in Riley, HT (ed.), *Chronica Monasterii S Albani* (London: Longman).

Vita Edwardi Secundi (2005) (Oxford: Oxford University Press).

Vita et Mors Edwardi Secundi Regis Angliae (1883) in Stubbs, W (ed.), *Chronicles of the Reigns of Edward I and Edward II*, vol ii (London: Longman).

Walsingham, T (1863) *Historia Anglicana*, vol i, Riley, HT (ed.) (London: Longman).

Walter of Guisborough, Chronicle of (1957) Rothwell, H (ed.) (London: Royal Historical Society).

Wright, T (ed.) (1839) *The Political Songs of England, from the Reign of John to That of Edward II* (London: The Camden Society).

Zeikowitz, RE (2003) *Homoeroticism and Chivalry: Discourses of Male Same-Sex Desire in the Fourteenth Century* (New York: Palgrave-Macmillan).

Notes

1 In recent years, scholars have started rehabilitating the king's performance (see, e.g., Musson, 2006).

2 These included sodomy, indecent kissing of the belly button and anus, and wearing a small cross next to the anus (*Annales Londonienses*, 1882: 187, 189, 193).

3 If this is the case, then the author of the *Vita* had simply forgotten his Homer when he classified Achilles' love for Patroclus as love of the moderate variety.

4 The book's concluding chapter is entitled 'Adoptive Brothers or Lovers?' (Chaplais, 1994).

5 Elsewhere we are told that Edward was '*amyable trop outre mesure as ceau quil amoit*' (*Scalacronica*, 2005: 64).

6 Ironically, Chaplais's adoptive brotherhood thesis, discussed in the text, actually adds plausibility to a reading of the fourteenth-century sources along the lines I have suggested. For if Edward and Piers did enter into a brotherhood pact, this makes it likely that their contemporaries would see it as a way of disguising an amorous (in fact, sexual) bond. In this connection, Boswell (1991: 262–263) argues that same-sex brotherhood pacts became suspect when, starting from the fourteenth century, a special preoccupation with the sinful quality of same-sex sexuality took hold in Western Europe. Compare Mills (2007: 11).

7 As Karras (2005: 147) notes, however, sexual elements must have been a frequent occurrence in passionate medieval same-sex pair bondings.

8 For example, some sources (Trokelowe, 1866: 65; *Flores Historiarum*, 1890: 139) state that he was granted the earldom of Cornwall, which properly pertained to the Crown.

9 Political songs may have been written by educated people rather than being the creation of the common folk (Phillips, 2010: 19).

10 The Trokelowe *Annales* (1866: 67, my translation) report that the king, 'who was bearing with much distress Piers's absence', had Piers marry his niece to make his return from Ireland more acceptable. According to the *Vita* (2005: 7) Edward arranged the marriage to improve his standing. Elsewhere the *Vita* (2005: 9) clarifies (albeit mistakenly: Hamilton, 1988: 19) that Piers was not of noble birth (the *Annales Paulini* (1882: 258, 259, my translation) even claim that he was 'raised from the dust' and 'elevated from dung'). Furthermore, Piers was an alien from Gascony and the *Vita* (2005: 5, 9) argues that his foreignness had much to do with his being disliked. For contemporary gay readers it is difficult not to speculate that Edward's marrying Piers to his niece also had something to do with a desire on the king's part to establish a formal kinship tie with the man for whom he had an 'unswerving love' (*Vita*, 2005: 9), akin to Alexander's marrying Stateira's sister to Hephaistion.

11 After Piers's return from Ireland, Edward and he, according to the *Vita* (2005: 17), indulged their desire for intimacy by spending Christmas at Langley – a place for which the king felt much fondness. The last remark, which the *Vita* makes in

passing, acquires a special poignancy after we learn that it is precisely to Langley that, after Piers's murder, Edward would have the remains of Piers translated (*Vita*, 2005: 103; *Flores Historiarum*, 1890: 153) and buried 'with the greatest honours' (*Annales Paulini*, 1882: 271, my translation), the body wrapped in a triple cloth of gold (Phillips, 2010: 241).

12 *Magna Carta* provided a legal basis for baron-led action against a monarch who failed to respect the agreements concerning his subjects' freedoms (Black, 1992: 151).

13 Probably, the barons chose a parliamentary context to circumscribe the king's powers less out of a regard for constitutionalism, than because being seen to act in the name of the community shielded them from accusations of self-interest (Dodd: 2006, 174–179).

14 According to the *Annales Londonienses* (1882: 202–203) Edward also wrote to the Mayor of London under the great seal to instruct him to publicly declaim a proclamation of Piers's loyalty.

15 The *Vita* (2005: 53), in reporting the king's reaction to the news of Piers's death, is characteristically discreet: on the one hand it assimilates the two men's relationship to one of kinship by blood, arguing that Edward mourned Piers like a father his son; at the same time it makes a veiled allusion to the homoerotic nature of their bond, where it likens the king's lament for Piers to that of David for Jonathan, which, famously, expressed a love surpassing the love of women. Interestingly, as we have seen, the *Vita* had begun by *contrasting* the unusualness of Edward's love for Piers with the (purported) usualness of David's love for Jonathan or Achilles' love for Patroclus; by the time of Piers's death, these relationships are considered analogous. If the relationships are alike in terms of the depth of feeling that characterises them (as expressed by Edward at the time of Piers's death), but nonetheless remain different, then it seems to me that the difference on which the *Vita* had initially insisted can plausibly mean only one thing: that the relationship between Edward and Piers went beyond the realm of platonic feeling and involved sexual intimacy.

16 The office of Chamberlain entailed an ability to control others' opportunities to have an audience with the king (Sponsler, 2001: 147).

17 This was completed three decades after Edward's deposition (Bruce, 1918: 7).

18 The *Vita et Mors* (1883) was probably originally written some decades after Edward's deposition. It has survived in altered and interpolated form from Elizabethan manuscripts (lvii–lxxv).

19 The *Flores Historiarum* (1890: 151), the *Annales Londonienses* (1882: 204) and the *Gesta Edwardi de Carnarvan* (1883: 34) (another source believed to be largely contemporary) apply the epithet 'seducer' to Piers rather than Hugh.

20 The transcript reports that the Younger Despenser used his influence to introduce his father into the royal circle, and how thereafter the Despensers proceeded to appropriate 'the leadership of the kingdom and royal power, to the king's dishonour' (*Gesta*, 1883: 66, my translation), and to usurp governmental functions, including by dismissing legitimate officials and appointing corrupt ones (66–67, my translation). The *Anonimalle Chronicle* (1991: 93) states that Hugh illegitimately assumed royal power leaving the king unwilling to resist him.

21 There are five versions of the charges against the Despensers. The one recorded on the parliamentary roll is the final official version (Phillips, 2010: 389–393).

22 The same theory of government appears, verbatim, in the *Annales Londonienses* (1882: 153–154) and, in Latin, in the *Gesta* (1883: 33–34, 65). In the *Annales Londonienses* (1882) it is presented as part of the case against Piers Gaveston in

the 1308 Parliament, which led to his exile; in the *Gesta* it appears both on the occasion of the 1308 Parliament indicting Piers and 1321 Parliament indicting the Despensers.

23 The Younger Despenser is said to have spent this time at sea, engaged in acts of piracy (*Scalacronica*, 2005: 91).

24 For a discussion of how the French historian Jean Froissart (writing probably towards the end of the fourteenth century) depicts Isabella and her heterosexuality as triumphant in the mission to secure the dynastic line for Edward III against the machinations of Hugh, who had estranged the queen from her husband, see Sponsler (2001: 148–151).

25 There is a romantic quality to the description in the *Vita et Mors* (1883: 309) of Lundy Island as a mythical land of plenty, where, additionally, an intriguing reference appears to the island being rich in a particular kind of fowl, 'which Alexander Neckam calls the birds of Ganymede'. Ganymede being the youth beloved by Zeus (who abducted him in the guise of an eagle to make him cupbearer of the gods), this might be a coded homoerotic allusion. Boswell (1980: 250–252) points out that the myth of Ganymede was well known in the Middle Ages. See also Karras (2005: 146) and Richards (1990: 137).

26 Hugh was hanged, decapitated, drawn and quartered (*Polychronicon*, 1871: 322).

27 An Anglo-Norman version of the sentence against Hugh appears in the *Chronicon Henrici Knighton* (1889: 437–441) and a better version in the same language in Holmes (1955: 261–270). According to the *Polychronicon* (1871: 318), the Despensers had got Edward to have the queen and his son (who at the time were in France – Isabella's native land – and refusing to return) publicly banished as traitors. Similarly, according to the *Anonimalle Chronicle* (1991), in 1325 Hugh successfully pleaded that Edward should stay in England with him (who would otherwise be in danger), rather than join his wife at the French court, where Queen Isabella had been sent to parley about the dispute over Gascony; accordingly, the queen was in distress as if she had 'lost her lord' (121).

28 An almost identical passage appears in the *Polychronicon* (1871: 298).

29 The last point vaguely portends one of the distinctive ways in which, as we will see, same-sex desire will be seen as a problem for the political order in the twentieth century – namely, through its tendency to 'radicalise' elite public officials by encouraging them to keep company with their social inferiors.

30 Interestingly, the *Scalacronica*'s (2005: 95) description of Edward's personality, in capturing the inevitability of his weakness as a political leader, also surprisingly resonates with what we tend to understand as relatively modern stereotypes about gay duplicitous subjectivities: 'affable in conversation but malevolent in deed'. Consider also Murimuth's (1889) statement that when Edward was called upon to abdicate the throne while in captivity, he tearfully replied that he was very sorry 'that this was the extent to which he deserved his authority in the eyes of the people; but he said that, since he could not be otherwise, he was pleased that his son was so acceptable to all the people as to succeed him' (51, my translation). The expression 'since he could not be otherwise' is enigmatic, for, being preceded by the question of the extent to which Edward had deserved ('*demeruit*') his authority to govern, one would expect the next clause to be 'since he could not have *done* otherwise'. Looking at the clause 'since he could not be otherwise' with eyes accustomed to the use of arguments about the innate nature of sexual orientation in support of gay-affirmative strategies, it is hard not to read in it the king's plea for the inevitability of his feeling sexually drawn to males. This interpretation would suggest that in the fourteenth century, sexual desire could be seen as marking subjectivities (the way one 'is'), rather than merely impelling one to action.

The *Prose Brut* – a popular text in later medieval England (Rajsic, 2013) – may also be seen as gesturing towards a wayward subjectivity in its insistence on the inverted orientation of Edward's affections, which it presents as lying at the root of Edward's poor government. Thus we are told of the discord between him and the people, and that he loved those his father had detested and bore ill will against the 'good and loyal' (*Prose Brut to 1332*, 2011: 186; compare the closely related *Anonimalle Chronicle*, 1991: 81, 83). The charges brought against the king when he was deposed beckon a similar construction where they conclude that the king was 'incorrigible', with no hope that he would improve ('Charges against Edward II', 1961: 37–38). Incorrigibility suggests that Edward's poor government, via his subjection to his favourites' bad advice, was due to ingrained character flaws.

31 The *Chronographia Regum Francorum* (1891), a fifteenth-century work from France, also explicitly mentions sodomy where it states that Edward, 'having abandoned his very own spouse, surrendered himself to sodomitical filth . . . preferring unnatural intercourse to natural desire' (285, my translation).

32 'Sodomy' could potentially apply to all sorts of non-procreative sexual behaviour, but often it was used to refer specifically to male same-sex anal sex (Karras, 2005: 134–135).

33 Karras (2005: 143) suggests that this may be due to the availability, in England, of the accusation of being a Lollard as a tool to delegitimise political opponents.

34 Edward was much criticised for being given to rustic pursuits (*Vita*, 2005: 69).

35 This is best illustrated by the essentially ceremonial functions to which the late medieval queen – whose household was separate from the king's – was relegated (Sponsler, 2001: 149).

Chapter 3

The Early Modern Age: King James, effeminacy and spineless policy

Introduction

The publication of *The Court and Times of James the I* in 1849 presented to the public for the first time in its entirety Robert Folkestone's eighteenth-century compendium of historically significant letters, written by different personalities that had moved about the court of Queen Elizabeth's successor. In the introduction, the book's editor, Thomas Birch (1849: viii) summarises the character of King James's reign as follows: 'In short, it was the age of the Gavestones and the De Spencers revived, without that energy in public opinion that pursued these minions with so signal a punishment.' James having died a natural death while still reigning, public opinion could be blamed for being unreasonably indulgent in sparing him the treacherous, sexualised and sadistic execution that it was reported had been inflicted on Edward. By the mid-nineteenth century, then, for some historians at least, the example of Edward II could function as a paradigm of all that could go badly wrong with government when rulers fell prey to same-sex desire.

The same perception was already circulating in James's own time, as illustrated in Christopher Marlowe's play *Edward II*. First published in 1594, the play deals with many of the themes I examined in the previous chapter, albeit with more nuance and moral complexity than contemporary historical accounts of Edward's reign. Gaveston is portrayed both as genuinely in love with Edward and interested in controlling him (Marlowe, 1995: 325–326); the queen is both a wronged wife robbed of her love by Piers (332, 338, 357) and an adulterous traitress who plots her husband's death (376, 387–388); and same-sex desire is presented at one time as both natural[1] and a problem for good government.[2] While the real villain and tyrant in the drama ends up being the queen's lover Mortimer – who becomes *de facto* ruler after the king's imprisonment (Marlowe, 1995: 393, 401) – the play also makes it hard not to blame the sorry state of the kingdom on Edward. For it is his blind devotion to his lover that acts as a catalyst for the tragedy. Nowhere is this best dramatised as when Edward, having been apprised of Piers's death, declares: 'O shall I speak, or shall I sigh and die?' (Marlowe, 1995: 365). The private commitments of the same-sex lover (mourning and dying of a broken heart) and the public commitments of the statesman (speaking to have his commands executed) are presented as mutually exclusive; the play makes it obvious that Edward's main failing as a ruler has been, throughout, his temperamental bias towards the former kind of commitments.[3]

Another illustration of the fact that Edward II's treatment of his male favourites had, by the time of James I, come to symbolise the dangers posed by same-sex desire to political rule can be found in John Hacket's *Scrinia Reserata* – a biography of Archbishop John Williams, adviser to the seventeenth-century king. In trying to explain why James's favourite George Villiers suffered a downfall despite being – in the author's relatively unorthodox view – of virtuous and honourable character, Hacket (1693: 39) explains that being a favourite is 'Inauspicious in almost all Examples'. This is because of the inevitable resentment and disappointment a king's favourite will engender when making difficult decisions about whom to advance. Therefore, Hacket (1693: 40) concludes, 'not only *Ahasuerus* his *Aman, Tiberius* his *Seianus, Edward* the Second his *Gaveston*, and such corrupt ones, must needs decline faster then they got up, but the most circumspect that possess such a room'. Three centuries after Edward's death, his reputation for weak rule was so well established that his favourite could be singled out as the epitome of a corrupt administrator.

Nonetheless, it is clear that for Hacket there is no necessary connection between same-sex desire and corrupt rule. Edward II – and the other two rulers Hacket mentions: Tiberius and Ahasuerus[4] – may have illustrated the potential for a ruler's same-sex desire to result into despotism. But Hacket (1693: 39) was adamant that, unlike them, James had been a good ruler regardless of the king's penchant for handsome males:

> I pray the Reader to consider the sweetness of the king's Nature, (for I ascribe it to that cause) that from the time He was 14 Years old . . . he began . . . to clasp some one *Gratioso* in the Embraces of his great Love, above all others.

Indeed, no sooner had the teenage James become King James VI of Scotland than he had singled out for special favour and affection the first such '*gratioso*' – Esmé Stewart, later Duke of Lennox. The king's partiality to Lennox – coupled with suspicions about the religious alliances of the latter – spelt the favourite's undoing soon enough. Scottish noblemen and the recently reformed Scottish Church became wary of his power and arranged for his exile (Croft, 2003: 15–16).[5] Marlowe's play – staged as it was after the Lennox affair had run its course – may well have been intended as a cautionary tale for, or about, James VI of Scotland.[6]

In sum, the story of Edward II appears to have been one of the mainstays – as James himself apparently well knew (Young, 2000: 58) – of the discursive repertoire on which early modern texts could draw when commenting upon the relationship between political authority and same-sex desire.[7] Alongside the case of Edward II, examples of famous same-sex bonds from antiquity also continued to be referenced. Thus *Corona Regia* (2010: 79–87) – a 1615 satire purporting to have been authored by the humanist Isaac Casaubon and published in London – expressly compared James to both Hadrian (for bestowing favours on his favourite merely because of his beauty) and Elagabalus (for his lack of sexual continence).[8]

As we have seen, Edward's rule has passed down to history as disastrous. James I has had his fair share of bad press and some of the arguments centred on same-sex desire that were used against Edward II's rule were redeployed by James's detractors. It does not seem, however, that James and Edward were particularly alike in their approach to governing and in the interest they took in public affairs.[9] Some of the charges levelled at James's government, rather than being justified by his own failings, may have been resuscitated against him simply because they could be. By the seventeenth century, certain understandings about the danger that same-sex desire posed for political rule – understandings that crystallised particularly vividly in historical accounts of Edward II's reign – had become part of 'common sense'. James being same-sex attracted provided a convenient excuse for his opponents to capitalise on these understandings. Even apart from any malicious intent, these understandings are likely to have provided part of the conceptual framework through which James's rule and conduct became intelligible (albeit in a distorted way) to many of his observers.

Elizabeth's legacy and James's subordination of public duties to private pleasures

James's seventeenth-century critics maintained that the king did not measure up to the standard set by his immediate predecessor Elizabeth (May, 1812: 3; *Tom-Tell-Troath*, 1809: 429).[10] In the 1650s, Weldon (1817) drew a subtle but eloquent contrast between the two monarchs in the very subtitle of his book, using the adjective 'ever-glorious' to describe Queen Elizabeth while leaving King James without the benefit of a qualifier. Importantly for our purposes, James's critics used his liability to same-sex desire as part of the explanation for why he failed to live up to Elizabeth's example. Thus, Osborne's 1658 *Historical Memoires* questions the legitimacy of James's and Elizabeth's reasons for public spending. Osborne (1689: 477) claims that James's weakness for handsome young men was not the '*lightest*' of his '*frailties*', as it doubled 'the *weight* of his *Oppression:* For the setting up of these *Golden Calves* cost *England* more than *Queen Elizabeth* spent in all her Wars'.[11] The fact that Osborne makes such an absurd charge in all seriousness speaks volumes about the ease with which James's same-sex desire could be manipulated for political ends.

In Osborne's passage, the idolisation of handsome (but false) objects of worship by this king ridden with 'frailties' stands in contrast with his female predecessor's martial spiritedness. If we are to judge by one of the comments with which

Birch intersperses Folkestone's collection of letters from James's own time, by the mid-nineteenth century this sexualised contrast between Elizabeth's rule and James's government was well established:

> Favouritism has often been urged against Queen Elizabeth as one of her worst faults; but ... those on whom she bestowed her favour held rank amongst the most gallant of her subjects; and ... we must not forget her position and celibacy, and the sex of her favourites. Her successor chose to gratify his inclinations by selecting from *his own sex* such as possessed personal recommendations only: for to handsome countenance and well-shaped limbs he was as sensitive as a schoolgirl.
>
> (Folkestone, 1848: 372)

Birch adds in a footnote: 'Raleigh [Elizabeth's favourite] was a living reproach to the effeminate coxcombs who clustered round their effeminate king' (Folkestone, 1848: 87). In these passages Birch's text explicitly establishes a relation of continuity between heterosexuality, gender conformity and well-considered political decisions, while linking same-sex desire and effeminacy with arbitrary and immature public decision-making. However, it is because these links emerge fairly clearly from seventeenth-century sources that Birch was able to articulate them so casually two centuries later.

One of the ways in which seventeenth-century sources establish an association between same-sex desire and immature decision-making is by depicting James (as had been the case with Edward II) as uninterested in government and devoted to pleasurable and whimsical pastimes, variously linking the pursuit of these to his sexuality. The satirical work *Corona Regia* – possibly the first text where James's sexuality was discussed in print (Schleiner, 2010: 12) – exemplifies this. After reproaching James for wasting his time on pleasures (*Corona Regia*, 2010: 87), the book mentions the king's passion for hunting, but goes on to clarify that the preys James favours are 'attractive and graceful and need not be tracked down' (91). There immediately follows an allegorical reference to same-sex intercourse, complete with an allusion to the king's erect penis poking around his lovers' hirsute backside regions: 'So you use a different kind of spear, you search through a different kind of underbush, and you capture different kinds of pleasure' (*Corona Regia*, 2010: 91). The text goes on to connect this passion for hunting to the birthmark James apparently sported on his chest, which some said resembled a lion (*Corona Regia*, 2010: 91); but it then suggests that the mark may look more like a toad or indeed is simply a 'formless blotch arising from a defect of nature' (93). Given the text's linking of the mark with the king's same-sex sexual activities, it seems that the argument here is that same-sex desire (which, as we have seen, causes a ruler to stint the time he devotes to public affairs) is grounded in a 'defect of nature'. This is indicative of a 'minoritising' understanding of sodomy as the vice of constitutionally defective males, which contrasts with the more usual 'universalising' early modern understanding of sodomy as debauchery, to which potentially we may all fall prey (Bray, 1995: 16).

Verse libels – a diverse genre of oral and printed material that frequently used sexual innuendo in the service of political critique (Bellany, 1994: 286, 292) – provide another illustration of the argument that James's same-sex desire inclined him to private pastimes rather than public affairs. In one of these libels, the relationship between James and his favourite George Villiers is sexualised by comparing it to that between Jove and Ganymede, suggesting that the king neglected public affairs to pursue the pleasures of the flesh (Bellany, 1994: 297).

Weldon's seventeenth-century historical work employs a similar strategy. He (1817: 16) claims that the king's ministers 'persuaded the king to leave the State affairs to them, and to betake himself unto some Country recreations, that they found him addicted unto, for the City, and business did not agree with him'. Crucially, James's preference for private pursuits over the public business of governing is described in terms of 'addiction' and the addiction is accounted for in terms of same-sex desire: James needed the leisure and seclusion of country life less to engage in rustic pursuits than to 'enjoy his Favourite with more privacy' (Weldon, 1817: 16).[12] Weldon (1817: 17) goes on to say that the king 'gloried in' enlarging the park of his country residence and stocking it with deer more than his predecessors did in conquering France – clearly meaning that James got the balance between private pursuits and public duties all wrong. He then reports that the king cared more for animals than for humans,[13] which revealed the 'weakness of his Judgement, and poorness of his spirit' (Weldon, 1817: 17). Taken together, these passages may be read as portraying the king's preferences (private pleasures over public duties, love of animals over love of people, and his enjoyment of male favourites) as expressions of generally poor judgement. Thus Weldon's text oscillates between representing same-sex desire as the cause of a lack of public spiritedness and presenting both homoerotic desire and the lack of commitment to public duties as symptoms of a certain kind of defective subjectivity.

The idea that James's bias towards both private diversions and same-sex desire is the result of a flawed temperament appears quite clearly in Hutchinson's (1848: 84) claim that James's son 'king Charles was temperate, chaste and serious; so that the fools and bawds, mimics and catamites, of [James's] court, grew out of fashion'. Here, same-sex desire (conjured up by the mention of 'catamites') is not the cause of James's lack of proper concern with public affairs, but a symptom of a flawed character – a lack of seriousness that also disables James from being a good ruler. Interestingly, however, the kind of mismanagement that same-sex attracted rulers like James will deliver is not necessarily the worst. For, as Hutchinson (1848: 84) clarifies, Charles turned out to be 'a worse encroacher upon the civil and spiritual liberties by far than his father' (primarily, it would appear, on account of his Catholic sympathies). Thus, for Hutchinson, the damage that can be wrought by a thoughtful and potentially virtuous ruler who deliberately chooses the wrong exceeds that which is merely the result of another ruler's temperamental bias towards levity and lasciviousness – even lasciviousness of the same-sex variety.

Same-sex desire as a cause of public wrongs

What is, for writers like Hutchinson, the nature of the acts of mismanagement of which James was guilty? What does it have to do with his same-sex desire? A range of answers to this question emerges from seventeenth-century sources. These include the idea that same-sex desire led James to make arbitrary distinctions among his subjects; that it set a bad example; that it was incompatible with the gravity of public work; and that (as an expression of a more general inclination towards sexual incontinence) it got the king and his officials to favour unduly permissive laws. Alternatively, in some cases, the link between poor government and same-sex desire is established rhetorically, without specifying particular acts of mismanagement and without articulating in what sense same-sex desire occasioned them.

Hutchinson (1848: 78) complains about James conferring honours to those who did not have 'blood', 'estates' or 'merit'. This imputation implies an attack on James's same-sex desire as the cause of this inappropriate conferral of privileges, for it was a general criticism of James that he bestowed favour on such irrelevant grounds as the physical attractiveness of the recipients. Thus, Hutchinson (1848: 84) later declares that the riches and titles acquired by James's favourite Villiers were granted 'upon no merit but that of his beauty and his prostitution'. For Hutchinson (1848: 78) James also ruled badly because he set bad examples: given the king's lack of seriousness, and the loose sexual morals that were evidence of it, his court was 'a nursery of vice and intemperance'.[14] Significantly, sexual misdeeds make up the lion's share of the crimes Hutchinson (1848: 78) lists as a consequence of James's bad example: '[T]hen began murder, incest, adultery, drunkenness, swearing, fornication, and all sorts of ribaldry, to be not concealed but countenanced vices, because they held such conformity with the court's example.' This is in accordance with her argument that the weakness of James's rule stemmed mainly from his loose morals and the example they set, rather than being, as in Charles's case, a matter of deliberately choosing the wrong kind of policies.

A concern with the king's oversexed attitude and lack of seriousness, and the bad example he hence set, is also evident in *Corona Regia* (2010: 89), which criticises James for being a king who made a show of his lusts, 'cast[ing] off severity'. The text goes on to imply that James's same-sex desire – or at least the fact that he acted on it – is incompatible with the gravity required for the task of government: 'You enjoy Alcibiades and you can philosophize; you are a king and you act like Socrates; you make love and you are pious' (*Corona Regia*, 2010: 91). James cannot hope, that is, to enjoy true wisdom (as displayed by those who truly 'philosophize') and virtue (being 'pious') *as well as* an Alcibiades at the same time. Indeed, sexually enjoying the beautiful

Alcibiades, when the youth had offered himself, was just the course of action dismissed by Socrates (Plato, 1994), the *true* philosopher (unlike James, whose work in political philosophy – discussed later – the text here implicitly dismisses as counterfeit). In any case, the gravity required of a ruler is of a different order from that typical of philosophers, the text implies; so that the oversexed James, who is not a Socrates but merely *poses* as one, is in fact twice removed from the task of successful rule.

Edward Peyton's *The Divine Catastrophe of the Kingly Family of the House of Stuarts* echoes some of Hutchinson's grounds for critique.[15] Peyton's (1811: 301) text establishes a connection between the Stuarts' sexual crimes and the injustice of their rule at the very outset of his book, through its use of polysemic terminology in the subtitle: 'wherein the most secret and chamber-abominations of the last kings are discovered, Divine justice in king Charles his overthrow vindicated'. The expression 'most secret and chamber-abominations' seems to allude at one time both to private sexual depravities and corrupt institutional processes. Both the reference to secrecy and the use of the word 'chamber' – a bedroom but also a room where official legal business is conducted – are key here. Other texts from the same period show that 'secrecy' is often associated with sodomy.[16] At the same time, secrecy, once read in conjunction with 'chamber', conjures up the inquisitorial proceedings of the dreaded Star Chamber. The idea of divine punishment reinforces this twinning of private vices and public crimes, for if God's retribution consists in debarring the Stuarts from ruling the country, it is all of their 'abominations' (including private sexual vices) that occasion God's ire. For readers steeped in biblical imagery, the mention of divine punishment must have immediately brought Sodom to mind, suggesting fairly clearly the nature of the Stuarts' crimes.

In fact, when referring specifically to James's sexual preferences, Peyton (1811: 346) is uncommonly direct, stating that he was 'more addicted to love males then females' and 'never lodged with [the queen] a night for many years'. Peyton (1811), after deploring James's scandalous relationship with Villiers (348), goes on to produce a list of public misdeeds under James's rule: 'divers incests were . . . pardoned', as was murder (Peyton specifically mentions that of a man who was killed by another he had rebuked for drunkenness and 'whoring'); people were allowed to dance around maypoles, thus 'breaking the Sabbath'; 'all impiety was incouraged'; and 'lawful marriages were divorced' (350–351). As in the case of Hutchinson, Peyton's puritanical sensibility emphasises public acts affecting sexual conduct. Even the murder case he refers to has a sexual element ('whoring'); and one of the grounds for Puritans' objections to maypoles was their phallic symbolism (Marcus, 1986: 155). The link between James's and his court's loose morals (with an emphasis on same-sex desire) and bad rule is apparent, although Peyton's account is slightly different from Hutchinson's because it adds an intentional element to James's poor government. While Hutchinson seems to suggest that under James's rule the country fell into waywardness because of James's bad example, for Peyton (1811: 364) the generalised 'licentiousness' and 'prophaneness' characterising all classes at the time was 'connived at by many debauched in authority' through 'want of ordinances'. In other words, poor government here consists in a penury of laws, which is the intended result of the government preferring licence over well-ordered liberty – with (sexual) 'licentiousness' figuring as the paradigmatic instance of licence.[17]

Osborne is possibly even more explicit in linking James's sexuality to poor government. At the beginning of his *Historical Memoires*, Osborne (1689: 412) states that the historian's task is to set down the cure for the 'Diseases of the Body Politik'; and he invokes the common good to justify the necessity 'to dissect and make inspection into the defects of a *dead king*' (409). In particular, providing a record of '*wicked, effeminate* and *ill-consulted Princes*' now dead acts as a restraining factor on those who are alive (Osborne, 1689: 409). The king's 'defects' are here portrayed as directly relevant to the common good; and effeminacy, alongside wickedness and being 'ill consulted', has pride of place among such defects. Importantly, the following passage makes it apparent that effeminacy – understood both in terms of gender presentation and as a gender-marked subjectivity – is, in Osborne's (1689: 476–477) view, not readily separable from same-sex desire:

> [T]he *love* the king shewed [his favourites] was as *amorously* conveyed, as if he had mistaken their Sex, and *thought* them Ladies. Which I have seen *Somerset* and *Buckingham* labour to *resemble*, in the effeminateness of their *dressings*. Though in w----- Looks and wantone Gestures they *exceeded* any part of *Womankind* . . . Nor was his love, or whatever else *posterity* will please to call it . . . *carried* on with *discretion* . . .; for the *kings* kissing them after so *lascivious* a mode in *publick* . . . prompted many to imagine some things done in *Tyring-house*, that exceed my *expressions* no less than they do my *experience*.

Because the text here constructs 'womankind' as sexually excessive, the effeminacy of James and his favourites seems primarily a charge of sexual intemperance. This is consistent with the argument that early modern constructions of effeminacy were centred, as in antiquity, on the idea of deficient self-control and a lack of moderation (King, 2004: 66–73).[18] However, it does not follow that effeminacy was unrelated to same-sex desire.[19] While for early modern writers there may have not been a necessary connection between effeminacy and same-sex desire (King, 2004: 64–67), I would argue that there was a logical one: sodomy was a characteristic vice of those excessively given to sensual delights (Bray, 1995: 16), but it was precisely effeminacy that marked the subjectivity of those who lacked moderation in the pursuit of bodily pleasure (King, 2004: 67–68). While Osborne is careful to distance himself from same-sex sexual experience – claiming he is literally at a loss for words to describe it – he makes clear that James's and his (male) favourites' intemperance was directed towards one another; and it was apparently the 'effeminateness' of their looks that elicited, or heightened, reciprocal sexual interest. Thus, gender presentation (effeminacy as the 'effeminateness' of one's looks), gender subjectivity (effeminacy as wantonness and intemperance) and same-sex sexuality co-implicate each other in Osborne's account.[20] If effeminacy implies same-sex desire (and vice versa) in Osborne's text, then his description of James as a prince that was '*wicked, effeminate* and *ill consulted*' rhetorically establishes a generic link between same-sex desire and dysfunctional rule, which – coming as it does at the very outset of the book – is foundational to the text as a whole. This results in an implicit (homo) sexualisation of all the different instances of poor government that Osborne imputes to the king. In some cases, however, the connection is articulated in more specific terms, as when Osborne (1689: 448) claims that the judges of the Star Chamber – 'that Den of Arbitrary Justice' – were in the habit of indicting those who 'refused to worship' James's favourites.

The pamphlet *Tom-Tell-Troath* (1809: 449) mirrors Osborne's approach (i.e. it links same-sex desire and bad rule both at a generic level and in more specific ways). Thus, the pamphlet *specifically* connects same-sex desire to poor government through *argument* in one instance, where it suggests that the king's male lovers were able to appropriate power and honours by blackmailing the king. Otherwise, it is through *rhetorical* flourish that the connection between private vices and public wrongs is established, and then only in *generic* terms. There are at least two instances of the pamphlet doing so. First, we are told that the king wished 'to make himself absolute and dissolute' (*Tom-Tell-Troath*, 1809: 449), the former adjective indexing public wrongdoing and the second private sinfulness. Secondly, there is an explicit reference to private vices specifically of the same-sex variety, where the pamphlet intimates that the king's relationships with other holders of public office are organised precisely around the principle of same-sex desire:

> Hee may solace himselfe as securely in his bedchamber as the Grand Signor in his Seraglio; have lords spirituall for his mates, lords temporall for his eunuchs, and whom hee will for his Incubus. There may hee kisse his minions without shame, and make his grooms his companions without danger.
> (*Tom-Tell-Troath*, 1809: 449)

The king's public spouse

Wilson's approach differs from that of the writers discussed so far. Instead of stating or implying that same-sex desire is a cause of poor government, Wilson contributes to a discourse – in which James himself participated – aimed at a rhetorical heterosexualisation of the relationship between the ruler and the ruled, conceived as a political marriage. Within the parameters of this discourse, James's male favourites figure as disruptors of marital harmony.

Writing in the mid-seventeenth century, Wilson is critical of James's reign, but he avoids drawing a necessary connection between same-sex desire and poor government. To begin with, Wilson's discussions of same-sex love read as non-judgemental. Thus, when talking about James's favourite Robert Carr and his female paramour, Wilson (1653: 59) treats same-sex and heterosexual love as functionally and morally equivalent ('thus did the Viscount get the *Conquest* of two, the *king*, and this *Lady*'). Wilson (1653: 59) even implies that Carr's primary duties as a lover should have been to James ('every hour the *Viscount* could steal from his *Royal Master*, he dedicated it to this disloyall *Mistris*'). He also makes it clear that same-sex love in itself is no bar to virtue, but that a heterosexual relationship with the wrong woman is ('if [Carr] had not met with such a *Woman*, he might have been a good man') (Wilson, 1653: 83). Wilson's text, then, treats same-sex desire as morally unremarkable in itself, conveying as much by exploiting the definitional ambiguity (Hammond, 2002) characterising much early modern discourse on same-sex bonds. This allows Wilson to couch his statements on same-sex desire in a way that makes them just about capable of being interpreted as observations on male *philia* (an ostensibly asexual form of close same-sex friendship) rather than same-sex erotic attachments. At the same time, for those willing to see, the erotic quality of James's same-sex bonds is never far below the surface of Wilson's text. Thus, occasionally Wilson (1653: 79) sounds like a veritable connoisseur of male-to-male love ('about this time the king cast his eye upon a Gentleman so rarely *moulded*, that he meant to make him a *Masterpeece*').

Wilson's non-judgemental attitude to same-sex desire does not mean, however, that he thought desire irrelevant to government. Indeed, in Wilson's (1653: 59) view, sexual passion posed distinct problems for political rule, for lust tends to be 'the *Consumption* of all *Reason*'. Even assuming that he shared the common early modern view that *sodomy* signalled a lack of moderation, Wilson did not claim that same-sex desire had a special ability to induce a loss of self-control. But Wilson (1653) – preoccupied with situations where 'the *sensitive* faculties get predominance over the *Reason*' (146) – did think that James's same-sex desire had got out of hand, causing the king's undoing:

> [T]here was a reciprocall Harmony between the king and the people because they courted one another; but when the king's Bounty contracted itself into private Favourites . . . bestowing the affection he *promised* the whole people, upon one man; . . . their passions flew higher than their hopes.
>
> (25)

This argument echoes one of the themes that had made Edward II's rule objectionable to his critics. Wilson's way of putting it is intriguing for two reasons. First, it draws attention to the erotic dimensions of the relationship between the rulers and the ruled, characterising them in terms of courtship, affection and passion. Secondly, it uses these erotic dimensions to provide an *ante litteram* psychological explanation of the displeasure which the king's subjects visited upon the king and his favourites.

James himself drew on erotic symbolism to characterise his relationship with the ruled. In *Basilikon Doron* and *The Trew Law of Free Monarchies* – his treatises on government, originally written without contemplating wide circulation (Worlmand, 1991: 48–49) – James I (1995a, 20; 1995c: 65) had depicted kings as fathers to their peoples. When addressing Parliament in 1604 (James I, 1995b: 136) and then again in 1621 and 1624, however, James's metaphor was not parenthood but marriage. In a speech directly addressed to the Lords in 1621 James spoke of a '*politique Marriage* betwixt me and my people' and – apparently sensing the jealousy of this political spouse – added somewhat defensively that he respected the public good more than any '*private person* whatsoever (were he never so dear unto me)' (Wilson, 1653: 156). Wilson (1653) reports that James ended up dissolving the 1621 Parliament over disagreements on institutional competence (182), foreign policy (173) and freedom of speech in the Houses (188–189).[21] It is again by resorting to erotic metaphors that Wilson (1653: 190) reprimands this act, declaring that James had 'pulled down such a *structure* of *Love* as was never built by the people for any of his *Predecessors*'.

In 1624, in an address to Parliament, James pursued the marriage metaphor further, saying that the people represented by Parliament were his wife and the king their husband, and that just as a husband performs his marital duty by 'visiting' his wife often, so the king did his duty to the people by administering justice; and just as a husband in extraordinary circumstances communicates with his wife on a matter of importance, so the king showed his love to the people by seeking their counsel (Wilson, 1653: 260). On this occasion the king had particularly strong reasons for trying to appease Parliament: the match of his son to the Spanish *infanta* – which Parliament largely opposed – had failed and the king was seeking a change of policy without losing face (Wilson, 1653: 259). It seems significant that in these circumstances James was especially careful to heterosexualise his relationship with the people.

The conceptualisation of the ruler-ruled relationship in terms of a marriage contract goes back at least to the Middle Ages. Like a husband tamed by marriage, so the medieval English monarch was domesticated by the common law and Parliament. If the monarch failed in his contractual obligation to govern in accordance with the law, he could be deposed (Sanchez, 2011, 11–12). The marriage metaphor, never abandoned, had experienced something of a revival under Queen Elizabeth. Elizabeth had declared herself wedded to the 'kingdom of England' – a metaphor that vindicated her unmarried status in real life and made her strong leadership more palatable by rhetorically masculinising the nation (Curran, 2009: 24–25). Elizabeth's emphasis was not on marital contractual obligations, but conjugal love. The love of her subjects was proof that, unlike Mary, she was no tyrant – evidence, that is, of the legitimacy of her rule (Sanchez, 2011: 15–16).

James no doubt appreciated the rhetorical advantages of his predecessor's use of the marriage metaphor and adapted the metaphor to his own needs. His deployment of the metaphor in 1624 enabled him to make leverage on an imagery of love and duty to attempt to consolidate his relationship with Parliament and the people: marital love is a source of duties, but it is itself conceivable as a duty – and one, of course, that is *mutually* owed by spouses.[22] At the same time, perhaps, the metaphor (reversing as it did the husband/wife roles as they had figured in Elizabeth's use of the metaphor) implicitly reminded the nation – too inclined to question its 'weak' consort's non-aggressive foreign policy – of who was rightfully in control of her destiny. For although James I (1995a: 42) argued that the reciprocal duties of spouses are grounded in love and hence willingly complied with, he was also clear about the asymmetrical organisation of marriage along gender lines, with the husband commanding and leading and the wife obeying and following. In other words, James's marital metaphor may be seen to have cunningly exploited the lag between the public rhetoric surrounding marriage, centred on spousal equality and mutuality, and its operational logic of subordination along gender lines.[23]

The lack of institutionalisation of same-sex love in early Modern Europe[24] and its more volitional quality compared to heterosexual marriage explain why a homoerotic metaphor could not have worked to the same effect. The metaphor of heterosexual marriage served the interest of the king, intent on establishing that the people *owed* (however 'willingly') their allegiance to him; but it also served the interest of the people, who would naturally prefer to conceive of the king's duties towards them as grounded in something more than the king's graciousness. This is just what a homoerotic metaphor, however, would not have allowed: without something like marriage to govern it, same-sex love was too *completely* dependent on the will of the parties to function as an appropriate symbol of the relationship between the king and the people.

Indeed, if criticism of James on the ground of his fickleness in changing favourites is representative of broader societal narratives about same-sex desire in early modern England, then same-sex relationships appear to have been perceived as being perilously at the mercy of the lovers' passing fancies.[25] Even Goodman (1839: 225), an apologist of James, felt compelled to justify the king's lack of constancy, explaining that the reason why Villiers replaced Carr in the king's heart is that 'love and affection, though they are the strongest passions for the instant, yet they are not of longest continuance, for they are not grounded in judgement, but are rather fancies that follow the eye'. It is not clear why Goodman felt the need to defensively account for James shifting his affections from Carr to Villiers through this theory of man's inconstancy.[26] James was no fickle lover, as demonstrated by the sheer length of his same-sex relationships and the fact that what spelt the end of each of them were dramatic events outside his control: the exile of Lennox; a public scandal involving Carr (accused of murdering his former secretary); and the king's own death, which cut short his ten-year involvement with Villiers. As Shakespeare's play *Much Ado About Nothing* indicates, however, there was a thriving discourse about love's inconstancy in Elizabethan and Jacobean England, and Goodman's theory of love's fickleness can be put into the context of this discourse.

The point is, in any case, that if all love is inconstant, then same-sex love is a poor candidate for serving as an allegory of the relationship between the king and the people; for it lacks the institutional structure (marriage) that can provide voluntary love with a firmer grounding and a little discipline. But there is another, more fundamental, reason why James or his contemporaries did not invoke same-sex love as a metaphor for the relations between the ruler and the ruled. Same-sex bonds from which desire was not disavowed could not be so invoked because the conventions of early modern legal, moral and political discourse made little room for the representation of same-sex eroticism in a positive light.[27] Early modern English society countenanced precisely the kind of extraordinarily intense homosocial bonds that encouraged same-sex sexual activity (Smith, 1994: 75). But given the stigma attached to sodomy at the time (Bray, 1995: 62, 75),[28] public discourse about same-sex *philia*, understood as the disinterested and egalitarian love of friends (Smith, 1994: 35–36),[29] generally required a discursive desexualisation of the *philic* bond. From this perspective, as Clarke (2002: 53–55) argues, an eroticised *philia* was a contradiction in terms, for same-sex *eros* was perceived to result in relational asymmetry, whereby one party's loss of masculine control made him subject to (desire for) the other. A same-sex relationship that had been desexualised in this way could have been conceivably used as an allegory of the bond between the ruler and the ruled; but precisely its non-hierarchical nature immediately explains why it was not.

Finally, if the king's bond with the people was of the heterosexual marital kind, and if, as Wilson suggests, James's same-sex fancies interfered with this marital harmony, so too did the king's love for Scotland. Weldon (1817: 16) states that James had great need of money 'to express his love, and his bounty to his Native nation'. Osborne (1689: 444) claims that the English were taxed so that money could be lavished on the Scots. He also casts aspersions on the sincerity of the king's loyalty to the English through an argument in which erotic metaphors and ethnocentric prejudice play equal parts. James, Osborne (1689: 447) argues, who was 'alien by birth' and an 'enemy in affection', should have been allowed to become king of England only with approval of both Houses of Parliament; for once they are secure in the throne, kings are ruled by their passions unless made to do otherwise. The king's '*too palpable partiality towards his countrymen*' meant he was just a '*king-in-Law*, not a king of any natural Affections to the People of this Nation' – Scotland being 'no les distant [than Spain] from the English in Nature and Affection' (Osborne, 1689: 422).[30]

Weldon's and Osborne's claim that the king's love for Scotland was a reason to doubt his loyalty to England, combined with James's insistence on his political marriage with the people and Wilson's argument that his male favourites interfered with their marital harmony, taken together, establish an equivalency between the objects of the king's misdirected love: his same-sex lovers and his native country. In so doing they make the legitimacy of political and institutional relations contingent upon their construction not only in heterosexual but also ethnically exclusionary terms.

God and war

James's failure to turn his back on Scotland, however, was not the main of his political faults. James's critics tend to agree that a worse shortcoming was his excessively indulgent treatment of Catholics at home and, on the foreign policy front, his failure to wage war against the (Catholic) Habsburgs.[31] Once again, same-sex desire is generally constructed – through the idea of effeminacy – as related to these poor political decisions.

James detested religious extremism of all brands, and his attitude to Catholics reflected this general stance. He also strongly opposed religious persecution. Imprisonment and execution rates of Catholic priests were far lower under his reign than under his predecessors, although fines against recusants continued – partly as a source of income for his chronically depleted coffers (Croft, 2003: 161–162). James also believed that a reunion of Christian churches – independently justifiable on account of the common bedrock of beliefs shared by all of them – was key to preventing the bloodshed of sectarian wars and bringing about a lasting peace in Europe (Patterson: 1997, 339–364). This idealism dictated his foreign policy choices, including negotiating a peace treaty in 1604 to put an end to the conflict with Spain, which had been wearing the country since the 1580s (Young, 2000: 24). It is, however, James's handling of what would become known as the Thirty Years War that met with his contemporaries' greatest criticism.

In 1603, James had married Elizabeth, his daughter, to Frederick V, the elective ruler of the Palatinate, a fragmented territory in central-western Germany. He had done so in a bid to position himself in a neutral, non-antagonistic relationship with Europe's powers, divided along religious lines (Curran, 2009: 4). However, 1618 marked the outbreak of the Thirty Years War. Frederick had accepted the crown of Bohemia following the overthrow of Archduke Ferdinand, the territory's recently elected ruler. Bohemia having a large Protestant population and Ferdinand being a staunch counter-Reformist, his election to the throne had proved divisive. After Ferdinand's election as Emperor of the Holy Roman Empire (to which both Bohemia and the Palatinate belonged), however, Frederick was ousted from both Bohemia and his hereditary territory, the Palatinate, at the hands of Catholic and imperial forces (the Austrian Habsburgs). James faced pressure at home to intervene on behalf of Frederick, but adequate funding to wage a war was not forthcoming from Parliament. James hoped to resolve the conflict by diplomatic means, particularly through a Spanish match for his son Charles (which, however, was never to eventuate). The Spanish match, James imagined, would enable him to pursue his agenda of religious reconciliation in Europe, as well as give him the leverage to get the Spanish Habsburgs to withdraw their support from, and even check, the Austrian branch of the Habsburg family. This would have allowed Frederick and Elizabeth's restoration to the Palatinate (Croft, 2003: 110–118).

Some seventeenth-century historians defended the king's decision not to embroil himself in a religio-political conflict in Europe. Goodman exemplifies this stance (1839: 58–61); he declared approvingly that 'neither the prince [his son], nor the duke [that is, his favourite Villiers], nor all his council could have prevailed with him to commence a war without just cause' (381). And Sanderson (1656: 319) recorded James's quite remarkable attempt at justifying a policy of religious tolerance to the 1604 Parliament. But Sanderson's and Goodman's treatment of these issues is atypical. Wilson (1653: 273), for example, called James's softness towards 'papists' a 'miscarriage' and explained that James was at fault in giving too much freedom to his agents, which amounts to poor government through 'carelessness'. He reported that when Parliament was keen on scrutinising these '*miscarriages* in *Government*', James's response was Parliament's dissolution (Wilson, 1653: 78). Later, the Commons, opposed to the proposed match of the heir to the English throne with the Spanish *infanta*, wrote a declaration inviting the king to be more aggressive towards Catholics, including by waging war on the Continent (Wilson, 1653: 167). James refused to do so, prompting Peyton (1811: 397) to declare that 'king James proved a coward to back a religious cause'. Wilson went so far as to blame James for the bloodshed that characterised his successor's reign and for the people becoming disaffected with the monarchy. He argued that these consequences could have been avoided if 'the king's spirit had been raised up to a War, when the voice of God (the voice of the people) called him to it' (Wilson, 1653: 172). May's (1812: 4) assessment amounted to the same: through his policies insufficiently severe against Catholics, James ended up jeopardising his own interests, those of his successors, of the Protestants and the 'honour of the whole nation'.

Hutchinson, May and Osborne identify the source of these policy choices in James's supposed lack of courage. In formulating this position, May's (1812: 3) tone is the least strident. He argues that James was 'of disposition mercifull and gracious', but too amicable with Rome and the Catholics, either because he feared for his own life or because he was 'a great seeker of peace, and abhorrer of bloodshed' even to the extent of seeking it by the wrong means. Hutchinson (1848: 80) is less forgiving: for her, through 'sloth and cowardice' James 'betrayed the cause of God and honour of the nation'. Osborne (1689) echoes Hutchinson's sentiment: James wrongly rushed into a peace treaty with Spain because of his 'pusillanimous Temper' (424) and 'upon [the] altar of [fear] he was not only ready to sacrifice his present *Honour* and future *Safety*, but the *Blood* of . . . his . . . *Children*' (484). Osborne (1689: 438) upbraids James for being too peaceful and for maintaining that 'he meant to spoil no people of their Honour, Lands, Felicity, Goods, or Laws'. Osborne (1689: 444–445) does not even spare James's dress choices, which he finds wanting in martial symbolism – ridiculing the king for failing to wear a sword on the first progress after coronation and preferring a green outfit with a horn and feathered hat. Recourse to the same phallic symbolism of swords was also made in political satire targeting James in Spain, where the king had apparently been depicted 'with a Scabbard without a Sword [or] . . . with a Sword that no body could draw out' (Wilson, 1653: 191).

In grounding James's religious tolerance and lack of belligerence in his purported constitutionally fearful disposition, these texts also establish a link between

James's 'soft' policies and his sexuality via the construct of effeminacy (which, as I argued above, has a logical affinity with sodomy in early modern England; and which Osborne, in particular, saw as inextricably linked to James's same-sex desire). These texts do not expressly say that James's 'fearful disposition' was part and parcel of a deficient virility or effeminacy, but the link between a peaceful foreign policy, cowardice and effeminacy is explicit in tracts appearing during James's lifetime. These include works by Thomas Scott as well as John Reynold's *Votivae Angliae* – part of a prolific production of printed material feeding the English people news and views about Catholic–Protestant conflicts on the Continent. Both these tracts attack James's attempts at a peaceful diplomatic resolution to the events of the Thirty Years War (Clegg, 2001: 173–176) and they do so by invoking the rhetoric of effeminacy. Reynolds denounced James's 'unmanly fear of Spain' (Cogswell, 1989: 289), while Scott advocated 'against effeminate peace and for a valorous war' (Peltonen, 1995: 252).[32]

Wilson's treatment of these issues is subtler, engaging in two parallel discourses – one stressing the king's peacefulness, and the other emphasising his fear. On the subject of James's fear, Wilson (1653: 271) claims that the king was 'of a fearful and tottering temper' and that, although he had great wisdom and knowledge, he was ruled mostly by '*Choler* and *Fear*' because these were not acquired but 'Naturall' (285). While Wilson (1653: 171) does not explicitly say that 'the king would be called *Rex Pacificus* to the last' because he was a coward, it is hard not to read his text as implicitly making that connection. On the subject of peacefulness, Wilson (1653: 91) first argues that this is not necessarily preferable to belligerence: '*Peace* is a great *Blessing*, if it bring not a *Curse* with it; but *War* is more happy in its effects' as peace tends to lead to 'feasting', 'debauchery' and an excessive focus on amusements (thus, the link between effeminate debauchery and peace here goes the other way round – from peace to debauchery). Secondly, Wilson (1653: 185) contrasts the crafty and devious processes of negotiation and diplomacy (favoured by James) to the good old honest ways of war to resolve international disputes. Thirdly, he associates a politics of peace with a vaguely sexualised and gendered imagery of decadence and decay: '*Peace* is a sort of *Soft Rayment, or Masking-dress*, not alwayes to be worne; *Standing lakes* beget *Corruption*' (Wilson, 1653: 190). A reader of this passage cannot fail to immediately picture James himself wearing those 'soft' feminine garments, given that Wilson (1653: 91) had previously stated that it was under the 'influence of our king's *peaceable* mind' that peace 'had almost a universall *operation*'. Fourthly, Wilson (1653: 190) alludes to the emasculation of British politics that James's pursuit of peace brings about: people started saying that 'they had lost strength by changing *Sexes*'. Elizabeth's manly femaleness had, in other words, been replaced by James's effeminate maleness. Fifthly, Wilson (1653: 266) reports a speech that James gave to the Houses in 1624, when Parliament was advising war, in which James declared that war was 'so farr from [his] *Naturre* . . . and so much against [his] *Heart*' that he would not enter it 'unless it be . . . (as some say it merrily of *Women*) *Malum Necesarium*'. This statement is significant not only for grounding James's peacefulness in his very being (a point reinforced later by Wilson (1653: 285) himself, who states that engagement in war was 'contrary to his very nature'); it also inadvertently links James's penchant for males (here taking a misogynistic turn) to his peaceful disposition: while both war and women are sometimes necessary, both of them are also an evil. Thus by the end of Wilson's treatment of the subject of peacefulness, not only are we left with an impression that James is peaceful because he lacks the courage to be otherwise, but a connection has been articulated between a misguided and mollifying politics of peace and decadent, homoerotic and gender-deviant subjectivities. This reading of Wilson's treatment of the question of peacefulness is only superficially in tension with Wilson's general treatment of same-sex desire in politics – where, as we have seen, he appears to take issue with same-sex desire only to the extent that it may lead to situations where reason is overpowered by lust. We have seen that Wilson seemed to think that in James's case this is precisely what had happened. Now, Wilson's discussion of peacefulness seems to suggest that the reason why in James's specific case same-sex desire happened to overpower his rational faculties is that the king's same-sex desire was grounded in a deviant subjectivity.

A different treatment of the link between same-sex desire and peaceful foreign policy appears in verse libel that draws a parallel between the purportedly poisonous smell of frankincense and myrrh (characteristic of Catholic Mass ritual) and Ganymede's (that is Villiers's) 'whorish breath', which leads the king wherever it pleases (Bellany, 1994: 298). Here the king is portrayed as being misguided by the bad counsel of his (crypto-Catholic) favourite, but what make James vulnerable to this bad advice is, of course, his sexual desire for Villiers – the seductive Ganymede-like male harlot. Albeit not brought to the fore, effeminacy here implicitly remains as part of the subtext, for the loss of self-control that makes the king subject to Villiers marks James as unmanly.

Robert Carr, Earl of Somerset: using favourites to rule poorly

'[A] slave was king James to his Favourites' declares the publisher of Weldon's (1817: 1) book in his note to the reader. One of the leitmotifs in critical accounts of James's rule closely tracks the argument against Edward II that the king gave too much heed to his favourites and entrusted them with too much power, even to the point that, in Wilson's words, 'our *Supreme Power* works by *second Causes*' (Wilson, 1653: 55; see also May, 1812: 4). Weldon (1817: 6) even appears to credit James with introducing the practice of favouritism in England, calling the first of James's favourites in England 'the first Meteor of that nature appearing in our climate'.[33]

As examined elsewhere in this chapter, there are few explicit references in the sources to James's same-sex physical intimacy with his favourites. More often, the references are implicit. *Corona Regia*, a satirical text circulating during James's life, is notable for unmistakably conveying the physical dimensions of James's relationship with his favourites without ever committing to an express statement to that effect. In addition to the hunting metaphor (discussed above) as a proxy for anal sex, there is an allusion to oral sex in a passage referring to the habit of eating 'acorns' (playing on the double meaning of the Latin word *glans*) (*Corona Regia*, 2010: 83). There is also a more generic, if vaguely disturbing, reference to same-sex sexual pleasures: 'The words of Christ were, "suffer children to come unto me". You summon boys – the very fair ones in particular – and appreciate the benefactions and miracles of nature into them' (*Corona Regia*, 2010: 89).

In any case, in James's times the very term 'favourite' seems to have strongly implied the possibility of physical intimacy between favourites and their patrons, while always maintaining a convenient ambiguity. This can be inferred from a passage in one of Sanderson's (1650: 2) texts, where, speaking about Queen Elizabeth, he states: 'Some say She had many *Favourites*, but in truth She had none. They were neer and dear to Her, and to Her affaires, as *Partners* of Her care; not *Minions* of phansey.' It seems from this passage that the term 'favourite', at least if unqualified and strictly understood, involves an erotic element. Being 'neer and dear' to one's patron is not enough to make one a favourite without the contribution of 'phansey', which suggests precisely erotic attraction, as other uses of this term in seventeenth-century sources indicate.[34] At the same time, as one of James's apologists, Sanderson (1650: 110) attempts to maintain some useful ambiguity when discussing the king's own favourites, stating that a favourite was '*one whom* the king *fancied, merely* for his *fashion*: upon no other *score*, nor *plot* of *design*'. It is possible that here Sanderson, in stressing the absence of further motives on James's part, is trying to say that James's attraction remained purely chaste.[35] Goodman (1839: 18) – being committed, like Sanderson, to rescue James's reputation – shows a determination to show James's attachment to his favourites in its best light, drawing on the conveniently ambiguous love-centred vocabulary of (ostensibly asexual) *philia*:

> [N]o man living did ever love an honest man more than he did. This I ascribe ... to his own goodness ... for as yet I never knew any man who had so great an understanding, and so great an affection, and such a violent passion for love as he had.

James's critics, however, exploiting James's vulnerability to the charms of his favourites to mount an attack against the king's government, seemed to have had an easier time of it. There is little ambiguity about James's favourites being objects of erotic desire in Osborne's (1689: 476) statement that they were '*younger Men ... of ... endearing Countenances*' chosen purely because of their '*handsomeness*'. Even more tellingly, Osborne (1689: 477) obliquely refers to certain unspecified '*conditions*' to which James's favourites had to subscribe to fill 'that *place* in his *Affection*'. Osborne (1689: 476) also argues that James's favourites 'were daily *interposed between* him and the *Subject*, multiplying the heat of *oppressions* in the *general opinion*, though in his own he thought they *screened* them from reflecting upon the *Crown*'. Peyton (1811: 355) makes a similar argument to the effect that the king used his favourites so as to lay the blame on them for his bad policies. These assertions go further than many parallel critiques of Edward II's favourites. Peyton implies that James deliberately used same-sex desire as a ploy to rule badly; the interposition of his favourites here figures as a technique of poor government, not just a poor technique of government.

Other grounds of complaint about the favourites and their hand in poor government suggest that same-sex desire turned out to be serviceable to arbitrary rule, even if not by design. For Peyton (1811), once James allowed his favourites – 'young counsellors, who had not vertue, but vanity' (364) – to rule instead of him (352), good government was inevitably compromised. These favourites 'being more addicted to pleasure and delights then the school of prudence and wisdome; looking more to their interest then the common good, or piety of life, gave so vast a liberty to their lives, as made an abordment of looseness in many' (Peyton, 1811: 365). Peyton (1811: 411) goes on to fault James's reliance on his favourites, rather than Parliament, to gauge the well-being of the people: these favourites 'for to encrease wealth (raised from nothing,) are like bloodsuckers'. The main idea here – plausible enough – is that in using same-sex desire and erotic attraction as the sole criterion to choose his closest officers, James was bound to govern poorly. Some of the texts emphasise this point in their treatment of Robert Carr, James's first high-profile English favourite, who made a dramatic entry into James's graces by breaking his leg while riding a horse before the king's very eyes at an official ceremony (Wilson, 1653: 54 55).

For Wilson (1653: 61) he was a 'Youth new started in the affair of the World, and mounted by the *wing* of *love*, not of *merit*', while Peyton (1811: 353) deplores his being elected to the Council, commenting sarcastically that with a library comprised of only 'twenty playbooks and wanton romances', he was 'very like to give wise counsel!' It is unclear that, in reality, when James decided to launch Carr's political career he was blinded by erotic passion;[36] but it was by making that choice appear dictated entirely by same-sex desire that James's detractors established its arbitrariness. In any case, the phenomenal rise of Carr – soon Viscount of Rochester and Earl of Somerset, as well as 'principal secretary to the king' (Wilson, 1653: 66) – undeniably lent itself to being made sense of in terms of same-sex desire facilitating the operation of dysfunctional political processes. Wilson (1653) describes Carr's appointment to public offices that empowered him to carry out many 'miscarriages' and grant or withhold positions and dignities at will (55, 79), so that 'the Lords themselves can scarce have a smile without him' (55).

The downfall of Carr – now Somerset – was occasioned by his involvement in the scandal of the poisoning of his former secretary, Overbury, who had made enemies of Carr's wife Frances Howard (Countess of Essex) and the powerful political faction with which she was affiliated. James apparently supported Somerset until catching vent of the rumours of Overbury's murder, at which point he instructed judges to fully investigate the matter and sent him off to be tried in London (Wilson, 1653: 80).[37] Somerset and the Countess were found guilty – though modern historians (Ashton, 1969: 109–110; Lindley, 1993) have doubted the correctness of the verdict with respect to the former – but were not executed thanks to the king's intervention. After a period of captivity in the Tower of London, they went on to spend the rest of their days in obscurity (Wilson, 1653: 82–83).

Sanderson (1650: 137, 138, 142) goes to great pains to show that James acted honourably towards Somerset in the circumstances, treading a fine balance between showing mercy and doing justice. Bacon's courtroom speech echoed the sentiment. The king had given special instructions that no innocent person should be punished or their reputation damaged, and Bacon concedes this was particularly important in the case because at stake were the reputation and liberty of a '*Nobleman* that his Majesty had favoured and advanced' (Wilson, 1653: 84). Nonetheless, Bacon stressed that the king 'to his great honour' showed to the 'World' that justice must be done, even to the extent that the case 'hath relation to my Lord of *Somerset*' (Wilson, 1653: 86). James's detractors, however, provide a different account of the events, playing up James's purported inconstancy, and portraying him as a ruthless ruler who manipulates institutional processes for his private ends, including personal gratification of the sexual variety. According to this account, James seized at the chance of being rid of Somerset as soon as it presented itself (all the while, in his personal relations with him, making an outward show of caring for him); for by then the king only had eyes for the new rising favourite, George Villiers (Weldon, 1817: 20–32).

George Villiers, Duke of Buckingham: forcing the king against nature

James I (1995a: 40) advised his son that beauty was a blessing in a spouse, as it would help him remain faithful to her, but added that it must be coupled, among other things, with wisdom, grace and honesty. James more or less practiced what he preached. On all accounts, 'incomparable beauty' (*Corona Regia*, 2010: 79) was a distinguishing feature of the 'sweet heart' to whom, anticipating their reunion after a period of separation, James spoke of renewing their 'marriage', and to whom he declared that he 'had rather live banished in any part of the earth with you than live a sorrowful widow's life without you' (Bergeron, 1999: 175). According to James's apologists, this sweetheart – George Villiers – was well endowed with virtues of the spiritual variety too. Even they, however, admitted he had some character flaws.

For Goodman (1839) 'he was the handsomest bodied man in England; his limbs so well compacted, and his conversation so pleasing . . . his intellectuals were very great; he had sound judgement' (225–226); he was capable of great love and 'truly just' and 'free of all cruelty and pride'; however he was also subject to outbursts of passion and rather careless in his deportment (91).[38] Peyton (1811: 359) too remarks upon Villiers's looks – but so as to show to full advantage, by way of contrast, his spiritual ugliness, as well as to make a case for James's subjection to him:

A lord of tall stature, amiable of countenance; who, like a ravenous kyte, ingrossed all into his hands, to inrich and advance his kindred, and to place and displace whom he listed, so that this lord grew so potent, his master stood in awe of him.

James's liability to same-sex attraction here becomes the reason why public policy starts being driven by personal interest. That liability means the king can't oppose an effective resistance to Villiers's ascendance: Villiers sat, Peyton (1811: 360) declares, like 'a gyant on the shoulder of king James, and drowned his power, limiting no bounds to his overflowing will'.

This account is in contrast with that of another contemporary observer. Describing Villiers, in private communication, as 'full of delicacie and handsome features', and adding that 'his hands and face seemed to mee especiallie effeminate and curious', the observer goes on to state that he undoubtedly did much harm to the nation; this was, however, probably the result of Jesuit influence, as 'his very countenance promised [his own nature] to be affable and gentle' (Nichols, 1828: 646–647). This remark shows the complexity of seventeenth-century discourses about the relationship between effeminacy (which I have argued above was often treated as entailing same-sex desire) and political power. On the one hand, as we have seen, effeminacy could be linked to poor government through the idea of effeminate statesmen preferring 'bad' policies dictated by fear (diplomacy over war, relative religious tolerance). On the other hand, effeminacy could be used – as it is here – to argue that effeminate statesmen could not do serious harm unless by falling prey to the wrong kind of influence.

For Weldon (1817: 28), Villiers's coming onto the scene was orchestrated by courtiers who were hoping thereby to gain some influence over the king; thus, to bring him into 'the king's eye', Villiers was made cupbearer. This office cannot fail to have called to mind, to spectators in the know, the myth of Ganymede, beloved of Zeus and abducted so he could serve as cupbearer of the gods. Weldon (1817: 29) is quick to clarify the nature of the king's attachment for Villiers: '[I]n his passion of love to his new Favourite . . . the king was more impatient then any woman to enjoy her love.' In early modern times, such a reference to a lack of self-control was a sure telltale sign of effeminacy. Weldon is outdone by Peyton (1811: 348), though, who declares that James 'sold his affections to Sir George Villiers, whom he would tumble and kiss as a mistress'. The early nineteenth-century editor of Peyton's (1811) book, in a footnote appended to this passage, felt compelled to remark upon 'the odd familiarities which James used with his favourites, and which were, to say the least, most disgusting and unseemly' (349). That we are indebted to James's harshest detractors for the most candid accounts of homoeroticism between him and his favourites speaks volumes to the link their texts implicitly, and sometimes expressly, draw between poor government and same-sex desire.

Villiers was quickly elevated to positions of honour, offered titles of nobility – culminating in the Earldom of Buckingham – and appointed to important public offices, including privy counsellor, admiral and master of the horse (Wilson, 1653: 104–105, 147). Wilson (1653: 147) explains that in order to make Buckingham master of 'his Heart also', James granted favours to the Earl's relations, allowing his female relatives to be brought to court, where they became popular matches for those seeking political and social advancement. According to Weldon (1817: 42), one of Buckingham's female relatives was married to an old nobleman who was, notoriously, sexually interested only in males – almost as if there were a race for men of his ilk to love women as much as the king loved Buckingham. This observation is paradoxical on many levels. Where Weldon tries to convey a sense of the absurdity of same-sex attracted men attaching themselves to women by comparing their attachment to James and Buckingham's bond, the analogy seems predicated on a belief in the 'unnaturalness' of James's attraction to Buckingham. At the same time, the remark naturalises same-sex desire by making it look innate or immutable – otherwise, of course, these men could simply make the switch to heterosexuality and there wouldn't be anything particularly remarkable about their marrying women. I am mainly interested, however, in what the passage says about the relationship between politics, kinship and desire. Weldon surely did not ignore that heterosexual marriage was routinely used for political purposes, despite the fact that he affects shock when reporting that Buckingham's party so used marriage. In fact, the custom of political marriages is one of the primary indicators of the elective affinity between the institution of heterosexuality and political institutions during much of European history. James himself made a conspicuous use of marriage and marriage celebrations to defuse political tensions, reconcile rival factions, and pursue a politics of national and religious unity (Curran, 2009). Weldon's pretended shock at the political uses of marriage by the Buckingham party is paradoxical because, in order to produce the effect it is aiming at, the text needs to implicitly invite its audience to disavow their knowledge that heterosexual marriage was regularly instrumentalised in the service of politics. But the passage is also paradoxical because, at the same time, it cannot fully do away with that knowledge. Indeed, the sarcastic statement about *same-sex attracted* males marrying women for political reasons seems to rest on a sense of outrage at same-sex desire fiddling with the time-honoured custom of making heterosexual marriage serviceable to politics. Presumably the cause of the outrage is that same-sex desire too unambiguously draws attention to the proverbial emperor's new clothes – the crude instrumentalisation of marriage for political ends.

James's apologists go to great lengths to establish that Villiers's 'first step into honourable *Office*' was justified and done in accordance with all due form (Sanderson, 1650: 169), and that the material advantages bestowed upon Buckingham[39] did not impoverish others (only the Crown itself) (Hacket, 1693: 187–188). They also argue that, Buckingham being from an ancient family with many members married into the gentry, it was only natural that they would appeal to him for 'preferment', there being nothing scandalous in his trying to help them (Sanderson, 1650: 175). James's critics, however, are quick to characterise

Buckingham's rise as unwarranted, pursued by ruthless means, and essentially resulting from James's inability to resist his every wish. Peyton (1811: 349) makes this inability immediately clear when, shortly after introducing Villiers, he relates how the favourite got James to break up Parliament for his personal gain. Wilson (1653: 104), characteristically, puts it more poignantly, informing us of James's physical indisposition when Buckingham was absent, and stating that the favourite 'now reigns sole *Monarch* in the kings affection; everything he doth, is admired for the *doers* sake'. Same-sex infatuation here is presented as potentially having the power not only to turn political arrangements on their head (one of the king's subjects becoming his sole 'monarch') but also to distort the judgement of the king, who becomes utterly incapable of objectivity.

Weldon's (1817: 43) way of putting it is equally compelling: 'this Favourite ... could force (by his Power over the king) though against Nature'. Because Weldon is not consistent or logical in his use of parentheses, it is unclear if the passage means that the king could be forced against nature or that the power of so forcing him was against nature. The former (being forced against nature) would suggest an unnatural effect on the king – the loss of the power of well-considered and objective judgement clearly qualifying as such. The latter (a power against nature) would suggest that the source of Buckingham's ascendancy was itself unnatural. On the one hand, this echoes arguments about Hugh Despenser 'bewitching' Edward II; on the other hand, it evokes the '*contra naturam*' terminology – which since medieval times had been used in connection with sodomy (Davies, 2001: 780–781).

James's apologists do not necessarily dispute Buckingham's formidable power over James. Hacket (1693: 187) says that 'this Beloved-Minion should be Wise to see what he ask'd, for his Master had no Power to say him nay'. Goodman (1839) speaks of Buckingham as 'the favourite of whom the king was so fond as that he could deny him nothing' (333–334), adding that 'it was impossible for a man to dote more upon another' (393). However, in denying, as we have seen above, that Buckingham was, to put it in Weldon's (1817: 43) words, 'insolent, cruel and a monster', these authors downplay the practical effect of his ascendancy over James. For example, where the critics deplore Buckingham's power to grant all honourable positions, offices and titles (May, 1812: 4; Weldon, 1817: 39–40), the king's defenders stress that Buckingham was magnanimous in his dealings, bestowing favours 'freely and nobly', without exacting 'gifts and presents' (Hacket, 1693: 39). They add that it is absurd to imagine that he had lavished titles and money to the extent that he was charged with by his detractors (Sanderson, 1650: 176). These interventions constitute an important counter-discourse. They do not (implausibly) deny that same-sex desire has the potential for disabling the rational faculties of rulers who are subject to it. Nor do they deny that this is precisely what happened in James's case. But they implicitly break the almost-necessary link – which most of the critics' texts tend to establish – between same-sex desire and villainy. In rejecting the proposition that same-sex attracted statesmen necessarily govern badly, the texts of James's apologists create a space for alternative understandings about the relationship between same-sex desire and political authority.

Conclusions

James's defenders – men who had known him and moved about his court – took on the task of responding point by point to what they saw as the unfair criticism to which his memory had been subjected.[40] Much of what they say is directly relevant to an assessment of the quality of James's rule. Thus, Sanderson (1656: 276) states that James was endowed with 'virtues and goodness' to a greater extent than is 'usual in *Princes*'; and Goodman (1839: 181) argues that James was learned and intellectually sophisticated and naturally surrounded himself with like 'privy councillors'; and he provides evidence of James's and Buckingham's disinterested liberality to counter allegations of their corruption (356–357). Even James's critic Weldon (1817: 57) at the end of his account brings himself to report that the king 'loved good laws and made many in his time'.

The dominant narrative – the one that until fairly recently left the greatest mark on mainstream historiography – is, however, very different. This narrative, emerging from accounts written by James's contemporaries mostly during the republican experiment of the Interregnum, reworks some familiar themes explored in our analysis of Edward II, while adding genuinely new elements. The most conspicuous novel element is the idea that same-sex desire is grounded (at least in James's case) in a constitutional effeminacy that makes it all the more problematic. The preoccupation with effeminacy and same-sex desire, understood as co-dependent, became conspicuous towards the end of the seventeenth century and in the eighteenth century (McCormick, 1997: 117). James himself became an archetypal figure around which this sort of concern congealed. Thus, 'Mundus Foppensis' (1997: 125), a 1691 poem satirising effeminate fops, before concluding that orally servicing twenty women is preferable to 'lick[ing] the bristles of one male dear *Dick*', recites: 'A most unmanly nasty trick;/One man to lick the other's cheek;/And only what renews the shame/Of J. the first, and *Buckingham*.' As we have seen, however, the link between unmanliness and same-sex desire can already be quite clearly detected in earlier sources. This is consistent with Smith's (1994: 76) persuasive argument that the lived experiences of same-sex attracted males in early modern England could take the form of 'gender-marked' homosexuality, even if social historians have commonly argued that this did not happen until the eighteenth century.

The sources examined use the idea of a deficient virility even to make sense of James's physical appearance. Thus, Peyton (1811: 332–333) describes him as 'weak in constitution', a 'spiny and thin creature', and 'unsuitable' for his wife, described – no doubt so as to further emphasise James's effeminacy – as a 'virago'. Weldon (1817: 50), who plays up James's cowardice, calling it his 'greatest blemish' (58), depicts James's physical weakness as going hand in hand with his poorness of spirit. Weldon (1817: 55) reduces his portrait of the king to a caricature, describing him virtually in the same breath as 'naturally of a timor-ous disposition', endowed with a 'Beard very thin', and plagued by a weakness in the legs which meant he was always supporting himself on other men, as well as by the habit of walking in circles while 'ever fidling about his cod-piece'! These details (from the sparse facial hair, through his need to be propped by other men, to his neurotic preoccupation with his crotch) bespeak a lack of bodily virility mirroring James's spiritual unmanliness – his effeminacy.

Feminist theorists have argued that although what is associated with feminin-ity varies from culture to culture, all cultures value the feminine less than the masculine, including when femininity, being attached to males, takes the form of effeminacy (Case, 1995: 30–34). This is consistent with James's critics grounding his same-sex desire in a constitutional effeminacy which they believed had blinded him to the good of the English people. According to this narrative, James's lack of manly courage meant that he refused to see that English interests consisted in aggressively opposing Catholic interests at home and abroad. Furthermore, his unmanly liability to same-sex desire meant that he was willing to let his favourites and their personal interests guide public policy. This is what Ashton (1969: 106) means where he says that for many of James's contemporaries his same-sex attrac-tion was the 'most disastrous of his vices' – 'disastrous' not on a personal level, but in what his critics thought were its implications for the good government of the country.

James I (1995a: 6) strongly opposed religious fanaticism, particularly where it preached that 'holy warres' were preferable to 'an ungodly peace'. He wanted resolutely (and in opposition to Parliament's much more belligerent attitude) to pursue a peaceful foreign policy (James I, 1995b: 133) and a policy of rela-tive religious tolerance in internal affairs. Because of this, but also because his favourites profited from Parliament not scrutinising too closely their activities, James governed too often without seeking the people's consent. May (1812: 4) argues that James's infrequent summoning of Parliament and his dissolution of those he did summon stemmed from his 'being loath, perchance, that the whole people should take notice of those waies in which he trod'. The expression May chooses is ambiguous – probably deliberately so – for, like Peyton's reference to the Stuarts' 'secret and chamber-abominations', it may allude both to corrupt public processes and questionable private practices. Among these private prac-tices, those of a physically intimate nature that the king might have engaged in with his favourites (which, as we have seen, were seen as directly related to some of James's governmental miscarriages) were clearly a matter of preoccupation for his critics.

Despite his public displays of affection with his favourites, however, it is unclear to what extent James countenanced sexual activities between males (though this, of course, raises the question of where the line should be drawn between displays of affection and sexual activity).[41] In any case, as often as not James's private practices were discussed in terms of what the king failed to do with the queen rather than what he did do with his male lovers – though it is fairly obvious what

James's critics were getting at. As Wilson (1653: 79) expressly noted, it was by '*Masculine conversation* and *intimacy*' that 'the king's love and company was alienated' from the queen. James I (1811: 332–333) himself made no mystery of having only a mild interest in women: having been criticised for taking too long to marry, he declared that he finally did it to produce an heir that would secure the reign, for he 'could have abstained langer'.[42] His critics clearly exploited his lukewarm heterosexual drive to their advantage. Thus, Weldon (1817: 55) writes that James was 'not very uxorious' and that 'he was ever best, when furthest from the Queen', so he often removed himself from their common residence. Peyton (1811) speaks of the queen as being 'deprived of the nightly company of a husband' (244) and consequently taking a number of lovers (334–339). Osborne (1689: 445) reports that James tried 'to show himself more uxorious before the People' than he actually was by publicly kissing the queen 'to the middle of her shoulders'.

Even Sanderson (a supporter of James's who otherwise appears to treat same-sex desire as in and of itself morally unremarkable) seems aware that an imputation of frigidity towards the queen would prove damaging to James and his memory – probably because it would lend credence to rumours of a consummated physical intimacy between the king and his male objects of desire. Thus, Sanderson (1650: 98) explains that James's removing himself to his country estates had to do with his health, '[w]ithout that Scandalous Intimation – *of leaving his Queen, without any love or liking*'. Similarly, Goodman (1839: 167–168) affirms that in the early years the king and queen 'did keep company' and 'had children', while defensively arguing that the greater distance between them in later years was due to the fact that the king 'was a very chaste man, and there was little in the Queen to make him uxorious'.

That James had some of the traits stereotypically associated with modern-day gay men is as undeniable as it is intriguing. Thus for Goodman (1839: 322) 'the king spent more in boots, silk stockings, beaver hats, than all the kings in Christendom did'. His favourites too are elsewhere described as 'extravagant' and as having a great 'love of dress' (Weldon, 1817: 6). To complete the picture, Weldon (1817: 57) styles James 'very witty' and for Wilson (1653: 289), 'If he had any predominant *Humour* to Ballance his *Choller* [it] was Sanguine, which made his *Mirth Witty*.' This characterisation of James as an *ante litteram* stereotypical gay man, however, comes at a cost. Just as modern-day gay identity carries its disciplinary implications, so the portrayal of James as a fashionable, humorous and sly conversationalist reinforces the argument that he failed as a political leader, enabling Weldon (1817: 58) to remark that the king was 'crafty and cunning in petty things . . . but a fool in weighty affairs'. James's treatises in political philosophy, however, as well as the speeches he made to Parliament, amply disprove Weldon's allegation of political foolishness; so too does the king's consistent championing of a peaceful foreign policy and comparative religious toleration.

James I (1995c: 72) believed in the divine right of kings and the associated view that the people owed obedience even to bad kings (unless their commands went directly against God), it being the sole province of God to judge and punish bad monarchs. However, the doctrine of the divine right of kings was not developed to justify arbitrary rule with impunity. It was a response to a tradition in political and religious thought which, having inherited from the Middle Ages the principle that monarchs derive their authority from God *and the people*, had developed (particularly in Jesuit hands) in the direction of justifying the people's killing of infidel kings in the name of true religion (Shuger, 1997: 141–142). Considering the cultural association in late medieval and early modern Europe between same-sex desire and heresy via the construct of sodomy, it is to be wondered if King James had especially compelling personal reasons for being concerned with discourses justifying religiously motivated regicide. In any case, the fact that the divine right of kings was not intended to justify tyrannical rule explains why James qualified his view that people owe obedience even to bad kings in important ways. For instance, he argued that there is a clear difference between kings, who govern for the public good, and tyrants, who rule driven purely by personal gain (James I, 1995a: 20); that although kings are above the law, good kings use the law to inform their conduct (James I, 1995c: 75); and that a 'righteous' king knows that he is 'ordained for the people, and not his people for him' (James I, 1995b: 143). As Sommerville (1991: 65) has argued, James was seeking neither to govern tyrannically nor to be hated by the people. An adequate understanding of why until about only three decades ago he regularly passed down as a detested despot in mainstream historiography needs to take into account his same-sex desire and the ways in which it was rhetorically exploited by his contemporary critics.

References

Ashton, R (ed.) (1969) *James I by his Contemporaries* (London: Hutchinson).

Auchmuty, R (2012) 'Law and the Power of Feminism: How Marriage Lost its Power to Oppress Women' *Feminist Legal Studies*, vol 20, 71–87.

Barker, N (2013) *Not the Marrying Kind: A Feminist Critique of Same-Sex Marriage* (Houndmills: Palgrave-Macmillan).

Bellany, A (1994) 'Rayling Rhymes and Vaunting Verse: Libellous Politics in Early Stuart England 1603-28' in Scarpe, K and Lake, P (eds), *Culture and Politics in Early Stuart England* (Houndmills: Macmillan) 285–310.

Bergeron, DM (1999) *King James & Letters of Homoerotic Desire* (Iowa City: University of Iowa Press).

Birch, T (ed.) (1849) *The Court and Times of James the First*, vol i (London: Henry Colburn).

Bray, A (1995) *Homosexuality in Renaissance England* (New York: Columbia University Press).

Case, MA (1995) 'Disaggregating Gender from Sex and Sexual Orientation: The Effeminate Man in the Law and Feminist Jurisprudence' *Yale Law Journal*, vol 105, 1–105.

Christianson, P (1991) 'Royal and Parliamentary Voices on the Ancient Constitution, c 1604–1621' in Peck, LL (ed.), *The Mental World of the Jacobean Court* (Cambridge: Cambridge University Press) 71–95.

Clarke, D (2002) '"The Sovereign's Vice Begets the Subject's Error"; the Duke of Buckingham, "Sodomy", and Narratives of Edward II, 1622–82' in Betteridge, T (ed.), *Sodomy in Early Modern Europe* (Manchester: Manchester University Press) 46–64.

Clegg, CS (2001) *Press Censorship in Jacobean England* (Cambridge: Cambridge University Press).

Cogswell, T (1989) *The Blessed Revolution: English Politics and the Coming of War, 1621–1624* (Cambridge: Cambridge University Press).

Corona Regia (2010) (Fyotek, T, trans) (Geneve: Droz).

Croft, P (2003) *King James* (Houndmills: Palgrave).

Crompton, L (2003) *Homosexuality and Civilization* (Cambridge: Harvard University Press).

Curran, K (2009) *Marriage, Performance and Politics at the Jacobean Court* (Farnham: Ashgate).

Davies, B (ed.) (2001) *The De Malo of Thomas Aquinas* (Oxford: Oxford University Press).

diGangi, M (1997) *The Homoerotics of Early Modern Drama* (Cambridge: Cambridge University Press).

Folkestone, R (1848) *The Court and Times of James the First*, vol 2, Birch, T (ed.) (London: Henry Colburn).

Friedeburg, R von (2011) 'Response to Introduction: "Ideology", Factions and Foreign Politics in Early Modern Europe' in Onnekink, D and Rommelse, G (eds), *Ideology and Foreign Policy in Early Modern Europe (1650–1750)* (Farnham: Ashgate) 11–28.

Gardiner, SR (1862) *Parliamentary Debates in 1610* (London: The Camden Society).

Goodman, G (1839) *The Court of King James the First*, vol 1 (London: Richard Bentley).

Hacket, J (1693) *Scrinia Reserata*, vol 1 (London: Samuel Lowndes).

Hammond, P (2002) *Figuring Sex between Men from Shakespeare to Rochester* (Oxford: Oxford University Press).

Houlbrooke, R (2006) 'James's Reputation 1625–2005' in Houlbrooke, R (ed.), *James VI and I: Ideas, Authority, and Government* (Aldershot: Ashgate) 169–190.

Hutchinson, L (1848) *Memoirs of the Life of Colonel Hutchinson* (London: Henry G Bohn).

James I (1811) 'Public Declaration' in Scott, IJ (ed.), *Secret History of the Court of James the First*, vol 2 (Edinburgh: Ballantyne) 332–333 (editor's note).

James I (1995a) 'Basilikon Doron' in Sommerville, JP (ed.), *King James VI and I: Political Writings* (Cambridge: Cambridge University Press) 1–61.

James I (1995b) 'Speech to Parliament of 19 March 1604' in Sommerville, JP (ed.), *King James VI and I: Political Writings* (Cambridge: Cambridge University Press) 132–146.

James I (1995c) 'The Trew Law of Free Monarchies' in Sommerville JP (ed.), *King James VI and I: Political Writings* (Cambridge: Cambridge University Press) 62–84.

Johnson, B (1729) *Sejanus: His Fall* in Johnson, B, *Ben Johnson's Plays*, vol 1 (Dublin: S Powell) 297–390.

King, TA (2004) *The Gendering of Men, 1600–1750: The English Phallus* (Madison: The University of Wisconsin Press).

Kuchta, D (1993) 'The Semiotics of Masculinity in Renaissance England' in Turner, JG (ed.), *Sexuality and Gender in Early Modern Europe: Institutions, Texts, Images* (Cambridge: Cambridge University Press) 233–246.

Lindley, D (1993) *The Trials of Frances Howard: Fact and Fiction at the Court of King James* (London: Routledge).

McCormick, I (ed.) (1997) *Secret Sexualities – A Sourcebook of 17th and 18th Century Writing* (London: Routledge).

McMullan, G (1994) *The Politics of Unease in the Plays of John Fletcher* (Amherst: University of Massachusetts Press).

Mager, DR (1994) 'John Bale and Early Tudor Sodomy Discourse' in Goldberg, J (ed.), *Queering the Renaissance* (London: Duke University Press) 141–162.

Marcus, LS (1986) *The Politics of Mirth: Jonson, Herrick, Milton and Marvell* (Chicago: University of Chicago Press).

Marlowe, C (1995) *Edward II* in Marlowe, C, *Doctor Faustus and Other Plays* (Oxford: Oxford University Press) 323–402.

May, T (1812) *The History of the Parliament of England, Which Began November the Third, M.DC.XL* (London: Robert Wilks).

'Mundus Foppensis; or the Fop Display'd' (1997) in McCormick, I (ed.), *Secret Sexualities – A Sourcebook of 17th and 18th Century Writing* (London: Routledge) 124–125.

Nichols, J (ed.) (1828) *The Progresses, Processions, and Magnificent Festivities, of King James the First*, vol 4 (London: JB Nichols).

Osborne, F (1689) 'Historical Memoires of the Reigns of Queen Elizabeth, and King James' in *The Works of Francis Osborn* (London: Bell & Howell, 9th edn) 405–487.

Patterson, WB (1997) *King James VI and I and the Reunion of Christendom* (Cambridge: Cambridge University Press).

Peltonen, M (1995) *Classical Humanism and Republicanism in English Political Thought, 1570–1640* (Cambridge: Cambridge University Press).

Peyton, E (1811) 'The Divine Catastrophe of the Kingly Family of the House of Stuarts' in Scott, IJ (ed.), *Secret History of the Court of James the First*, vol 2, (Edinburgh: Ballantyne) 301–466.

Plato (1994) *Symposium* (Oxford: Oxford University Press).

Purkis, J (2011) 'Attributing Authorship and Swetnam the Woman-Hater' in Traister, BH and Starner, JW (eds), *Anonymity in Early Modern England: 'What's in a Name?'* (Farnham: Ashgate) 113–128.

Russell, C, Cust, R and Thrush, A (2011) *King James VI and I and his English Parliaments* (Oxford: Oxford University Press).

Sanchez, ME (2011) *Erotic Subjects: The Sexuality of Politics in Early Modern English Literature* (Oxford: Oxford University Press).

Sanderson, W (1650) *Aulicus Coquinariae* (London: Henry Seile).

Sanderson, W (1656) *A Compleat History of the Lives and Reigns of Maria Queen of Scotland, and of Her Son and Successor James* (London: Humphrey Mosley).

Schleiner, W (2010) 'Introduction' in *Corona Regia* (Fyotek, T, trans) (Geneve: Droz).

Sedgwick, EK (1990) *Epistemology of the Closet* (London: University of California Press).

Shepard, A (2003) *Meanings of Manhood in Early Modern England* (Oxford: Oxford University Press).

Shuger, DK (1997) *Habits of Thought in the English Renaissance: Religion, Politics, and the Dominant Culture* (Toronto: University of Toronto Press).

Smith, BR (1994) *Homosexual Desire in Shakespeare's England: A Cultural Poetics* (Chicago: University of Chicago Press).

Sommerville, JP (1991) 'James I and the Divine Right of Kings: English Politics and Continental Theory' in Peck, LL (ed.), *The Mental World of the Jacobean Court* (Cambridge: Cambridge University Press) 55–70.

'Tom-Tell-Troath or a Free Discourse Touching the Manners of the Time' (1809) in *The Harleian Miscellany*, vol 3 (London: Robert Dutton) 428–452.

Weldon, A (1817) *The Court and Character of King James* (London: Smeeton).

Wilson, A (1653) *The History of Great Britain, Being the Life and Reign of King James the First* (London: Richard Lownds).

Worlmand, J (1991) 'James VI and I, *Basilikon Doron* and the *Trew Law of Free Monarchies*: The Scottish Context and the English Translation' in Peck, LL (ed.), *The Mental World of the Jacobean Court* (Cambridge: Cambridge University Press) 36–54.

Young, MB (2000) *King James and the History of Homosexuality* (New York: New York University Press).

Notes

1 For example, in describing a show that he plans to set up for the king, Gaveston titillates the play's audience through a bucolic imagery involving a cross-dressing boy hiding with an olive branch 'those parts which men delight to see' (Marlowe, 1995: 326). Edward's relationship with Gaveston is also normalised by comparing it with such historical antecedents as Alexander and Hephaistion (344).

2 For example, Edward declares to Piers that 'but to honour thee is Edward pleased with kingly regiment' (Marlowe, 1995: 329); and he contemplates giving up his kingdom and retiring to a private life shared with Gaveston (335).

3 Marlowe's play is frequently discussed in queer scholarship on early modern England: diGangi (1997: 108–115); King (2004: 56–61); Smith (1994: 209–223).

4 In 1603 Ben Jonson had staged his play *Sejanus*, an allegory of despotic rule, describing the eponymous villain of the play as a former prostitute and 'the noted *Pathick* [that is, sexually passive male] of the Time' (Johnson, 1729: 309), who had managed to win the favour of Tiberius – 'Emp'ror, only in his Lusts' (361) – and become 'The Partner of the Empire' (309). It is conceivable, too, that Hacket and his contemporaries had a sense of the homoerotic undercurrents of the biblical relationship between the Persian king Ahasuerus and his evil favourite Aman, from whom Queen Esther saves him, remedying through her intervention the deficient 'heterosexual buffering of the inexplicit intensities between them' (Sedgwick, 1990: 82).

5 On James and Lennox's relationship, see Bergeron (1999) 32–64.

6 *Edward II*, however, cannot have been intended as social commentary applicable to James I of *England*, as by the time it was staged James had not acceded to the English throne. This is true also of Jonson's *Sejanus*: although it was staged in the year when James became king of England, that was well before the king's involvement with his most notorious favourites, Robert Carr and George Villiers. Jonson's play aside, there is evidence that comparisons between James and Tiberius – Sejanus' imperial patron – did circulate during his time as king of England. In the 1650s Wilson (1653: proeme) wrote that '[s]ome *Parallel'd* James to *Tiberius* for *Dissimulation*'. More than two decades after the Lennox affair, a biography of Sejanus (Pierre Matthieu's *The Powerful Favorite*), translated into English from the original French, was widely interpreted as an allegory of the tyrannical power wielded by James's favourite Buckingham, who had no less influence on James's son Charles than he had had over the father (Friedeburg, 2011: 23).

7 Hammond (2002: 121–124) discusses a poem on Edward II and Gaveston, which the author, Michael Dayton, repeatedly revised out of fear that it could be interpreted as a critique of James I.

8 References to same-sex attracted rulers from Graeco-Roman antiquity could be invoked also without malicious intent. Hammond (2002: 128) reports an incident in which, during a masque performed on New Year's Day in 1604, the performers drew an erotically charged analogy between James and Alexander, clearly intended both to flatter and titillate the king. In general, early modern discourses about same-sex desire engaged both liberally and imaginatively with literary materials from antiquity (Hammond, 2002: 44; Smith, 1994: 20).

9 For brief illustrations of James's leadership in matters of both domestic and foreign policy see Croft (2003: 20–21, 82, 174).

10 Writers sympathetic to James, however, were suggesting even at the time that Elizabeth's virtues may have 'now become Torches in the dark, which appear greatest afar off, as his Vices (made so by some writers) do neer at hand' (Sanderson, 1656: proeme).

11 The king's misspending of money on his male favourites was a ground of complaint against Edward II too. Osborne's work has been described as 'full of prejudice and inaccuracy', Houlbrooke (2006: 172).

12 Sanderson (1650: 98) disputes this and claims that James spent time in the country because he loved sports and was advised to live where the air was wholesome owing to an 'unwildines or weaknes in his *Limbs*'.

13 This point was echoed by Osborne (1689: 424), who mocked James as a 'Sylvan Prince' 'intent upon *Ease* and *Pleasure*'.

14 James I (1995a: 20) himself believed in the idea that kings govern as much by making and executing laws as by setting examples.

15 The editor of the 1811 edition of Peyton's (1811: 307) work describes Peyton as a 'prejudiced enemy' of the Stuarts and a supporter of Cromwell who probably 'expected a theocracy similar to that of the Jews under the laws of Moses'.

16 For instance, speaking of Bacon's sodomitical practices, Sir Simonds D'Ewes states that it is a 'secret sin' that should be buried 'in silence' (McCormick, 1997: 52, reproducing a passage from *Sir Simonds D'Ewes Life*, written by himself, 3 May 1621).

17 According to Peyton (1811: 353–355), for example, Villiers's chief delight was deflowering virgins, and James assisted in procuring the opportunity for him to so do.

18 Thus, in Renaissance England a commoner who dressed above his station could be accused of effeminacy, but so too could an aristocratic male whose attire

failed to navigate the correct course between sobriety and extravagance (Kuchta, 1993).

19 Young (2000: 69–77) has provided a compelling counter-argument to the conventional scholarly view that early modern discourses tended to distance effeminacy from same-sex desire (particularly sodomy) – and he has done so precisely in the context of a discussion of James.

20 Other contemporary sources associate effeminacy with same-sex desire. D'Ewes, for example, in making a case for sodomy being Bacon's worst sin, informs us that the jurist used to keep 'a very effeminate-faced youth, to be his catamite and bedfellow' (McCormick, 1997: 52). Here the effeminacy (which, evidently, is not merely accidentally linked to the youth's status as a 'catamite') has to do with gender presentation, but it seems likely that his effeminate face is intended to signal an effeminate subjectivity too.

21 For a discussion see Christianson (1991: 91–94).

22 See also Sanchez (2011: 21–22) noting that, for James, 'affection is a duty' and drawing the implication that subjects cannot ever justly rebel against their king. Sanchez is correct, but the marriage analogy works both ways: the monarch too cannot abandon his subjects and has a duty to love them and do justly by them (James thought kings had a responsibility to exercise power benevolently).

23 For discussions of this logic in the contemporary context see Barker (2013); Auchmuty (2012).

24 By this I mean the lack of an equivalent to heterosexual marriage. Others have argued that same-sex desire was 'institutionalised' in early modern England, but it is apparent that by 'institutionalisation' they mean the routine practical integration of practices of same-sex desire into certain social institutions, rather than the publicly endorsed formalisation of certain practices of same-sex desire as an institution in its own right (which is just what marriage does for different-sex desire). Thus Bray (1995: 33–57) has argued that same-sex desire was 'institutionalised' not only through prostitution, but also in the household (for instance through master/servant or labourer/apprentice relationships) and the school (particularly tutor-pupil relationships). But see Shepard (2003: 116–122), qualifying Bray's arguments. King (2004) has taken this institutionalisation argument further. He speaks of erotic relationships between males in seventeenth-century England in terms of 'pederasty', to highlight their hierarchical organisation around the power (but not necessarily the age) differentials of the partners.

25 While the facts seem to speak to James's long-lasting loyalty to his favourites Lennox, Carr and Villiers, James's detractors deplored his supposed inconstancy. An uncritical acceptance of their accounts made Birch (1849) style James, in the mid-nineteenth century, a 'fickle king' (375) and a 'Christian Pacha' enjoying a 'male hareem' (viii). Weldon (1817) is representative of James's seventeenth-century detractors, asserting that the king quickly tired of his favourites (47, 56); that he welcomed Carr's involvement with the Countess of Essex because his eye had begun 'to wander after a new Favourite [Villiers]' (24); and that later, secretly grown tired of Villiers himself, he had hoped to lose him in Spain, even at the cost of the loss of his own son Charles (they had both gone to Spain on a mission to bring off Charles's match with the *infanta*) (45). Weldon's exaggerations and inaccuracies are rebutted by Sanderson (1650; 1656), Goodman (1839) and Hacket (1693). On the point of the king tiring of Villiers see Sanderson (1650: 182–183), Hacket (1693: 115) and Goodman (1839: 385).

26 Carr alienated the king's feelings by quarrelling and starting to refuse physical intimacy (Crompton, 2003: 386–387; Bergeron, 1999: 80–91). But the evidence

is in James's private letters and Goodman would not necessarily have been aware of it.

27 An equivocal and inexplicit representation of same-sex desire in a positive light was however possible in the context of drama, literature and poetry (Smith, 1994: 267–270; Hammond, 2002: 6–7, 16–20). The difference between these discourses and those that made no room for this representation is that the latter (legal, political and moral discourses) claimed a connection to rationality – although they may have only *postured* as rational discourses. In this connection Mager (1994: 158–159) argues that from the early Tudor period a standard feature of public discourses about sodomy was their masquerading as rational.

28 Bray (1995: 24–32) argues that the early modern popularity of the myth of Sodom and Gomorrah is the reason why same-sex sexuality was associated with ideas of social disorder (causing divine retribution) and hence was regarded as an abomination.

29 See also Shepard (2003: 22–25) testifying to the widespread presence of a discourse of 'perfect friendship' between two males – a relationship modelled on the Aristotelian idea of *philia* between equals. Bray (1995: 40–61) argues that a relationship of *philia* could became socially intelligible – and hence abhorred – as sodomy if one had reason to doubt its egalitarian and non-mercenary nature. The ease of manipulation of the distinction between sodomy and *philia*, alongside the fact that both could involve public displays of affection, made sodomy accusations a formidable weapon. diGangi (1997: 1–2, 12, 16–17), arguing that the distinction between the homosocial and the homoerotic is hard to draw in the Renaissance, prefers to speak of 'orderly' (socially countenanced) homoerotic practices and 'disorderly' (sodomitical) homoerotic practices.

30 Similar arguments had been used against Edward II and his interest in Gascony.

31 These charges take up virtually all of the pamphlet *Tom-Tell-Troath* (1809), apparently dating from 1622. Variants of the pseudonym Tom-Tell-Troath appear in several early modern texts (Purkis, 2011: 115).

32 For further evidence of the link drawn by James's contemporaries between pacifism, cowardice and effeminacy see Young (2000) 77–80. Young (2000: 85–101) has plausibly argued that James's peaceful policies generated national anxiety about English manhood and that England's eventual involvement in the Thirty Years War was partly due to an urge to prove that the nation was capable of living up to the ideal of chivalric manliness by rescuing James's daughter Elizabeth.

33 It is possible that Weldon means that this was the first of James's *English* favourites.

34 See, for example, McMullan's (1994: 140) discussion of a passage in the *'Brief Lives,' Chiefly of Contemporaries, set down by John Aubrey between the Years 1669 and 1696.*

35 Alternatively, Sanderson was trying to counter the charge, examined below, that James surrounded himself with favourites in order to hide behind them when intent on governing badly.

36 Even Weldon (1817: 19–20), a harsh critic of James's, describes Carr, at the time he entered into the king's favour, as someone 'that was observed to spend his time in serious studies, and did accompany himselfe with none but men of such eminences, as by whom he might be bettered'. Thus, James's decision to advance Carr may have not been as arbitrary as we are generally led to believe.

37 Croft (2003: 90–91) has defended James's conduct in relation to this incident.

38 Hacket (1693) points out that even Wilson, who opposed all 'Regians', called Buckingham 'our English *Alcibiades* for Beauty, Civility, Bounty' (39); but he concedes that Villiers had a 'fault too patent against all Apology', being 'of very

desultorious Affection' (40). Hacket presumably means Villiers's social allegiances (not his affection for James, which appears to have been genuine and enduring).

39 Wilson (1653: 185–186) states that the king asked for money, but all that Parliament could see was that it would be lavished on Buckingham. In reality James had inherited a massive debt from Elizabeth (Russell, Cust and Thrush, 2011: 3–13). The absence of effective supervision on ministerial expenditure, coupled with James's prodigious liberality, made it impossible for the situation not to get worse (Gardiner, 1862: ix–xx). In a 1604 speech to Parliament, James I (1995b: 144–145) apologised for the burden on the public purse caused by his liberality in according honours and rewards, while at the same time eloquently articulating their rationale.

40 Goodman's and Hacket's works, both conceived as responses to Weldon's unsympathetic account, were not published until the nineteenth century, giving perhaps a clue to the relatively disinterested motivations of their authors in writing them.

41 While James I (1995a: 23) generally thought strict application of the laws should be tempered by the imperative of substantively doing justice in particular cases, he made an exception for certain 'horrible crimes', including 'sodomie'. This comment is found in *Basilikon Doron*, which James VI of Scotland wrote before his accession to the English throne. Scotland, however, had no civil offence of sodomy at the time; and the breadth of the traditional meaning of 'sodomy' (Bray, 1995, 14; Hammond, 2002: 8–9) means that James could have had any number of things in mind when making his comment about strictly enforcing it. These things almost certainly included sexual activities between males, but James may well have had in mind only penetrative ones. Compare Young (2000, 36–50) (also arguing that James almost certainly had sex with men). James addressed the issue again eleven years later, in 1610, instructing Lord Chancellor Burleigh not to extend to those guilty of sodomy the pardon customarily issued at the end of a Parliament session (Crompton, 2003: 386). In early modern England 'sodomy' was more typically a category of moral discourse; the law preferred the term 'buggery'. Henry VIII had made the crime against nature a civil offence for the first time in the Buggery Act 1533 (25 Henry 8, Chapter 6), which, as Smith (1994: 43–45) conclusively demonstrated, was enacted as a political and economic weapon against the Catholic Church. By the time of Elizabeth's reign, the Act (which had been variously repealed, re-enacted and modified) had reconfigured the offence in ways that separated it from considerations of political expediency. Indictments, however, were extremely rare and convictions even more so, essentially targeting only the anal penetration of a non-consenting male, generally underage (political uses of the law did away with these requirements, but they were exceptional) (Smith, 1994: 45–53; see also Bray 1995: 71–74). It is possible that James had this non-consensual scenario in mind when he provided that no pardon should be accorded to those convicted of sodomy in 1610.

42 James I (1995a: 39) also advised his son that if a man expects (as men do) to marry a virgin, than he himself should keep chaste until marriage.

Chapter 4

The Victorian Age: The rhetorical conflation of homosexuality and poor government in the Cleveland Street and Dublin Castle scandals

Introduction

The number of men prosecuted and punished for same-sex sexual activity rose dramatically in the nineteenth century (Cocks, 2007: 109). In the 1880s, two same-sex political scandals, known as the Dublin Castle scandal and the Cleveland Street scandal, rocked the United Kingdom. These coincided with what is generally regarded as a seismic shift in the problematisation of same-sex desire in Europe. As I argued, the idea that same-sex desire (or some form thereof, like a desire to be penetrated) not merely impels one to action but marks one's subjectivity can be traced back to antiquity. It was not until the late Victorian age, however, that subjectivities marked by same-sex desire were specifically understood in terms of 'homosexuality': an object of sustained scientific study for the newly established discipline of sexology and, some twenty years later, psychoanalysis (Foucault, 1998; Weeks, 1991: 69–74). Indeed, it was in 1886 – a mere two years after the Dublin scandal – that Krafft-Ebing published the first German-language edition of *Psychopathia Sexualis*, to whose subsequent editions the popularisation of the term 'homosexuality' is generally credited.[1] And only about half a decade after the Cleveland Street scandal, Havelock Ellis published *Sexual Inversion*.

Because the work of sexologists was still in the making at the time when the Dublin and Cleveland Street scandals occurred, however, their discourse appears to have had a very limited effect, if any, on the treatment of these scandals in the sources I discuss in this chapter. Indeed, Kaplan (1999: 84) argues that no contemporary treatment of the Cleveland Street scandal discussed homosexuality in terms of pathology. As to the Dublin scandal, homosexuality was pathologised to the extent that it was represented as a form of leprosy, but this differs from the way in which sexological discourse pathologised homosexuality. The universalising representation of homosexuality as leprosy drew attention to the risk of contagion that it posed. The pathologisation of homosexuality in sexological discourse, however, was primarily (although not exclusively) linked to the minoritising idea of a congenital inversion of sexual desire grounded in a constitutional degeneracy (Mondimore: 1996: 35–36).

The lack of engagement with new sexological knowledge, however, does not mean that public discussion of the Cleveland Street and Dublin Castle scandals unimaginatively reiterated previous centuries' *topoi* on political authority vis-à-vis same-sex desire. Some continuity can be detected, but the case for same-sex desire interfering with the good exercise of public powers does not primarily hinge on arguments deployed in previous centuries to discredit same-sex attracted rulers. Furthermore, parallels with King James and Edward II are absent, while those with classical antiquity are scarce and as a rule do not specifically refer to Graeco-Roman same-sex attracted *statesmen*. For example, a source commenting on the Cleveland Street scandal makes no more than a very generic reference to the wickedness of the 'Greeks or Romans, in the days of their greatest degradation and debasement' (NA-18), without singling out, for example, the emperors Elagabalus or Tiberius.

In the context of the Dublin Castle affair, *United Ireland* – the newspaper responsible for precipitating the scandal – in one of its attacks against a homo-sexual public official did make a reference to the classical myth of Pythias and Damon (RMA-12). But this was simply a stratagem aimed at clarifying the same-sex nature of the allegations against the official. The myth of Pythias and Damon was routinely understood to allude to same-sex relationships in the nineteenth century (Kaye, 2002: 64), and it was a convenient metaphor for *United Ireland* to convey the idea of same-sex sexual conduct. Some such stratagem was all but necessary as, in the 1880s same-sex desire was deemed capable only of oblique reference by many of those publicly discussing it (Adut, 2005: 222–223). The medieval 'namelessness' of same-sex desire had, in the late Victorian age, been taken to the extreme that 'unmentionability' or 'unspeakability' – generally aided by such words as 'horrific' or 'abominable' or, as is the case with *United Ireland*'s article, some appropriately coded reference – stood in for the thing itself (see Cocks, 2007: 107, 113; Murphy, 2010: 187–188).

United Ireland was the propaganda machine of the nationalist party of Charles Stewart Parnell (O'Brien, 1976: 14–15) – the Irish nationalist leader advocating home rule for Ireland. Dublin Castle, the seat of the British administration in Ireland, had become a powerful symbol of colonial oppression. *United Ireland*'s director William O'Brien was doing his unrelenting best to attack Castle officials and it was his nationalist newspaper that ignited the Dublin scandal by making revelations about the homosexuality of two such officials. *United Ireland*'s deci-sion to denounce Castle officials' homosexuality through the Damon and Pythias metaphor to discredit the tyrannical government of Dublin Castle was, however, deeply ironic. For not only do Damon and Pythias figure in the myth as paragons of manly virtues, but also, at least in the most popular Irish recounting of the myth, as defenders of political freedom.

The myth tells of how a Greek man pledged his person with Dionysius, tyrant of Syracuse, as security for his bosom friend, who, albeit sentenced to death, temporarily evaded custody to attend to some vital affairs, but returned in time to release his companion and face his own execution. The story is told in classical sources, including Cicero and Valerius Maximus, but it seems more than likely that the author of the article in *United Ireland* became acquainted with it through the Irish playwright John Banim's popular recounting of the myth in his 1821 play *Damon and Pythias.* In addition to its portrayal of same-sex love as on a par, and capable of happily coexisting, with different-sex attachments, what is distinctive about Banim's version of the story is that it makes the play's namesakes champions of political freedom. Banim's Damon and Pythias are, like Harmodius and Aristogeiton, sworn enemies of tyrannical rule. In Banim's (1860) play, the reason why Damon – who calls Pythias his 'gallant soldier' and 'halved heart' (12) – is condemned to die is his attempt to kill Dionysius, who plots to become king and sole ruler of Syracuse with the complicity of the senate. Himself a senator and one who deeply cares for 'all the noble rights that freemen love' (Banim, 1860: 23), Damon is outraged by the senate's voting for its own dissolution and for trading its right to political participation for the prospect of increased security and a supposedly wiser and better rule at the hand of the tyrant (24).

In short, Banim's *Damon and Pythias* all but relocated to Syracuse the founding myth of Athenian democracy. In doing so, it provided a counterpoint to prevailing discourses about the relationship between same-sex desire and political rule. It demonstrated, that is, the possibility of weaving counter-truths even after centuries of conventional wisdom that had put same-sex desire at odds with legitimate authority and the good exercise of public powers. At the same time, the fact that the author of *United Ireland*'s article could so easily overlook – or treat as inconsequential – the myth's tyrannicidal associations suggests that Banim's counter-discourse about the relationship between same-sex desire and political freedom was just that. It was a discourse that ran *counter* to prevailing understandings of that relationship.

While the felicity of his use of the Damon and Pythias metaphor may be open to question, O'Brien's general tactic of using the homosexuality of Castle officials as a way of attacking British rule in Ireland was everything but inapt. He clearly realised the potential that a virulently anti-homosexual rhetoric had for exerting a powerful leverage on public opinion – and he made sure to exploit it to full effect. Half a decade later, the Liberal MP Henry Labouchere would adopt a similar strategy in the context of the Cleveland Street scandal, this time in a bid to attack the Conservative government of Lord Salisbury.

Dublin Castle and the cases against French and Cornwall

Established in 1204, Dublin Castle – the seat of the English, and later the British, administration in Ireland – is virtually as old as the history of Irish colonisation. That history had begun three decades before, with thousands of English and Welsh settlers hoping to improve their social status by relocating to the neighbouring island. Only six years after the Castle was established, King John created the British administrative structure that would operate from it and instituted a judicial system based on the English common law (Bartlett, 2010: 36–46). By

Tudor times, the English Crown held an area called the Pale, extending northwards and eastwards of Dublin; the rest of Ireland was under the control of either Irish rulers or powerful English barons. The Tudors and Stuarts started a more systematic and aggressive policy of colonisation. They did so by suppressing rebellion; by substituting the common law for the authority of Irish rulers; and by encouraging further (Protestant) settlement, which eventually led to a concentration of the most desirable land in settlers' hands (Lockyer, 2005: 162–172). The Act of Union of 1801 – conceived both as a way of consolidating British control and leading to the 'emancipation' of Catholics, who had hitherto not enjoyed full political rights (Jackson, 2010: 24–26) – hailed the birth of the United Kingdom of Great Britain and Ireland. It abolished the Irish Parliament, instead providing for Irish representation within the British Parliament.

Even after the union, however, the Castle continued to rule Ireland according to an imperialist logic. For one thing, the Castle administration lacked representativeness. As nationalist politician Justin M'Carthy (1885) explained in a newspaper piece entitled 'On Dublin Castle and Irish Discontent' (published shortly after the Dublin scandal had run its course), the Lord Lieutenant ('absolute master of the political rule of the country'), the Chief Secretary (who, in practice, had responsibility for the country's government) and all 'permanent officials' were almost invariably either English or Scottish and Protestant. As to Dublin Castle itself, M'Carthy (1885) described it as 'an absolute anomaly in a civilisation like ours' – one where 'despotism', rather than the constitutionalism characterising other parts of the United Kingdom, reigned.

Economic deprivation, religious sentiment and political disempowerment contributed to considerable unrest throughout the nineteenth century and the Castle's repressive responses exacerbated the people's discontent (Jenkins, 2006: 10–21). In 1879, the Irish National Land League, created to protect and advance the interests of tenant farmers vis-à-vis landlords, gave impetus to the nationalist movement led by Charles Stuart Parnell. The ensuing 'land war' – centred on 'boycott' against non-cooperative landlords – had the effect of waking up the British political class not only to issues of Irish land tenancy (legislation was passed to meet some of the farmers' grievances), but also to the question of home rule (Pelling, 2003: 37–47). Through the Irish National League and the Home Rule League (later renamed the Irish Parliamentary Party), Parnell's promotion of the home rule cause became more systematic in the 1880s.

Delegitimising the Castle was integral to the campaign for home rule. *United Ireland*, the press organ of Parnell's party, played a vital role in doing so (O'Brien, 1976: 17). The newspaper, launched in 1881, was an overnight success, with a readership estimated at 500,000. O'Brien, the newspaper's director, was a passionate nationalist and a staunch Parnellite (O'Brien, 1976: 15). Having suffered imprisonment with other nationalist leaders, O'Brien must have welcomed the opportunity specifically to target, by denouncing their homosexuality, James Ellis French and Gustavus C Cornwall. French, as Detective Director of the Royal Irish Constabulary and County Inspector, played an important role in the detection of crime; so did, to some extent, Cornwall, who, as Secretary of the General Post Office, could intercept and monitor correspondence. O'Brien made no mystery of the fact that, in denouncing these officials' sexuality in both *United Ireland* and in the House of Commons, where he sat as an MP, his design was to inflict a blow on the British administration in Ireland as a whole. These men, *United Ireland* declared, 'do the work of Government in Ireland . . . With the poor wretch himself we have no quarrel beyond the disgust of ordinary humanity against his crimes. Our war is with his masters' (RMA-13).

United Ireland's revelations about French's and Cornwall's homosexuality spawned a number of civil lawsuits for libel as well as criminal proceedings. French failed to take forward in a timely fashion the civil action against O'Brien, and his suit was unsuccessful. He was found guilty of unnatural practices in the criminal trial and sentenced to two years' imprisonment, after enduring trial three times because the jury could not agree on a verdict ('The Dublin Scandals', 1884b). In the original libel action instituted by Cornwall against O'Brien, the verdict was for the newspaper's director. Cornwall was then arrested and committed for trial in the criminal case for 'unnatural offences'. In August 1884 he was acquitted of the felonious charge of buggery, but there was no jury agreement on the mis- demeanour charge – that is, on the charge that he had 'conspired, confederated and agreed to procure young men and boys . . . to commit certain lewd and filthy acts to wit masturbation and mutual pollution, against the peace and the statute' (RMA-11). A second trial on the misdemeanour charge followed in October of the same year. Cornwall was acquitted again. The judge, summing up the case for the jury, had indicated that the investigator paid by O'Brien to collect evidence against Cornwall 'resorted to any contrivance to procure evidence' and that one of the 'tainted witnesses' on whose testimony the prosecution case rested had 'admitted he had the strongest possible reason for trumping up a case against Cornwall' ('The Dublin Scandals', 1884a). The *Freeman's Journal* argued that the acquittals were due to the prosecution putting forward their case in a 'lame and abortive way' (RMA-7). Being acquitted of all the criminal charges, Cornwall applied to have the verdict of the jury in the civil action set aside and the case re-tried. Judge Murphy, turning down the application in the Common Pleas, declared that there was sufficient evidence that Cornwall belonged to 'a vile gang' consorting 'for the pursuit of unnatural depravity and vice' (RMA-7). Cornwall appealed the decision. The Court of Appeal ruled that the only portion of the verdict against Cornwall that should be set aside was that which related to the commission of the felony; but this was a ground for damages worth only 'one farthing, or any smaller coin, if such existed' (RMA-2). Cornwall declined to appeal the case to the House of Lords for want of means (RMA-1).

Apart from the personal and financial consequences for the accused, the broader political significance of the scandals was plain to everyone. In the immediate aftermath of the scandal M'Carthy explained: '[T]he Irish peasant . . . knows that these men were paid officials and the Castle's favourites . . . Dublin Castle is, in the Irishman's experience, the place which imprisons the men he loves and keeps in its pay persons of atrocious character' (M'Carthy, 1885). Similarly, when Cornwall's libel action against O'Brien failed, the National League told the crowds celebrating in Cork that now 'a little more determined resistance and co-operation on the part of the Irish people would root out Dublin Castle and leave the government of the country in their own hands' ('The Dublin Scandals' 1884c).

Unspeakability and exceptionality

O'Brien's offensive began on 25 August 1883, when *United Ireland* threatened to lay 'bare to the universe' French's 'life and adventures and . . . private character'. On 6 October, the newspaper declared that 'an official intimately connected with the detection of crime in Dublin [had] been suspended from his functions under circumstances that are likely to create profound sensation when they are revealed'. Five days later *United Ireland* took credit for driving the 'foul bird' to flight when it had threatened to expose 'his detestable crimes'; it added that a 'filthier wretch was not in the hire of the Castle', emphasising the connection between him and the higher orders of political authority by calling him 'a special Viceregal pet' ('Action against "United Ireland"', 1883).

For twenty-first century readers it may be hard to believe that anyone, having no previous knowledge of French's homosexuality, could have understood the nature of the charges made against him in these newspaper articles. But *United Ireland* was almost certainly following well-established semantic conventions to convey the idea of homosexuality, by using such terms as 'private character' and 'detestable'. As already mentioned, the standard way of referring to same-sex sexual activity at the time involved a failure to mention it directly, accompanied by a number of strategies drawing attention precisely to that failure. The most effective of these strategies involved the actual use of the words 'unspeakable', 'nameless' or 'unmentionable'. In two 1884 *United Ireland* articles, French and Cornwall themselves are called 'the unspeakables' (RMA-22; RMA-23).

O'Brien launched his attack on Cornwall in May 1884. The charges levelled at the Secretary of the General Post Office, while still in keeping with the idea that homosexuality is unspeakable and can only be referred to obliquely, were worded in a more revealing way compared to those initially made against French. Not only did *United Ireland*, in this opening attack on Cornwall, deploy the Pythias and Damon metaphor, but it also conjured up the spectre of effeminacy. In announcing, on 10 May 1884, that Cornwall was apparently planning to leave the country, *United Ireland* sarcastically commented that they agreed about 'the unsuitability of our humid climate to an official of his tastes' (RMA-12). Two weeks later, it was reiterated that 'Mr Cornwall is finding the Irish Climate trying to one of his delicate organisation' (RMA-13).

Unlike its deployment in case studies from previous centuries, it is unclear that the imputation of 'softness' and, hence, effeminacy is made here with a view to discrediting the competence with which a public official carries out his duties. In the case of King James, for example, his effeminacy was considered to be bound up with his cowardice, which in turn was deemed to account for his excessively peaceful and conciliatory policies. Cornwall's effeminacy, in contrast, is simply used as a device to convey the idea of his homosexuality, which cannot be directly mentioned. His homosexuality, in turn, is assumed to disqualify him *ipso facto* from public office; but the reader will look in vain for some underlying rationale as to why this should be the case. Unlike the case studies from previous eras, there is no suggestion that same-sex desire makes a statesman liable to being badly counselled, favouring the undeserving, or choosing certain kinds of (undesirable) policies. Rather, same-sex sexual activity is a crime – indeed, the worst crime imaginable – and that in itself disposes of the need for adducing any reasons why it is incompatible with public office.

The exceptional gravity of same-sex sexual conduct (and its consequent ability automatically to disqualify from public office those who practise it) is made apparent in the same *United Ireland* article that imputes effeminacy to Cornwall. In describing French, Cornwall and Bolton – another Castle official accused of criminal conduct – as 'rats in the Castle cellars', and in taking credit for driving them out, *United Ireland* referred to them as 'fraudsters, adulterers or worse' (RMA-13). Adultery and fraud were Bolton's crimes (he had perpetrated fraud, incidentally, at the expense of his own wife); French and Cornwall, however, were guilty of a 'worse' crime. The sentiment was echoed by an Irish MP, Arthur O'Connor, who stated that compared to French's crimes, 'the delinquencies of Bolton were venial' (*Hansard*-4: 684).

One week later, on 31 May, *United Ireland* almost appeared to retract this statement. In an article entitled 'Is This One of George [Bolton]'s Jokes?' it ridiculed Bolton for suing the newspaper for libel for six times as much money in damages than Cornwall had done. The newspaper sarcastically commented: 'Bad as Mr George Bolton's character is, it is worth six times as much as that of Mr. Gustavus Cornwall' (RMA-16). The point was elaborated upon the following week. The newspaper stated that they had 'carefully discriminated between the mere swindler, adulterer, forger, and bankrupt and the beasts in comparison with whose performances [Bolton] evidently regards fraud and adultery with pardonable complacency'. It went on to characterise Bolton's crimes as 'of the blunt, natural, honour-among-thieves, penal-servitude-for-life order of human imperfections' (RMA-17).

While the sarcasm so effectively used in the 31 May article has the effect of de-exceptionalising homosexuality in the context of this specific text, the idea of homosexuality's exceptional gravity, among all other offences that public officers could conceivably commit, is a leitmotif of the Dublin scandal. M'Carthy, for example, seemed altogether serious when he stated that the offences of Cornwall and French outdid those of Bolton, whom he described as 'guilty, not indeed of offences anything like those which were brought out in what are called distinctively the Dublin scandals' (M'Carthy, 1885). It was homosexual offences – not any criminal offence – that exposed the political apparatus of Dublin Castle in all its scandalous corruption.

Mr Trevelyan, the Chief Secretary for Ireland, agreed: in the Commons, he declared himself shocked at *United Ireland*'s calling Bolton, French and Cornwall a 'precious trio', thereby implying that Bolton too was guilty of the 'atrocious crime' attributed to Cornwall and French (*Hansard*-4: 698). He reiterated the point a few months later, stating that 'a general allegation of breach of trust or forgery against some well-known public official' could safely 'be neglected'; but it was 'a very different matter' when such charges 'of a very grave nature' as those appearing against French and Cornwall in *United Ireland* were made (*Hansard*-2: 1813). In these cases, according to Trevelyan, the appropriate response was for the government to ask the officials concerned to either clear their names or resign. Timothy Healy, for the nationalists, retorted that this was not an adequate course of action in response to such crimes, purporting to show through an analogy that the government should have proceeded to investigate the matter as soon as an allegation had been made:

> Suppose the charge ... had been one of murder, made by a landlord's paper–supposing that The Daily Express had stated that the hon. Member for Mallow (Mr. O'Brien) had killed the Chief Secretary in the Phœnix Park ... would [the Government] have made no further answer, and ... allowed [O'Brien] to clear himself by means of trial by way of an action for libel?
>
> (*Hansard*-2: 1819)

Plainly, Healy saw no difference between homosexuality and murder.

As for *United Ireland* itself, it missed no opportunity to drive the same message home, referring to same-sex sexual activities as 'infamies more appalling than death itself' (RMA-18), a 'conspiracy against the very existence of society' (RMA-21) and 'infinitely more repulsive to human nature than most felonies' (RMA-25). Cornwall himself was 'a person more dangerous to human society than a wild beast in the streets' and 'a monster whose guilt exceeds that of nine-tenths of the wretches' in jail (RMA-25). For the *Freeman's Journal*, the Dublin scandal involved 'the greatest questions of public morality' (RMA-6). When Cornwall appealed the Common Pleas' decision in the libel case in which he had impugned *United Ireland*'s attacks, the Court remarked that there would be 'few who would not take the chance of the first felon who might happen to be discharged from any felon's prison in the country as an associate rather than the owner of such a reputation as the plaintiff's' (RMA-3).

The rhetorical status of homosexuality as the worst crime one could possibly commit strongly indicates that these late Victorian political scandals did not simply happen to be about homosexuality. Rather, the exceptional opprobrium attached to homosexuality in public discourse in the late Victorian age made imputations of homosexuality a particularly powerful resource for those seeking to discredit particular individuals and the institutions to which they were attached with a view to advancing contingent political ends. This enabled O'Brien and

Labouchere to escalate the Dublin Castle and Cleveland Street affairs into full-blown political scandals.

The Castle's 'homosexuality'

I argued above that the point of attacking the sexuality of Cornwall and French was to discredit the Castle as a whole. The argument here – central to virtually all the contributions made by O'Brien and his supporters on the matter of the scandal, whether in print or in the House of Commons – was that the Castle was doing its utmost to protect its officials (RMA-15). Importantly, this argument enabled O'Brien to metaphorically 'homosexualise' the Castle itself:

> Mr Trevelyan [the Chief Secretary] has now confessed that . . . [they] had *prima facie* evidence that the charges against [French] were true, but deter-mined to observe a benevolent neutrality . . . because (at [the Castle's] instigation) he had brought an action for libel against this journal. Was there ever an admission that so completely identified the Irish Government as accessories to the fact to nameless crime?
>
> (RMA-15)[2]

Similarly, the *Freeman's Journal* opined that 'for months, if not years, the author-ities must have been acquainted with the unspeakable horrors and are to a certain extent *participes criminis*' ('The Dublin Scandals', 1884c).[3] Thus, the government was guilty not only of 'screening' (RMA-20; RMA-18) homosexual suspects and failing 'to deliver Dublin from the horrors of the sink of depravity in which these men lived' (*Hansard*-4: 694); but also, in so doing, it turned *itself* into a homosexual.

The homosexual character of the Castle is further consolidated through the use of language that echoes the treatment of same-sex attracted rulers in historical work from previous centuries. Thus *United Ireland*'s article on 24 May 1884 refers to 'French and his Castle patrons' and to 'a moral gangrene, murderous to the very existence of society . . . eating its way unchecked among the minions and favourites of [Lord Lieutenant Earl Spencer's] own entourage' (RMA-14). On 12 July 1884 the newspaper speaks again in terms of patronage: 'the devilish ministers [of this crime] were the very officers of justice and their patrons of the ruling castle' (RMA-18). For anyone familiar with the historical accounts of Edward II's and James I's reigns – discussed in chapters 2 and 3 – it is impossible not to read these passages, with their terminology centred on patronage and favouritism, without implicating the highest orders of the British government in Ireland in same-sex desire. Note that there is no argument here to the effect that first, the Castle is a den of sodo-mites and, secondly, that this results in poor government. There is, instead, a crafty *rhetorical* homosexualisation of the Castle as a seat of poor government.

A rather more crude exercise in homosexualising the Castle following the French and Cornwall scandals appears in an article published in the *Irish Citizen and Industrial Advocate* on 14 June 1884, entitled 'Earl Spencer and his Criminals'. According to the article, the Lord Lieutenant for Ireland 'is a man who employs criminals, *knowing* them to be criminal, and prefers them on that account' (RMA-8). Considering the nature of the crime at issue, this reads very much like a straight imputation of homosexuality on the head of the British government in Ireland. Interestingly, there is also at least one instance of the British government being deliberately homosexualised by O'Brien's political opponents. When they attempted to shame the government into energetically responding to *United Ireland*'s accusations of jury tinkering in one of the trials spawned by the Dublin scandal, they suggested that inaction would be taken as an indication that the government was lacking in heterosexual manliness. The government, they sarcastically argued, 'is at perfect liberty to . . . exhibit itself to the world as effete and cowardly', but it should at least protect jurymen exercising public functions (RMA-5).

Pollution and national sentiment

The 'homosexualisation' of the Castle, and, through it, of tyrannical rule, is also accomplished through the deployment of a bluntly nationalistic rhetoric that presents homosexuality as a quintessentially English vice (Walshe, 2005). According to Hanafin (2000), this rhetoric was an attempt to respond to the sexualised connotations of colonisation: casting doubt over England's masculinity meant shaking off the effeminacy associated with Ireland's submissive position in the configuration of imperial relations. *United Ireland* had already foreshadowed this rhetorical strategy in an article dating to May 1884, where it had referred to 'the seamy side of English Government in Ireland' (RMA-15). The strategy becomes particularly evident in July of the same year, following O'Brien's victory in the libel suit brought against him by Cornwall. Decrying the fact that the British government in Ireland was run by men 'bitterly alien to us in blood, creed, and sympathy', *United Ireland* speaks of 'the whole fabric of English rule within which the dark brood of the Cornwalls and Frenches have had their births and nurture' (RMA-18). It goes on to call the two Castle officials 'propagators of the horrible English leprosy' (RMA-18) and the 'foulest brood of monsters that English rule in Ireland ever produced' ('Second Edition', 1884).[4] Even Sir Patrick O'Brien, albeit a member of the Parliamentary majority, spoke of the need of 'preserving the purity of Ireland from being offended by acquaintance with abominable practices' (*Hansard*-1: 938).

This nationalistic rhetoric constructing homosexuality as a foreign import may have been particularly powerful because the inner logic of homosexuality as pollution – manifest in much public discourse about same-sex desire in the late nineteenth century – mirrored the imagery associated with concerns of foreign forces impinging upon the purity of national integrity: one set of images, thus, lent strength to the other. Unsurprisingly, the representation of homosexuality as a polluting force is ubiquitous in the context of the Dublin scandals. French drenched 'society with unnameable pollutions' (RMA-13). Cornwall was 'a monster of uncleanness' (RMA-24), 'whose depravity poisoned the air of Dublin', as well as 'carrion . . . [who] sickens society . . . with the odour of his filthy vice' (RMA-25). The 'pure air of Ireland' was said to urgently require delivery 'from unspeakable pollution', and to have been 'cleansed' by O'Brien's victory in the libel action (RMA-18). Homosexuality itself was a 'hellish crime . . . smoking in the midst of us, poisoning the very source and sweetness of human society, spreading its fearful ravages all the wider because it raged unseen' (RMA-18).[5]

This inflated rhetoric, centred on ideas of pollution and uncleanness, was not the exclusive province of popular journalism. It pervaded institutional settings too. M'Carthy stated in Parliament that the 'charge was that there was a mass of corruption festering round Dublin Castle' (*Hansard*-4: 722), and reported the (purportedly) popular opinion that Dublin was being converted 'into a foul Gehenna like the waters of the Sea of Sodom' (*Hansard*-2: 1850). In the Commons, O'Brien spoke of Cornwall as 'breeding the foul leprosy in Dublin' (*Hansard*-2: 1808). Similarly, in charging the jury, the trial judge in Cornwall's libel action against *United Ireland* explained that Cornwall was 'in danger . . . of utter and complete banishment from all decent society as a loathsome and impure person' (RMA-9). He added that the jury should not, however, hesitate to find 'a true verdict' if Cornwall indeed 'debauched and corrupted others until the wicked evil has spread to a circle whose limits no man may circumscribe, no more than he can stop a conflagration – if he has been the fountain and author of the immoral poison that festers and spreads unseen in the night' (RMA-9).[6]

This over-the-top treatment of homosexuality as pollution establishes a rhetorical connection between homosexuality and poor government. Just as the nationalistic rhetoric makes the 'English vice' and the Castle's poor government go hand in hand, so the pollution-centred terminology, repeated *ad nauseam*, conjures up an imagery of disease eating away at the Castle from the inside out, making poor government appear as an inevitable consequence of this corrupting influence. The inflated rhetoric is not an invitation to *reflect* about the real plausibility of any connections between homosexuality and poor government. Rather, it establishes those connections (which would not bear a test of rational scrutiny) as a matter of unreflective common sense. The effect of establishing these connections was – as much for the audience of these rhetorical flourishes as for their authors – to compound the sense of the illegitimacy of British rule in Ireland.

Thus, the representation of homosexuality as pollution takes the place of argument in articulating a link between homosexuality and poor government. In particular, if homosexuality contaminates those with which it comes into close proximity, it will corrupt governmental functions as much as anything else. Unsurprisingly, some MPs tried to rescue the reputation of the Castle by arguing that French's and Cornwall's *physical* connection with it was tenuous (so their crime could not possibly be due to a 'contaminating' effect on the part of the Castle itself):

> It was too often said in reference to these wretched charges in Dublin that they were due to the Castle. That was not so. . . . French's office was in one of the buildings in Lower Castle Yard . . . Cornwall's office was altogether outside the Castle; and he had nothing whatever to do with the Castle or the Executive Government
>
> (*Hansard*-5: 237)

While this passage shows a concern about the public viewing the Castle as a breeding ground for homosexuality among its officers, at other times the preoccupation was the reverse – that Cornwall's and French's homosexuality would corrupt that which they touched, particularly their public functions, and hence the work of government. Consider the treatment afforded by Healy to Bolton and French in the Commons, when in June 1884, a motion was made to appoint a Select Committee to inquire into the conduct of the government with regard to the criminal charges against Castle officials:

> This man Bolton – forger, adulterer, wife swindler – he who procured evidence and manipulated prisoners in their cells – did the in-door work of the Government; the out-door work was done by Mr. James Ellis French; they were the two branches of crime detection in Ireland. On the right of the Government there was George Bolton, and on their left James Ellis French. And [the Irish] were asked to have confidence in the administration of justice!
>
> (*Hansard*-4: 710)

As far as Bolton is concerned, the relevance of his wrongdoings to his inaptitude for public functions is either immediately clear (his crimes, involving as they did fraud of some kind or another, told against his trustworthiness as Crown Prosecutor) or explicitly articulated (he 'manipulated prisoners'). For French, however, a reference to his homosexuality is thought to be sufficient to discredit his work as Detective Director and County Inspector, despite the actual irrelevance of same-sex desire to the nature of French's public tasks. It is, furthermore – and in accordance with the conventions about homosexuality's unspeakability – an entirely phantasmatic reference, for it is conjured up in the reader's mind without the need for Healy's speech to supply it. Homosexuality (indeed, the phantasmatic shadow of it) can do this formidable work of accounting for what it does not in fact *rationally* explain (namely, that a homosexual Detective Director is unfit for his tasks) because the rhetoric of pollution and of exceptionality takes the place of reasoned argument.

The same dynamic can be appreciated one month later, when the Commons were debating public expenditure. Arthur O'Connor stated that French, given his position, must have surely controlled large sums of money, yet 'it had been discovered that French was absolutely unfit to be intrusted with anything of the kind' (*Hansard*-2: 1768). French's homosexuality, for O'Connor, made him *ipso facto* unable to manage public funds properly. Timothy Harrington, apparently alive to the *non sequitur* in his colleague's speech, tried to construct a contrived argument articulating why French's homosexuality was relevant (albeit in a highly mediated way) to his unsuitability for managing large sums of money:

> French himself was in the habit of writing to his friends, who were participators in his crime, sending messages to the detectives under him to observe the actions of those who were employed to spy upon his movements, in an endeavour to bring him to justice. . . . Could it be believed that they were carrying on their operations out of their own private resources?
>
> (*Hansard*-2: 1771–1773)

Harrington's contribution, striving to *logically* connect homosexuality to misadministration, was the exception. In general, those participating in these debates were satisfied that homosexuality *automatically* tainted the public work of same-sex attracted public officials. Thus, a few months later it was stated in the Commons that Irish inmates had been committed to prison on the basis of information which, being derived from Detective Director French, 'came from a foul and corrupted source' (*Hansard*-1: 935); and that the Irish government should have promptly investigated rumours of homosexuality against people in its pay to ascertain that the government's work was not being carried out by 'contaminating and vile officials' (*Hansard*-2: 1845).

Unequal justice

Approximately at the same time as the Dublin scandals were unravelling, the staunchly unionist (Dicey, 1886) AV Dicey (1915: 189) was formulating his famous definition of the rule of law, making the neutral enforcement of the law one of its main tenets:

> In England the idea of legal equality, or of the universal subjection of all classes to one law administered by the ordinary Courts, has been pushed to its utmost limit. . . . A colonial governor, a secretary of state, a military officer, and all subordinates . . . are as responsible for any act which the law does not authorise as is any private and unofficial person. . . . The idea of the rule of law in this sense implies, or is at any rate closely connected with, the absence of any dispensing power on the part either of the Crown or its servants.

Interestingly, the Castle's failure to energetically follow up on the allegations made against its officials in *United Ireland* gave the Irish nationalists an opportunity to argue precisely that the law was not being enforced neutrally. The discrimination was between, on the one hand, Castle officials and, on the other hand, nationalist leaders and the Irish people, whom the government had proved all too willing to target for minor offences. As Healy put it, 'there was such a thing as a little want of keenness [in being indulgent] where one's opponents were concerned, and a little overplus of charity where one's friends were concerned' (*Hansard*-2: 1826). The nationalist leader Parnell plainly stated that the government's conduct rightly incurred 'the imputation of one-sidedness and unfairness in the execution of their duty as the upholders of the law and the punishment of offenders in Ireland' (*Hansard*-4: 717).

The conduct of the trials that followed provided further fodder for the argument that the government was failing to uphold the rule-of-law principle according to which the law should be administered equally. The acquittal of Cornwall from criminal charges in August 1884 was received by *United Ireland* with the statement that '[t]he tribunal which is warranted to bring doom to the Western peasant would lose half its usefulness if it could not be relied upon to deliver high officials in distress'. The article went on to argue that no evidence was independently sought by the prosecution; that the indictment was framed so that much of the evidence that had been relied upon in the civil trial for libel became unavailable in the criminal trial; and that the jury had been packed with people 'closely allied with the prisoner in rank and sympathy' (RMA-19).

The same charges were made by the *Freeman's Journal* at about the same time (RMA-6). Some days later *United Ireland* reiterated them, while enriching them with a sexualised imagery involving 'the prostitution of the machinery of justice for the purpose of securing impunity . . . for the Castle Criminals'. A reference was made to the 'worst depth of degradation of which civilised Government is capable' (RMA-20). Albeit ostensibly not of the same-sex variety, the sexualisation of the activities of the British government in Ireland in connection with the trials is redolent of its *homo*sexualisation, effected, as we have seen, through other means. In particular, the expression 'worst depth of degradation' recalls the idea of homosexuality's exceptionality.

In response to the Court of Appeal's decision, in Cornwall's libel action against *United Ireland*, to set aside the verdict against Cornwall in respect of the felony charge, the newspaper deplored the 'rules of legal pedantry' that produce results at odds with 'eternal justice' and systematically disadvantage the poor and those who fight for the national cause (RMA-25). Cornwall had been granted a retrial 'for having been described as a felon when his true description is that of a beast. Felony might be only the theft of a loaf; it is frequently in Ireland only fearless high-souled patriotism' (RMA-25). This is not an argument that formal rules are deliberately created by the government to promote sectional interests. Rather the underlying idea is that even within the framework of neutral rules, the Castle is capable of carrying out a 'policy of persistently obstructing . . . justice', engaging in 'disgracefully-doctored prosecutions' (RMA-25). This makes the newspaper look a little like an *ante-litteram* propounder of the legal realist doctrine about law's inherent indeterminacy.

An article in *United Ireland* from November 1884 ties similar concerns about the unequal administration of the law to concerns about same-sex desire, moving from the allegation that the Castle had protected homosexual criminals to the proposition that it *was* one such criminal. The article comments on the disparity of outcome for Cornwall, who had been acquitted, and other defendants in the criminal proceedings for unnatural crimes, who had been convicted.[7] *United Ireland* observed: 'The mind sickens in contemplation of the official turpitude which connives at the scandals of its own set and frowns with stern saintliness on the sins of the meaner instruments of criminality' (RMA-22). Unlike its cognate 'to wink at', which is capable of bearing either the more active meaning of 'silently approving' or the more neutral one of 'turning a blind eye', 'to connive at' suggests more clearly the former meaning. The moralistically charged term 'turpitude' and the choice to refer to homosexual Castle officials as the government's 'own set' do the rest; once again we are left with the impression that the government's arbitrary conduct – which in this case takes the form of disregard for the rule of law – is the conduct distinctive of a homosexual subject.

In July 1884, Gladstone, the Prime Minister, deplored in the Commons the 'frightful' accusation that 'all these gentlemen connected with the government of Ireland and with the administration of justice in Ireland' were 'capable of . . . such horrible contempt of duty' (*Hansard-2*: 1858–1859). Gladstone's terminology reveals the transitivity of the horror and fright associated in public discourse with homosexuality, which is transferred from the crime itself to the charge that the government failed in its duty to prosecute it. At the same time, Gladstone's shocked protestation that 'a more frightful charge never was launched . . . against a whole body of men' (*Hansard-2*: 1859) constructs official tolerance of homosexuality as the paradigm of poor government.

19 Cleveland Street

It is widely speculated that the Dublin scandals prompted or facilitated the introduction, in 1885, of the famous 'Labouchere amendment', providing for a new offence of 'gross indecency' between males (Kaplan, 2005: 178; Edsall, 2003: 114; Dettmar, 2001: 138). The radical Liberal MP Henry Labouchere declared that he had introduced the amendment out of a concern that homosexuality was on the increase and to make it easier to secure convictions, as the traditional offence of buggery did not capture sexual activities that did not amount to sodomy, and had to be proven by an accessory to the act (*Hansard-7*: 1534–1535).[8] The text of the legislative provision, as passed by Parliament, read as follows:

> Any male person who, in public or in private, commits, or is a party to the commission of, or procures or attempts to procure the commission by any male person of, any act of gross indecency with another male person shall be guilty of a misdemeanour.

The penalty was imprisonment for up to two years with or without hard labour (NA-1). It has been argued that the amendment provided a new conceptual vocabulary for thinking about homosexual crime, which was now assimilated to prostitution and age-of-consent offences, in contrast to the medieval association between sodomy and bestiality, which had survived legal redefinitions of sodomy earlier in the nineteenth century (White, 1999: 3; Weeks, 1991: 52). As we will see, however, the ancient medieval rhetoric of unnameability and abomination was not displaced by this reconceptualisation.

As editor of the periodical *Truth*, Labouchere was chiefly responsible (alongside Ernest Parke, editor of a less well-known newspaper called *The North London Press*) for the revelations that made the Cleveland Street scandal erupt. He did so by denouncing the government's inaction or half-hearted attempts at prosecuting homosexual men of high social station who patronised a male brothel in Cleveland Street. Labouchere argued that there was a very good reason for his zealotry, and that it had to do precisely with the recent introduction of the new criminal offence of gross indecency:

> I am determined that my clause shall run against all . . . If Parliament is to make laws, and the Executive is to exercise a dispensing power whenever any one connected with the "classes" is thought to have contravened them, it is clear that Parliament wastes its time in legislating
>
> (NA-29)

Ostensibly, Labouchere's statement shows a preoccupation both with institutional efficiency and egalitarian principles. An analysis of the materials, however, suggests that he was also motivated by a puritanical (though he disclaimed this characterisation) determination to stamp out homosexuality, which he regarded as 'revolting to every man with a vestige of manly feeling' (NA-28). Indeed, Labouchere, despite his radical politics, was ferociously hostile not only to homosexuals, but also to Jews and feminists (Donovan and Rubery, 2012: 137). Although the *Times* was oversimplifying the matter where it stated that the rumours were being 'put about for political purposes' (NA-24), it is obvious too that Labouchere's goal was to damage the credibility of the Conservative government headed by Lord Salisbury.

The genesis of the scandal had to do with a telegraph boy being questioned about a sum of money in his possession and declaring that he had got it in exchange for sex with men, which had taken place at a house kept by one Charles Hammond at 19 Cleveland Street, in London's West End. The boy had been introduced to Hammond by a young post office co-worker, Henry Newlove. Investigations revealed that men from the upper classes, including Lord Arthur Somerset (LAS), patronised the house. The foreign press, revealing information often absent from the domestic coverage, provided numbers of the people involved. Some gave it as a fact that the authorities were in possession of the names of more than eighty 'prominent' people ('A Beastly Scandal', 1889). Herbert John Ames, a boy who escaped with Hammond to the United States after the scandal erupted, later stated that according to Hammond 'about twenty men' had been in the habit of visiting the establishment ('Unmentionable Crimes', 1891).

The scandal centred on the question of LAS's prosecution. The case was conducted under the direction of the Attorney General (Sir Richard Webster) who, like the Director of Public Prosecutions (Sir Augustus Stephenson) and the Chief Commissioner of the Metropolitan Police (James Monro), believed that LAS should be prosecuted.[9] The Home Secretary (Henry Matthews) disagreed, at least initially. The case was referred to the Prime Minister (Lord Salisbury), who sought the Lord Chancellor's (Lord Halsbury) opinion (NA-6). Lord Halsbury argued that if penal servitude for life were the penalty and a successful prosecution could be secured, then he would advise that proceedings be instituted. But there was a lack of corroborative evidence and LAS was only accused of the new misdemeanour of gross indecency, which carried with it light punishment. Therefore, he wrote, a prosecution was not in the public interest: given LAS's notoriety, much publicity would be given to 'matters of the most revolting and mischievous kind', and 'enormous evil' would thereby follow without any compensating benefit (NA-7).

When failing to issue a warrant against LAS became increasingly untenable, Lord Salisbury consented to see Sir Dighton Probyn, from the Prince of Wales's household, to which LAS also belonged as assistant equerry to the prince. Salisbury gave Probyn to understand that developments could be expected with respect to LAS (*Hansard-7*: 1543). In Salisbury's own words he told Probyn that there was:

> no vestige of evidence against anyone except one person . . . and . . . the evidence was not thought to be sufficient in the judgment of those whose business it was to decide. I think I added . . . that rumours had reached me that further evidence had been obtained, but I did not know what its character was. . . . I am quite certain that I never said, as has been imputed to me, that a warrant was about to be issued the next day.
>
> (*Hansard-6*: 1618)

Be that as it may, by the time a warrant was issued against LAS, he had fled the country. Newlove and a man called George Daniel Veck – who was described as Hammond's 'confederate' (NA-31) – were convicted and sentenced to a few months' hard labour. None of the well-to-do patrons of the brothel, however, was prosecuted. In *Truth*, Labouchere started a crusade denouncing the conduct of the authorities in allowing LAS to escape justice. He also brought the issue up in the Commons, making much, among other things, of the fact that LAS had been allowed an honourable discharge from the regiment of the Royal Guards and that he had retained two county magistracies (*Hansard-7*: 1545; see also *Hansard-3*). He concluded his parliamentary intervention by declaring: 'I think that this House ought to disconnect itself from any condoning of abominable offences of this kind, and ought to stand up for the principle of equal justice between man and man' (*Hansard-7*: 1549). The implication was that neither the government nor the Upper House was doing either. The similarities with the

Dublin scandals did not pass unnoticed (NA-14; NA-16). Interestingly, *Truth* itself opened the first article in which it denounced the affair with the statement 'The law must be equally administered – if not in Ireland, at least in England' (NA-26).

Even before *Truth* took up the story, a relatively little-known radical newspaper called *The North London Press* had been covering the affair, using it as an opportunity to denounce the governmental establishment. Its editor, Ernest Parke, was sued for libelling Lord Euston, whom the newspaper had identified as one of the patrons of 19 Cleveland Street. The *North London Press* met the suit with the rallying cry 'God defend the Right!' (NA-9). The main witness, on whose evidence Parke's case rested, however, was John Saul – or 'the creature Saul' as he was contemptuously referred to during the scandal.[10] Saul – who had stated that Euston was not 'an actual sodomite', as he just liked 'to play with you and then "spend" on your belly' – described himself as a 'professional "mary-anne"' who had 'lost [his] character' (NA-13). He said he could not 'get on otherwise' and occasionally did 'odd jobs for different gay people' (NA-13).[11] The value of his testimony was discounted as 'utterly unworthy of credit' (NA-37) and Parke lost the case.

Newton, solicitor to LAS, was also prosecuted and imprisoned on the charge of conspiring to defeat the ends of justice. Newton had assisted Hammond, who had initially fled to continental Europe, in leaving Europe for the United States. Newton had also approached one of the main witnesses, offering him financial incentives to emigrate to America. In an article that, ironically, seems deliberately designed to provide homoerotic titillation, the *North London Press* described this witness, Algernon Allies, as 'a good-looking, curly haired youth of twenty, who was at one time employed at the Marlborough club' (NA-12).[12] Accused of dishonesty, Allies had lost his employment at the club, and had been thereafter financially supported by LAS (NA-4). After leaving Cleveland Street, he had regularly received letters from his aristocratic lover (NA-12). By the time of Newton's trial, the *Pall Mall Gazette* – and with it no doubt many who did not share the radical politics of Labouchere and Parke – had come to the conclusion that the government had interfered with the administration of justice: 'Nominally, Mr Newton will be on his trial; really, it will be Ministers who will stand in the dock.' (NA-17) Newton was found guilty. The judge declared that Newton was acting in the interest of wealthy clients; if he fined him, the clients would pay his fine, so the judge must sentence him to imprisonment as 'an attempt to defeat the law is a matter which throws too much scandal on the administration of justice' (NA-25).

Exceptionality and its transitivity

Perhaps even more so than in the Dublin scandals, drawing attention to the unnameability of homosexuality was a constant element in the treatment of the Cleveland Street scandal: 'a very serious offence that need not be specifically described' (NA-15); 'a scandal . . . that . . . would be better unmentioned' (NA-10); 'it is, of course, impossible to allude to the details that were revealed'

(NA-26); 'unutterable and abominable crime' (NA-22); 'the vague talk about "hushing up" . . . is simply foolish. All cases of this particularly vile and unmentionable kind *are* "hushed-up" . . . from a regard for public decency' (NA-21); 'the intimate relationship . . . became of a character that cannot be particularised' (NA-12). Even a French newspaper that covered the scandal combined the rhetoric of unnameability with nationalistic point-scoring, stating that, as to what happened between LAS and Allies at 19 Cleveland Street, the details would not be disclosed '*á cause de leur precision trop anglaise*' (NA-5).

As in the Dublin scandal, there are also instances of newspaper articles and parliamentary debates constructing homosexuality as a crime of exceptional gravity. The *Echo* spoke of the 'blackest scandal with which London has had to deal for many years' (NA-3). An article entitled 'Our Old Nobility – Charges of Infamous Conduct against Peers', appearing in the *North London Press*, started by reporting the case of Lord Galloway sexually molesting a 10-year-old girl in broad daylight, but reserved the most strident notes ('horrible and repulsive') to describe the Cleveland Street affair (NA-11).

Labouchere insisted on the exceptionality of homosexuality on several occasions while commenting on the scandal. He stated, for example, that, compared to Hammond's house, a heterosexual brothel was 'respectable' (*Hansard-7*: 1541) and that homosexuality was a 'foul' crime that could not be tolerated 'unless London is to be regarded as the disgrace and opprobrium of modern civilisation' (NA-26). He also declared: 'The fall of Louis Philippe was to a great extent due to the Duc de Praslin having murdered his governess, but the Duc's crime compares favourably with that of these titled miscreants' (NA-26). Labouchere got his history wrong: the Duke had killed his wife, not his governess (the governess had been dismissed by the Duchess, on suspicion, among other things, of being her husband's mistress). But the comparison was on point because, as in the Cleveland Street affair, the Praslin case in France had been widely held to exemplify the unequal administration of the law: it was believed that the Duke was deliberately allowed to commit suicide instead of having to face trial like a person of lower station (Latimer, 1893: 102–107). The crucial point, in any event, is Labouchere's statement that homosexuality is a crime worse than murder – an opinion whose intransigence goes even further than a contemporary newspaper's observation that homosexuality is 'the foulest offence short of murder' (NA-18). Labouchere voiced this opinion repeatedly. Thus, lamenting the leniency with which Veck had been sentenced, he said the man should have been 'publicly flogged' and 'put into a dark cell' and that '[m]any murderers who have been hanged were respectable citizens in comparison with him' (NA-31). He also asked whether the government would have allowed the parties to a 'dynamite conspiracy' in Ireland to flee the country as they had done with LAS – implying that terrorism, with its potentially fatal consequences, and homosexuality were entirely commensurable (NA-31).

These statements, apparently made in all earnestness, both exploit and re-install the exceptionality of homosexuality. The political usefulness of insisting on the exceptionality of homosexuality was in the transitivity of that exceptionality: if the crimes of the noblemen who slept with telegraph boys were exceptionally grave, the conduct of the government in shielding them partook of that gravity. This dynamic can be seen in another observation made by Labouchere: 'Ministers are now accused of action far worse than was ever charged by the Times against Mr Parnell.' (NA-30) Among other things, Parnell, the Irish nationalist leader, had been unjustly[13] accused of applauding the 1882 murder, in Dublin's Phoenix Park, of the Permanent Under-Secretary to the Lord Lieutenant of Ireland (Thomas Henry Burke) and the newly appointed Chief Secretary (Lord Frederick Cavendish). The logic of Labouchere's point is based on his belief that homosexuality is a crime worse than murder: if it is, then governmental tolerance of homosexuality was 'far worse' than Parnell's (purported) endorsement of murder. Indeed, official tolerance of homosexuality was worse than murder itself, as the Leader of the House of Commons suggested during debates about the conduct of the government in the Cleveland Street affair:

> The most grave charges are made which could be made against any public man – [A Voice: "Murder"] – well, I am not sure that this is not worse than murder, which might possibly be committed under provocation; but we are charged with deliberately hindering the course of justice.
>
> (*Hansard*-7: 1579)

These quotes illustrate the political function of driving home the message of homosexuality's exceptional gravity, for judgements about the enormity of homosexuality readily transferred to the government's protection of homosexual men in high stations.

The game of equivalencies

As in the treatment of the Dublin Castle affair, so in debate about the Cleveland Street scandal we encounter a preoccupation with uncleanness and pollution – as when the *Star* talked of homosexuality in terms of 'foul, loathsome, slimy things that are hidden out of sight' (NA-22); or when the *North London Press* spoke of the Cleveland Street establishment as involving a 'foul and widespread plot to poison the morals of the community' (NA-9). On the whole, however, the rhetoric of pollution and contamination seems less prominent than in the Dublin Castle scandals. One of the main functions that this rhetoric, in conjunction with nationalistic sentiment, had performed in the Dublin Castle affair – namely, discrediting political adversaries through their homosexualisation – was accomplished, in the Cleveland Street affair, through a strategy more attuned to the circumstances. This strategy involved establishing three equivalencies – between the government and the aristocracy, between the aristocracy and homosexuality and, consequently, between the government and homosexuality.

Establishing the first equivalency did not require a great deal of effort. A number of circumstances produced a close identification between the government headed by Lord Salisbury and the aristocratic class. These included Salisbury's high Toryism; his championing the constitutional role of the House of Lords (Steele, 1999: 66; Marsh, 2003: 91); his running his government (the last Prime Minister to do so) from the Upper House, where the Conservative party enjoyed an aristocracy-backed majority; and his eloquent defence of aristocratic life (Green, 1995: 85).

Labouchere and other radicals were then able to concentrate their efforts on the second equivalency (that between the aristocracy and homosexuality), sure in the knowledge that this would amount to a homosexualisation – and hence an indictment – of the government itself (the third equivalency). The strategy of aristocratising homosexuality is evident in a number of newspaper articles and contributions in the Commons. Thus, *Truth* first described the goings-on at 19 Cleveland Street as a 'gathering of the "gentlemen of England"', and the frequenters of Hammond's house as 'titled miscreants' (NA-26). The *North London Press*, in an article entitled 'Our Old Nobility – Charges of Infamous Conduct against Peers' underscored the social station of the patrons of 19 Cleveland Street by calling them 'rich and influential' and 'high-born' (NA-11). One of *Reynolds's Newspaper*'s headlines promised 'Horrible Revelations about the Aristocracy' (NA-19). Other issues spoke of the 'abominable institution frequented by aristocrats' (NA-20), the 'damnable doings of the Cleveland-street gang of aristocratic sodomites' ('Salisbury, the Shuffler', 1890) and 'the aristocratic Cleveland-Street scandals' ('The Radical Benches', 1890).

An even cruder exercise in aristocratising homosexuality is evident where same-sex attracted noblemen are compared to their non-aristocratic counterparts. Thus, the *Echo* (whose editor was the Liberal MP John Passmore Edwards, champion of the working classes) called the 'aristocratic individuals' who had absconded 'principals' in the crime, while Veck and Newlove were merely 'minor suspects' and 'accomplices' (NA-3). Likewise, the *Referee*, describing the Cleveland Street affair as 'one of the most loathsome and horrible scandals the "higher civilisation" has been able to produce', entirely denied Newlove and Veck any sexual agency (NA-18). They were 'low-class criminals' made to commit crimes by 'high-class tempters', whose elitism the newspaper underscored by visualising them as being 'dragged before the unhallowed gaze of an indignant multitude' (NA-18). Veck and Newlove were 'bred in sin and suckled on wickedness' and hence had 'every excuse when they [went] wrong'; they were 'the miserable victims of [the] baleful lusts and unnatural passions' of 'blue-blooded beasts' (NA-18). The *Star* followed the same line of argument, commenting on the 'unhappy creatures on whose innocence and whose poverty these miscreants were able to play' (NA-22). So did Labouchere in the Commons, speaking of 'poor and wretched creatures [who] live to minister to the vices of those in a superior station' (*Hansard*-7: 1548); and in *Truth*, where he pitted the 'poor tempted wretch' to the 'well-born tempter' (NA-28; see also NA-29). The article in the *Referee* concluded by contrasting the 'toil and sweat and starvation and houselessness in the East-End of London' with the affluent West-End, presented as a stage for scenes of *fin-de-siècle* aristocratic ennui and decadence. It spoke of 'heinous offenders, some of who are still young, but who have drunk pleasure's cup to the dregs' and who are 'so tired of every natural enjoyment . . . that they band together for the exact purpose of doing that which is unnatural' (NA-18).

Unequal justice and the prince

Conceivably, the homosexualisation of the government could have been effected even without additional recourse to an argument about its discriminatory administration of the law. But the fact that the government's conduct offered an opportunity to deploy that argument made Labouchere's case all the more powerful, both in the Commons (*Hansard-7*: 1546, 1548) and in the press. In any case, there is no good reason to doubt that Labouchere was genuinely troubled by inequality in the administration of the law. Even pro-establishment publications were obliged to concede that it 'would be monstrous . . . that what is punished in one class of life is condoned in another' (NA-21).

'Why are the minnows to be imprisoned, and the sharks to be allowed to go scot-free?' Labouchere asked (NA-27). One week later he was explicitly charging the government with conspiring 'to usurp the functions of the Magistracy, and to shield the rich and the high-born from having to stand, like humbler mortals, their trial' (NA-28). He also deployed the rhetoric of homosexuality's exceptionality to strengthen his point: 'The administration of the law – and in cases like these more than in any other – must be equal to all.' (NA-28) The following March he was still ramming the message home, denouncing that 'Lord Chancellors, Attorney Generals and Prime Ministers were putting their heads together' (NA-34) to shield 'the nobleman' guilty of the same offence for which 'the man of low estate' was tried (NA-35).[14] In the meantime, Newton's prosecution for his attempt at removing witnesses had given Labouchere a further opportunity to argue that there was no equality in the administration of the law. This time the discrimination was not between peers and commoners guilty of gross indecency, but between Newton on the one hand and Lord Salisbury and Matthews (the Home Secretary) on the other – the latter two, according to Labouchere, being more guilty than the former of attempting to defeat the ends of justice (NA-32; NA-33; NA-35).

Several commentators explicitly merged the argument that the government was failing to uphold equality in the administration of justice with the idea that homosexuality was a quintessential aristocratic practice. This, coupled with the fact that Salisbury's government was very much a government of and for peers, resulted in a particularly powerful rhetorical homosexualisation of the government. For example, Labouchere argued that putting noblemen guilty of buggery or gross indecency – the government's 'friends', as he called them – on trial 'would deal a blow to the reign of the classes and to the social influence of the aristocracy' (NA-26). He added: 'It would be really too monstrous if crimes, which, when committed by poor ignorant men, lead to sentences of penal servitude, were to be done with impunity by those who the Tory Government delights to honour' (NA-26). This statement casts a homoerotic slant on the relationship between the government and aristocratic homosexual men, whom it portrays as Salisbury's protégés through the use of such expressions as 'friends' and 'delights to honour'. An analogous rhetorical move had been performed by the *Pall Mall Gazette*, which under the editorship of Stead was pioneering investigative journalism (Mitchell, 1988: 757) and which had covered the Cleveland Street affair in its early stages. In drawing attention to the harsh treatment reserved for the 'wretched agents' compared to 'the lords and gentlemen who employ them', the *Gazette* declared that the latter were 'even welcomed as valuable allies of the administration of the day' (NA-15).

Even more eloquent was Labouchere's statement, on another occasion, that the government was endeavouring 'to hush up what they thought would tell against that portion of Society that they specially represent' (NA-31). This wording leaves the reader with the distinct feeling that Salisbury's government may have been the designated representative not just of the aristocracy, but specifically of a homosexual aristocracy. *Reynolds's Newspaper* conveyed that very idea in a more definite way when it upbraided the Lords for failing to question Lord Salisbury when, in the House of Lords, he was forced to account for his conduct by Labouchere's revelations in the Commons. The newspaper stated that the Lords 'fully adhered to that conspiracy of silence . . . to hush up the scandalous and horrible revelations concerning the Cleveland street den, the frequenters thereof being mostly members of their own order, and moving in the highest classes of society – peers, &c.' ('Salisbury, the Shuffler', 1890).

US newspapers could dwell on these themes at even greater length:

> The Tory Government of England may be overthrown by a whirlwind of popular indignation excited by the vices of its own supporters . . . born nobles, earls and viscounts, the heirs of the dukedoms and the darlings of society. The ruling class in England realizes that aristocratic institutions could not survive the disgrace of the imprisonment of the proudest nobles of the land for a crime the most detestable and infamous, and therefore, it is said, Lord Salisbury himself has stayed the hand of justice until the criminals should have the opportunity to escape. But what will the commons say when parliament meets?
>
> ('Unmentionable Crimes', 1891)

Without quite saying as much, the statement constructs the British Upper House, from which Salisbury governed, as a relic of the past, enfeebled and corrupted by the decadent homoerotic practices of its aristocratic members – all but doomed to give way to the greater (heterosexual) legitimacy of the Commons. The same kind of picture could be rendered even more effectively by drawing into it Prince Albert Victor, the eldest son of the future King Edward VII and heir presumptive to the throne.[15] References to the prince were generally absent from

British newspapers or parliamentary debates on the scandal, other than to deny that he was in any way connected to it (even then his name was not actually mentioned).[16] US newspapers, however, made much of the prince's supposed involvement, constructing an argument about the superiority of (heterosexual) democratic republicanism to (homosexual) monarchical government. This argument is still relatively implicit in the *New York Times* article that closely followed the revelations made in *Truth* in November 1889. The *New York Times* ridiculed the prince, calling him a 'long-necked, narrow-headed young dullard' and a 'stupid, perverse boy' generally reputed to have been 'mixed up in the scandal'; it foretold 'that such a fellow' would 'never be allowed to ascend the British throne' ('Excitement over the London Scandal', 1889). (The influenza pandemic, rather than any royal palace conspiracy, proved the prediction correct.)[17] The same article pointed out that the government's conduct in the Cleveland Street scandal was doing 'enormous damage, not only to the Government, but to the aristocratic social structure generally' and predicted that the effects of the scandal would be 'prodigious upon the whole political and social edifice of contemporary England' ('Excitement over the London Scandal', 1889).

The argument was much more clearly (and crudely) drawn out in another US newspaper ('Prince Victor', 1890). After declaring that the prince had returned from a trip to India where he had sailed to avoid being brought into the Cleveland Street scandal, the newspaper indicated that the British people would prefer his younger brother George as heir apparent. Albert Victor was 'physically and mentally . . . something of a wreck and not half the man in all the attributes of manly make-up that characterizes George'. Having constructed homosexuality and effeminacy as incompatible with the role of a monarch, the article went on to state that the prince's involvement in the scandal was 'only another indication of the debauchery that too conspicuously tinctures European royalty'. Homosexuality was then incorporated into a broader narrative of degeneracy – typical of early sexological discourse – affecting monarchical government. The paper argued that the 'inbred crowd of royal stock of all Europe is becoming sadly deteriorated both bodily and mentally'. Finally, the degeneracy of the monarchy was contrasted with 'the strength of a higher order of governmental civilization which the common people are attaining' ('Prince Victor', 1890).

Conclusions

The Dublin and Cleveland Street scandals employed a number of rhetorical strategies to construct a relationship of radical incompatibility between same-sex desire and good government. Virtually all these strategies are eloquently pulled together in an unidentified newspaper cutting preserved at the National Archives at Kew, which is worth quoting at length:

> The crime with which these noblemen are charged is one beyond the pale of mercy . . . a crime that the most degraded, violent, and licentious members of

the lowest classes would look upon with loathing and with scorn. . . . A man guilty of that crime would be considered a contamination . . . If a king were guilty of such an atrocious offence as that alleged against our Peers he would be utterly unfit to reign. If the cleverest statesman . . . were found guilty of such a crime it would be the duty of the nation to cast him forth; to strip him of his honours; to erase his name and title from the public records, and to exile him for ever . . . And it is alleged that men of the highest nobility, statesmen and public officers of trust and repute, *are* guilty of this nameless and inhuman horror. And it is alleged that the Home Office is hiding and screening them . . . [T]hese men are wealthy and educated and of high rank. For them there is no excuse. No degree of ignorance, or bad training, or evil conditions will avail them. They are of the class that monopolises the dignity and the wealth and the pomp of the land . . . [I]f they are screened by those who should convict and punish them, they are screened because the rotten-ness, the villainy, the dissipation, an the utter, irredeemable, unpardonable baseness of these numerous titled scoundrels would so rouse the rage and stir the disgust of the British people as to endanger the existence of the House of Peers and the snug monopoly of the land and revenues of the idle . . . [T]his mockery of justice and subversion of the law; this prostitution at the service of the basest criminals must not be allowed . . . And if the Government can be proved guilty of complicity in the rascally attempt to shield these moral lepers from justice, that Government is thereby proved unworthy to rule this country and should be at once dissolved and sent to receive sentence at the hands of the constituencies (NA-36).

As this article demonstrates, by the late nineteenth century the discourse about same-sex desire and its relationships with political authority had undergone a significant shift. In particular, in the late Victorian age – unlike the Middle Ages and the early modern period – same-sex desire was constructed as *ipso facto* disqualifying same-sex attracted statesmen from public office. The treatment of Edward II's and James I's same-sex desire included a number of arguments *rationalising* these rulers' unsuitability for their public role. Their same-sex desire turned them into poor rulers because it exposed them to the bad advice of their favourites, drove them to drawing arbitrary preferences among their subjects, dis-tanced them from the people, encouraged them to waste public money on their lovers, or made them too lenient and peaceful, or uninterested in public affairs, etc. These or equivalent rationalisations are absent from the Cleveland Street and Dublin Castle scandals. In the place of these rationalisations we observe a discourse about homosexuality's exceptionality, constructing homosexuality as a crime worse than murder.

The logic of exceptionality forecloses any debate about whether or not toler-ating homosexual statesmen or public officials could even be contemplated. It removes any need to articulate *why* a statesman's homosexuality poses a prob-lem for the good exercise of public powers. The rhetoric of homosexuality's unspeakability, which at this time is particularly powerful, pushes in the same direction, for it suggests that references to, let alone public debate and open discussion about, homosexuality are generally undesirable and counter-productive. Likewise, the imagery of pollution and contamination, suggesting as it does that homosexuality is endowed with a special power to corrupt that which it touches (another novel element compared to case studies from previous centuries) replaces rational argument about the incompatibility between same-sex desire and public office. In short, the more homosexuality is constructed as unnameable, abominable and polluting, the larger it looms. And the larger is looms, the more it absolves those who want to use it for political purposes from the need to *justify* why it disables public officials from carrying out their functions well or why it is incompatible with public office.[18]

In both the Dublin and Cleveland Street scandals the main target of, respectively, the nationalists' and radicals' attacks were not the homosexual public officials themselves, but the government who had employed them and had mobilised to prevent the conflagration of the scandals from blowing. All scandals, because they function in accordance with a collectivist logic and the paradigm of popular justice, have the potential for negatively reverberating over institutions to which the offender is affiliated (Adut, 2005: 220). In the Cleveland Street and Dublin Castle scandals, however, the attack on the government was the main driver of the scandal (rather than merely a contingent externality) and was expressly identified as such both in the Commons and in the radical press. Furthermore, this attack proved particularly powerful because of the transitivity of homosexuality's exceptionality: if homosexuality is the worst crime anyone – including a public official – could commit, shielding homosexuals from legal punishment is the worst a government could do.[19] The nationalists and the radicals, moreover, were able to make their case even more powerful by rhetorically constructing homosexuality as quintessentially English, in the one case, or aristocratic, in the other, and by relying on the equivalency between either the English and the Castle administration or the aristocracy and Salisbury's government. In either case, these rhetorical strategies were connected to a rule-of-law-informed argument about the government protecting 'their own' and deliberately failing to administer justice equally.[20] It is sometimes remarked that the Cleveland Street scandal precipitated the construction of homosexuality as an aristocratic vice, but perhaps it is not always appreciated what were the contingent political drivers behind this construction.

Particularly in the Dublin scandal, the rhetoric of homosexuality's pollution was harnessed for the purpose of homosexualising the government. It has been argued that sex scandals generally have a special 'polluting "viscosity"': purely by virtue of being about sex, they have the power to contaminate third parties (even audiences), and this is a reason why sex is so often involved in scandals which are otherwise so different (Adut: 2005: 221). Once again, however, the express construction of homosexuality *as* pollution – as one of the strategies tending to homosexualise the government in the Dublin scandal – seems to go above and beyond this. Contamination here is not just one of the attributes of a sexual construct that is essentially centred on something else, but is construed as the very essence of that construct. The discourse of homosexuality's exceptionality arguably facilitates this construction of homosexuality as the paradigmatic case of sexual pollution.

To the extent that efforts were occasionally made to unravel the logic behind the attacks – at *explaining*, that is, *why* an imputation of homosexuality reflected negatively on the public official or the government employing him – the attempts were remarkable failures. Consider the following passage from an article in the *North-Eastern Gazette*:

> But it must not be assumed that the Dublin Nationalists have interposed out of mere malice or ill will. Their standing charge against the Irish executive is that its officials are entrusted with arbitrary and personal powers such as cannot safely be given even to men of admitted integrity and morality, and hence they establish these terrible charges of immoral practices against a man who was permitted to open and study all letters addressed to Nationalist members and agitators [and] against another Government official upon whose words scores of men, standing high in the public estimation, where committed to gaol . . . these revelations disclose something more than human depravity – they indicate the corruptness and fallibility of the Irish executive.
>
> ('London Notes', 1884)

This passage is confusing because it purports to explain something it does not actually explain. The idea is that revelations about French's and Cornwall's homosexuality were made because they illustrated particularly powerfully just how dangerous the virtually unrestrained powers wielded by Dublin Castle officers could be. But the Dublin Castle affair does not illustrate anything of the kind. The article does not *show*, it merely assumes or claims as obvious that either French or Cornwall must have exercised those powers badly by virtue of their 'depravity'.

Both the Dublin Castle and Cleveland Street affairs were almost entirely built on rhetoric rather than rational argumentation. This, while putting them at odds with deliberative democratic values, apparently did not hamper the pursuit of the political goals sought by the radicals and nationalists. It has been argued that 1883–1884 was an unproductive period in Irish nationalist politics, during which little was being done to advance home rule, and that O'Brien's journalistic invective against the tyranny of Dublin Castle filled this void (O'Brien, 1976: 24–25; Cocks, 2007: 129). In this context, the significance of the Dublin scandals in the fight for home rule has been downplayed, even ridiculed (O'Brien, 1976: 25). However, in a study focusing on scandal in the Georgian period, Clark (2004: 1–2) demonstrates that, far from being trivial, sex scandals can become symbolic of broader political causes and mobilise social forces around them. The Dublin scandal may be an illustration of this. If we are to believe a contemporary observer, it may well have contributed to a change of heart in Gladstone, who, after losing the premiership in 1885, ended up in favour of home rule (unionist Liberals then defected to Salisbury's Conservatives):[21]

> As a consequence of the exposures . . . many Englishmen of eminence publicly pronounced in favour of giving Ireland some measure of home rule. As an evidence of the change in thought which these disclosures were influential in bringing about, a brief quotation from . . . Matthew Arnold will be of interest: '. . . those hateful cases which have been tried in Dublin courts this last year suggest the dark and ill-omened world which applies to the whole state of Ireland – anti-natural. Anti-natural, anti-nature – that is the word which rises irresistibly in my mind . . . It is unnatural that Ireland should be governed by Lord Spencer . . .'.
>
> (Mahoney, 1885: 108)

In Arnold's quote we witness, once again, the transitivity of homosexuality's exceptionality – in particular, of its exceptional unnaturalness, which turns from a quality of the crime committed by Castle officials into a descriptive feature of the British government in Ireland. The exceptionality attributed to homosexuality partially accounts for why imputations of homosexuality became a privileged strategy of political delegitimisation in the late Victorian age. The incident, mentioned above, of Lord Galloway molesting a young girl, for example, seems to have attracted nowhere near the same amount of attention as the Cleveland Street scandal, despite the fact that in his case too the government was proving less than eager to bring him to justice.

This rhetoric implacably hostile to homosexuality, however, does not completely exhaust the treatment of the scandals by contemporary commentators. George Bernard Shaw, in a letter he wrote to *Truth*, objected to the sensationalistic coverage of homosexual scandals. Shaw's (1899) letter normalises homosexuality by historicising it, by appealing to moral pluralism and by arguing that the level of acceptance of homosexual people in practice does not live up to society's 'overcharged protestations of horrors'. Shaw (1899) points to the harm of having these issues 'darkly hinted at and gloated over as filthy, unmentionable, abominable' instead of openly and sanely discussed. He concludes by taking a stand – which he makes subject to protecting children from sexual abuse[22] – 'against the principle of the law under which the warrants have been issued' and against enforcing 'its outrageous penalties in the case of adult men' (Shaw, 1889). The kind of rational treatment of the scandal advocated by Shaw, however, neither conformed to Labouchere's deeply held contempt for homosexuality nor did it lend itself to the political aim of discrediting Salisbury's government. Because Labouchere's case essentially consisted in a sequence of rhetorical moves, it did not invite – indeed, it deliberately attempted to bypass – that kind of rational treatment. Unsurprisingly, Shaw's views on the scandal and the criminalisation of consensual homosexual sex between adults were to remain an example of what critical scholars call 'subjugated voices': the letter was never published.

The use of anti-homosexual rhetoric in these late Victorian scandals has a familiar contemporary resonance in the leaders of some non-Western states defending their countries' adoption or retention of laws or policies hostile to homosexuality. While the anti-gay views expressed by these leaders may genuinely convey their personal stance, it is apparent that they are also instrumentalising homosexuality in order to make some points about Western imperialism. The target of these anti-gay interventions is both cultural and political imperialism. Cultural imperialism here concerns the exportation of Western homosexual 'lifestyles', as well as the imposition of supposedly Western values through human rights-based appeals to repeal (or desist from enacting) anti-gay laws and policies. An analogy with the late Victorian scandals suggests that these representations of homosexuality as a Western practice and of gay rights as a Western value may be intended to enact a homosexualisation of the West directed at undermining its moral authority (and consequently its political legitimacy) in the international arena. Ironically, it is precisely that moral authority that the Western actors may be seen as trying to consolidate where they censor these non-Western countries' anti-gay laws and policies.

Related to this charge of Western cultural imperialism is one of political imperialism. This is essentially an allegation that the West, by interfering with non-Western countries' sovereign right to determine the way in which they should deal with homosexuality, is failing to treat them as equal partners in the international community. This charge throws into relief the similarities between these contemporary uses of homophobic rhetoric on the part of some non-Western states and the case studies analysed in this chapter – where, as we have seen, hostility to homosexuality was similarly harnessed in the pursuit of egalitarian agendas. The inflated anti-gay rhetoric often displayed in these contemporary interventions parallels the Victorian discourses analysed in this chapter. Now, as in the Victorian age, it is largely by constructing homosexuality as a crime of exceptional gravity that those who exploit it for political goals manage to turn it into a powerful symbol around which broader political concerns are engaged.

References

'A Beastly Scandal' (1889) *Ogden Standard Examiner*, 20 November.

'Action against "United Ireland"' (1883) *Freeman's Journal and Daily Commercial Advertiser*, 5 November.

Adut, A (2005) 'A Theory of Scandal: Victorians, Homosexuality and the Fall of Oscar Wilde' *American Journal of Sociology*, vol 111, 213–248.

Aronson, T (1994) *Prince Eddy and the Homosexual Underworld* (London: John Murray).

Ball, S (ed.) (2008) *Dublin Castle and the First Home Rule Crisis: The Political Journal of Sir George Fottrell, 1884–1887* (Cambridge: Cambridge University Press).

Banim, J (1860) *Damon and Pythias* (New York: Moore and Bernard).

Bartlett, Y (2010) *Ireland: A History* (Cambridge: Cambridge University Press).

Clark, A (2004) *Scandal: The Sexual Politics of the British Constitution* (Princeton: Princeton University Press).

Cocks, HG (2003) *Nameless Offences: Homosexual Desire in the 19th Century* (London: IB Tauris).

Cocks, HG (2007) 'Secret Crimes and Diseases, 1800–1914' in Cook, M (ed.), *A Gay History of Britain: Love and Sex between Men since the Middle Ages* (Oxford: Greenwood) 107–144.

Cohen, E (1993) *Talk on the Wilde Side* (London: Routledge).

Cook, M (2003) *London and the Culture of Homosexuality, 1885–1914* (Cambridge: Cambridge University Press).

Dellamora, R (1990) *Masculine Desire: The Sexual Politics of Victorian Aestheticism* (Chapel Hill: University of North Carolina Press).

Dettmar, K (2001) 'Vocation, Vacation, Perversion: Stephen Dedalus and Homosexual Panic' in Gillespie, MP (ed.), *James Joyce and the Fabrication of an Irish Identity* (Amsterdam: Rodopi PV) 132–150.

Dicey, AV (1886) *England's Case against Home Rule* (London: John Murray).

Dicey, AV (1915) *An Introduction to the Study of the Law of the Constitution* (London: MacMillan).

Donovan, S and Rubery, M (eds) (2012) *Secret Commissions: An Anthology of Victorian Investigative Journalism* (Calgary: Broadview Press).

Edsall, NC (2003) *Toward Stonewall: Homosexuality and Society in the Modern Western World* (Charlottesville: University of Virginia Press).

'Excitement over the London Scandal' (1889) *New York Times*, 17 November.

Foucault, M (1998) *The History of Sexuality, vol 1: The Will to Knowledge* (London: Penguin).

Green, EHH (1995) *The Crisis of Conservatism: The Politics, Economics and Ideology of the British Conservative Party, 1880-1914* (London: Routledge).

Hanafin, P (2000) 'Rewriting Desire: The Construction of Sexual Identity in Legal and Literary Discourse in Postcolonial Ireland' in Stychin, C and Herman, D (eds), *Sexuality in the Legal Arena* (London: The Athlone Press) 51–66.

[*Hansard*-1] Amendment (Mr. Sexton) – Composition of Juries (Ireland). *HC Deb 4 November 1884 vol 293 cc910–959.*

[*Hansard*-2] Class II. – Salaries and Expenses of Civil Departments. *HC Deb 21 July 1884 vol 290 cc1759–1895.*

[*Hansard*-3] Lord Arthur Somerset. *HC Deb 25 March 1890 vol 342 cc1804–1805.*

[*Hansard*-4] Motion for a Select Committee. *HC Deb 17 June 1884 vol 289 cc679–722.*

[*Hansard*-5] Supply. – Report. *HC Deb 7 August 1884 vol 292 cc232–249.*

[*Hansard*-6] The West End Scandals – Personal Explanation – The Marquess of Salisbury. *HL Deb 3 March 1890 vol 341 cc1618–1619.*

[*Hansard*-7] Vote on Account. *HC Deb 28 February 1890 vol 341 cc1523–1611.*

Hyde, HM (1976) *The Cleveland Street Scandal* (London: WH Allen).

Jackson, A (2010) *Ireland 1798–1998: War, Peace and Beyond* (Chichester: Wiley-Blackwell, 2nd edn).

Jenkins, B (2006) *Irish Nationalism and the British State: From Repeal to Revolutionary Nationalism* (Montreal: McGill-Queen's University Press).

Kaplan, M (1999) 'Did My Lord Gomorrah Smile? Homosexuality, Class, and Prostitution in the Cleveland Street Affair' in Robb, G and Erber, N (eds), *Disorder in the Court: Trials and Sexual Conflict at the Turn of the Century* (New York: New York University Press) 79–99.

Kaplan, MB (2005) *Sodom on the Thames: Sex, Love and Scandal in Wilde Times* (Ithaca: Cornell University Press).

Kaye, RA (2002) 'The Return of Damon and Pythias: Alan Dale's "A Marriage below Zero", Victorian Melodrama, and the Emergence of a Literature of Homosexual Representation' *College Literature*, vol 29, 50–79.

Latimer, E (1893) *France in the Nineteenth Century* (Chicago: AC McClung).

Lockyer, R (2005) *Tudor and Stuart Britain, 1487–1714* (London: Routledge, 3rd edn).

'London Notes' (1884) *The North-Eastern Daily Gazette*, 16 July.

Loughlin, J (1986) *Gladstone, Home Rule and the Ulster Question, 1882–1893* (Dublin: Gill and Macmillan).

Mahoney, JS (1885) *Charles Stewart Parnell and What He Has Achieved for Ireland* (New York: Excelsior Publishing House).

Marsh, P (2003) 'Salisbury's Definition of the Powers of the Lords' in Davis, RW (ed.), *Leaders in the Lords, 1765–1902* (Edinburgh: Edinburgh University Press) 91–100.

M'Carthy, J (1885) 'On Dublin Castle and Irish Discontent' *Freeman's Journal and Daily Commercial Advertiser*, 29 January.

Mitchell, S (ed.) (1988) *Victorian Britain: An Encyclopaedia* (London: Routledge).

Mondimore, FM (1996) *A Natural History of Homosexuality* (Baltimore: Johns Hopkins University Press).

Moran, LJ (1996) *The Homosexual(ity) of Law* (London: Routledge).

Murphy, JM (2010) 'Disgusted by the Details: *Dr Jekyll and Mr Hyde* and the Dublin Scandals of 1884' in O'Connor, M (ed.), *Back to the Future of Irish Studies* (Bern: Peter Lang) 177–190.

O'Brien, J (1976) *William O'Brien and the Course of Irish Politics, 1881–1918* (Berkeley: University of California Press).

Pelling, N (2003) *Anglo-Irish Relations: 1798–1922* (London: Routledge).

'Prince Victor' (1890) *Daily Northwestern*, 26 May.

'Salisbury, the Shuffler' (1890) *Reynolds's Newspaper*, 9 March.

'Second Edition' (1884) *Western Mail*, 18 July.

Shaw, GB (1889) 'Letter to *Truth*', 26 November, retrieved 13 September 2014: www.bbk.ac.uk/deviance/sexuality/shaw/18-7-1%20shaw.htm.

Steele, D (1999) *Lord Salisbury: A Political Biography* (London: Routledge).

'The Dublin Scandals' (1884a) *The Belfast News-Letter*, 30 October.

'The Dublin Scandals' (1884b) *The Belfast News-Letter*, 22 December.

'The Dublin Scandals' (1884c) *Western Mail*, 9 July.

'The O'Brien Fund' (1884) *Freeman's Journal and Daily Commercial Advertiser*, 5 August.

'The Radical Benches' (1890) *Reynolds's Newspaper*, 2 March.

'Unmentionable Crimes' (1891) *The Omaha Daily Bee*, 19 January.

Walshe, É (2005) 'The First Gay Irishman? Ireland and the Wilde Trials' *Éire-Ireland*, vol 40, 38–57.

Weeks, J (1991) *Against Nature: Essays on History, Sexuality and Identity* (London: Rivers Oram Press).

White, C (ed.) (1999) *Nineteenth-Century Writings on Homosexuality: A Sourcebook* (London: Routledge).

Press cuttings and other material from 'Prosecution of Gustavus C Cornwall, Secretary to the General Post Office, Dublin' (POST 120-58 to POST 120-65), file held at The Royal Mail Archive [RMA] (Freeling House, London):

[RMA-1] Cornwall's letter to Blackwood, 18 August 1885 (120–65).
[RMA-2] *Daily Express*, 8 December 1884 (120–64).
[RMA-3] *Dublin Evening Mail*, 11 May 1885 (120–64).
[RMA-4] *Dublin Evening Mail*, 11 May 1885, 'The Case of Cornwall v O'Brien: A New Trial Granted' (120–64).
[RMA-5] *Evening Mail*, 21 August 1884, 'What Will the Government Do?' (120–61).
[RMA-6] *Freeman's Journal*, 25 August 1884 (120–61).
[RMA-7] *Freeman's Journal*, 4 December 1884 (120–64).
[RMA-8] *Irish Citizen and Industrial Advocate*, 14 June 1884, 'Earl Spencer and His Criminals' (120–59).
[RMA-9] *Irish Times*, 8 July 1884 (120–59).
[RMA-10] Letter 24406, signed Hamilton, 18 November 1884 (#24406) (120–64).
[RMA-11] 'Report of Trial', 26 October 1884 (120–63-3).
[RMA-12] *United Ireland*, 10 May 1884 (120–59).
[RMA-13] *United Ireland*, 24 May 1884 (120–59).
[RMA-14] *United Ireland*, 24 May 1884, 'From the Irish Benches' (120–59).
[RMA-15] *United Ireland*, 24 May 1884, 'Official Compounders of Felony' (120–59).
[RMA-16] *United Ireland*, 31 May 1884, 'Is This One of George's Jokes?' (120–59).
[RMA-17] *United Ireland*, 7 June 1884 (120–59).
[RMA-18] *United Ireland*, 12 July 1884, 'Justice at Last!' (120–59).
[RMA-19] *United Ireland*, 21 August 1884, 'A New Glory for Green-Street!' (120–61).
[RMA-20] *United Ireland*, 30 August 1884, 'How It was Done' (120–61).
[RMA-21] *United Ireland*, 30 August 1884, 'The Week's Work' (120–61).
[RMA-22] *United Ireland*, 1 November 1884, 'Stainless Green Street' (120–64).
[RMA-23] *United Ireland*, 13 December 1884 (120–64).
[RMA-24] *United Ireland*, 13 December 1884, 'A Bolt from the Blue' (120–64).
[RMA-25] *United Ireland*, 16 May 1885, 'The Newest Phase of the Castle Plot' (120–64).

Press cuttings and other material from '"The Cleveland Street Case" re Lord Arthur Somerset and Others' (DPP 1/95/1 to DPP 1/95/7) and 'The Cleveland Street Scandal – A Residuum of Notes' (HO 144/477/X24427 to HO 144/477/X24427A), files held at The National Archives [NA] (Kew, London):

[NA-1] Criminal Law Amendment Act 1885 [48 & 49 Vict Ch 69], s 11 (DPP1/95/6).
[NA-2] DPP's letter to Monro, 22 October 1889 (DPP1/95/1).
[NA-3] *Echo*, 11 November 1889, 'The Painful Society Scandal – The Minor Suspects in Custody' (DDP1/95/2).

[NA-4] Elizabeth Alley's statement, 3 September 1889 (HO144/477/X24427A).

[NA-5] *La Lanterne*, 2 January 1890 (DPP1/95/2).

[NA-6] Leck's synopsis of case, 7 December 1954 (DPP1/95/1).

[NA-7] Lord Halsbury's opinion, circa 7 October 1889 (DPP1/95/3).

[NA-8] Monro's letter to the DPP, 1 October 1889 (DPP1/95/1).

[NA-9] *North London Press*, 23 November 1889, 'The West End Scandal' (DPP1/95/2).

[NA-10] *North London Press*, 28 September 1889 (DPP1/95/2).

[NA-11] *North London Press*, 28 September 1889, 'Our Old Nobility – Charges of Infamous Conduct against Peers' (DPP1/95/2).

[NA-12] *North London Press*, 11 January 1890, 'At Bow Street' (DPP1/95/2).

[NA-13] Original statement of Saul (DPP1/95/4).

[NA-14] *Pall Mall Gazette*, 15 July 1889 (DPP1/95/2).

[NA-15] *Pall Mall Gazette*, 12 September 1889 (DPP1/95/1).

[NA-16] *Pall Mall Gazette*, 20 November 1889 (DPP1/95/2).

[NA-17] *Pall Mall Gazette*, 24 January 1890 (DPP1/95/2).

[NA-18] *Referee*, 24 November 1889, 'Pendragon's Handbook' (DPP1/95/2).

[NA-19] *Reynolds's Newspaper*, 12 January 1890, 'The West End Scandals' (DPP1/95/2).

[NA-20] *Reynolds's Newspaper*, 19 January 1890, 'Lord Euston's Case' (DPP1/95/2).

[NA-21] *St James Gazette*, 25 November 1889 (DPP1/95/2).

[NA-22] *Star*, 25 November 1889, 'What We Think' (DPP1/95/2).

[NA-23] Stephenson's letter to Lushington (Home Office), 17 October 1889 (DPP1/95/1)

[NA-24] *Times*, 1 March 1890 (DPP1/95/2).

[NA-25] *Times*, 21 May 1890 (HO144/477/X24427A).

[NA-26] *Truth*, 14 November 1889 (DPP1/95/2).

[NA-27] *Truth*, 21 November 1889 (DPP1/95/2).

[NA-28] *Truth*, 28 November 1889 (DPP1/95/2).

[NA-29] *Truth*, 5 December 1889 (DPP1/95/2).

[NA-30] *Truth*, 12 December 1889 (DPP1/95/2).

[NA-31] *Truth*, 19 December 1889 (DPP1/95/2).

[NA-32] *Truth*, 2 January 1890 (DPP1/95/2).

[NA-33] *Truth*, 6 February 1890 (DPP1/95/2).

[NA-34] *Truth*, 6 March 1890 (DPP1/95/2).

[NA-35] *Truth*, 20 March 1890 (DPP1/95/2).

[NA-36] Unidentified newspaper cutting, 28 November 1889, 'The West End Scandal. Is the Law to Be Evaded?' (HO 144/477/X24427A).

[NA-37] Webster's opinion (DPP1/95/4).

Notes

1 In the first edition Krafft-Ebing had spoken of same-sex desire in terms of 'antipathic sexual instinct' (Mondimore, 1996: 36). For a discussion of Krafft-Ebing's terminology in later editions of *Psychopathia Sexualis*, see Moran (1996: 6–7).

2 'Irish Government' here means the British government in Ireland.

3 The *Western Mail* quoted the *Freeman's Journal* on this point.

4 The *Western Mail* quoted *United Ireland* to this effect.

5 The general public quickly picked up this barrage of clichés – a letter sent to the *Freeman's Journal* in 1884 in support of O'Brien spoke of 'purify[ing] the filthy atmosphere of Dublin castle' ('The O'Brien Fund', 1884).

6 Likewise, one of the judges that heard Cornwall's appeal from the decision of the Common Pleas refusing a retrial of the libel case expressed concerns about Cornwall 'court[ing] the society of the young to corrupt them by his contaminating influences' (RMA-4).

7 The latter were described as 'one old man sentenced on his own confession to what is practically life-long imprisonment' and 'two men taken from the very dregs of the population, undefended, and whose guilt was practically unquestioned, sentenced each to two years' imprisonment' (RMA-6).

8 Labouchere was worrying unnecessarily, as the common law had developed an imaginative array of 'unnatural offences' that were used to target homosexual men; sexual activities between males that did not amount to sodomy could in any case be punished as the attempt to commit the act itself (Cocks, 2007: 110–112). For a discussion of Labouchere's radical politics, flamboyant persona, insider/outsider position within the aristocracy, ambivalence towards the bohemian world, and possible strategic motivations for introducing the amendment, see Dellamora (1990: 201–203).

9 A letter from Monro to the Director of Public Prosecutions (DPP) laments the press undeservedly critiquing the inaction of the police and asks for an urgent reply to his previous enquiries about how to proceed (NA-8). Stephenson, in a letter addressed to the Home Office, states that he had 'been of the opinion that proceedings should be instituted against several persons, including LAS' but the Attorney General instructed him 'to take proceedings against Veck only' (NA-23). In a letter to Monro the DPP declares that the case was 'entirely out of [his] hands' because he had been acting entirely under the direction of the Secretary of State for the Home Department and the Attorney General (NA-2).

10 Kaplan (1999: 92) points out that the judge referred to Saul repeatedly as 'that creature'. So did the newspapers reporting on the case. Cook (2003: 60–61) argues that Saul and other homosexual men in high-profile, *fin-de-siècle* same-sex scandals became the object of intense voyeuristic interest on the part of journalists and their readers, and journalistic descriptions of their bodies (stressing their fleshiness and unwholesomeness) consolidated and redefined stereotypes about the homosexual population.

11 Kaplan (1999: 87) argues that the term 'gay' refers to female prostitutes, as it had not come into use to refer to homosexuals yet.

12 A picture inserted midway through this statement shows the Greek profile, framed by wavy locks, of a slightly languid-looking, sleepy-eyed young man.

13 The murder was roundly condemned by nationalist leaders (O'Brien, 1976: 22).

14 According to Hyde (1976: 215–231), Labouchere was labouring under a misapprehension when he insisted that the government had connived at hushing up the scandal and defeating the administration of justice.

15 It has been argued that the prince did in fact frequent the Cleveland Street establishment (Aronson, 1994: 162–177; Hyde, 1976: 59).

16 Labouchere said that LAS's claim that he had fled England in order to 'screen a highly-placed person' was 'a falsehood of the basest and most baneful description' (NA-31).

17 Prince Albert Victor contracted influenza shortly before his twenty-eighth birthday and died of pneumonia one week later (Hyde, 1976: 244).

18 This is illustrated in a letter by Robert George Crookshank Hamilton, who was Under-Secretary to the Lord Lieutenant (Mahoney, 1885: 103). Despite Cornwall's acquittal in the criminal trials, Hamilton invokes the moral enormity of his sexual preferences to dispose conclusively of the question of whether Cornwall should be granted a work-related benefit. The letter states that Cornwall (who had been about to retire shortly before the scandals erupted and who had been ruined by legal expenses) could not be offered a pension while the civil action verdict stood. His character was 'so disgraceful and differing so little, if at all, in moral enormity from the actual felony, that a person proved to be guilty of it, should not . . . receive a pension' (RMA-10).

19 Cocks (2003: 67) argues that, in cases of either heterosexual or same-sex prostitution, the Home Office policy was to prosecute only where unavoidable. It might be, then, that in the Cleveland Street affair the 'minnows' (Veck and Newlove), who by any account obtained what were regarded as light sentences, were prosecuted because there was little else that could be done, rather than because of a policy to systematically shield the rich while targeting the poor. Through an analysis of Lord Somerset's fate, at any rate, Kaplan (1999: 95) persuasively argues that laws on homosexual offences, even if unenforced, produced considerable adverse consequences in practice.

20 Cohen (1993: 124) and Kaplan (1999: 88) have argued that the distinctive feature of the press coverage of the Cleveland Street scandal was its representation of homosexuality only insofar as this proved serviceable to constructing an argument about unequal justice.

21 Gladstone's decision to throw his weight behind home rule was apparently dictated by a mixture of considerations. These included pragmatic concerns – namely, staving off Irish republicanism, as well as giving up the increasingly unmanageable task of governing Ireland in the context of regular cycles of disorder and repression. Gladstone was also actuated by idealistic motives (the Irish people's right to self-government) and ones that sat midway between pragmatism and idealism (concerns over an impendent revolution and social anarchy) (Ball, 2008: 1–5, 74–77; Loughlin, 1986: 35–52).

22 Kaplan (2005: 188) demonstrates, however, that the telegraph boys involved in the Cleveland Street affair were not 'sexual innocents'.

Chapter 5

Late Modernity: Homosexuality, disloyalty and falling below the standards of public life

Introduction

Since the Dublin and Cleveland Street scandals of the late Victorian age, authorities had continued to target homosexual men for unnatural offences. In the post-war period, however, prosecutions were carried out with renewed zeal (Houlbrook, 2005: 34–37), culminating in the Montagu trials – reportedly the first time in history 'a peer of the realm' was made 'to stand trial for felony before a judge and jury' [LAG-21].[1] It may not be entirely accidental that, following the 1948 abolition of the right enjoyed by peers to be tried for felony in the House of Lords, it was precisely on charges of committing homosexual offences that the first peer stood an ordinary trial. It is plausible to see this as the culmination of a centuries-old discursive tradition that had variously supposed or articulated a special incompatibility between a statesman's same-sex desire and his suitability for public office, constructing same-sex desire as a problem for good government. As I argue in this chapter, however, in the mid-twentieth century this construction acquired, if only for a brief period, a distinctive cold-war flavour.

As we have seen, the 1884 Dublin scandal is believed to have prompted the criminalisation of gross indecency between males through the Labouchere amendment of 1885. Conversely, the Montagu trials – which took place seven decades later – are widely regarded as pivotal to the decriminalisation, in England and Wales, of consensual same-sex sexual activities between adult males in private (Lafitte, 1958–1959: 8; Montagu of Beaulieu, 2000: 97, 124; 'Lord Montagu on the Court Case Which Ended the Legal Persecution of Homosexuals', 2007).[2] The trials attracted much publicity and in their immediate aftermath the *Sunday Times* ran an editorial arguing that the case for decriminalisation was 'very strong' [LAG-25]. In August of the same year, the Home Secretary appointed the Departmental Committee on Homosexual Offences and Prostitution. In its 1957 report – known as the Wolfenden report – the committee recommended the decriminalisation of consensual same-sex sexual activities in private between males over 21. Ten years later the legislature gave legal effect to this recommendation in the Sexual Offences Act 1967.

As we will see, in the Montagu trials and the debates on homosexuality that surrounded them there are echoes of some of the assumptions and contentions made in the context of the Dublin Castle and Cleveland Street scandals – particularly the idea of the exceptional gravity of homosexual offences. Novel elements, however, also appear – especially a new scientific vocabulary to aid (or indeed undermine) the construction of homosexuals as poor public officials. The Montagu case must also be put into the context of a new discourse, imported from the United States, casting homosexual statesmen and governmental employees as either inclined to disloyalty or as security risks.

In this chapter I also discuss the case of Ian Harvey, a junior minister who, only four years after the Montagu trials, resigned his post after being caught red-handed while engaged in sexual conduct with a guardsman in London's St James's Park. Harvey's case is interesting for reasons of its own. First, it is evidence of widespread societal assumptions that homosexuality disqualifies one *ipso facto* from public office. Secondly, it is indicative of the power of these assumptions, to which Harvey – epitomising modernity's docile citizen engaged in self-management and self-discipline – responded by tendering his resignation from public office.

Importing the lavender scare

In 1951 Guy Burgess, member of the Foreign Office staff and formerly employed by the Security Agency, mysteriously disappeared with diplomat Donald Maclean, amid rumours of political disloyalty and homosexuality. The latter charge was repeated with 'vociferous intensity' (Driberg, 1956: 108) over the following five years, when it was learnt the two had indeed defected to Moscow. The disappearance sparked concerns both domestically (*Hansard*-3) and across the Atlantic (Johnson, 2013: 66; Carlston: 2013: 181), where the FBI had apparently been investigating Burgess even prior to his disappearance (Vargo; 2003: 98). Significantly, by 1951, in the United States the systematic dismissal of homosexual governmental employees, who were considered 'security risks', enjoyed cross-party endorsement (Johnson, 2004: 117).

A full history of the US 'lavender scare' has been reconstructed by Johnson (2004). Both lesbian and gay governmental employees were targeted, but those who ignited and stoked the anti-homosexual hysteria tended to treat male homosexuality as the paradigmatic case, as suggested by the way in which they couched their contributions to the debate. The scare had started four years earlier, at the beginning of the cold war period, when Republican congressmen had voiced concerns about homosexuals employed in the State Department (Johnson, 2004: 4). In response, the Secretary of State instituted a new security programme that would enable it to weed out, alongside those guilty of disloyalty (Communists and spies), so-called 'security-risks'. These were individuals of bad character – habitual drunks, the morally depraved, the financially irresponsible, criminals and sexual perverts – whose poor judgement was believed to make them more likely to associate with subversives (Johnson, 2004: 21). Johnson notes that although 'security risk' could mean several things, more often than not it was used to imply homosexuality (8). While alcoholics and excessively loquacious individuals raised concerns, they did not require full congressional investigations, specialised security officers or the maintenance of specific records. Indeed, these three types of security risk were often rhetorically conflated through the representation of gay men as both given to excessive drinking and being incapable of keeping secrets (Johnson, 2004: 8–9).

In 1950, Senator McCarthy drew a fairly explicit connection between homosexuality and political disloyalty, effectively claiming that homosexuality, as a mental or physical disorder, inclined homosexuals to Communism (Johnson, 2004: 16).[3] Later – after Republicans cornered the State Department into admitting that it had dismissed ninety-one homosexual employees – the emphasis shifted. The idea that homosexuality predisposed one to Communism was overtaken by the notion that their sexual perversion made homosexuals particularly vulnerable to being blackmailed into providing classified information (Johnson, 2004: 23). Republicans denounced previous Democratic governments as the 'New Deal and Fair deal and *fairy* deal administrations' (Johnson, 2004: 30). Aided by tabloid journalism and the popular press, they insisted that homosexuality was significantly over-represented in the New Deal bureaucracy (Johnson, 2004: 84–89). As a result, in 1950, the 'problem' of homosexuals in the public administration at times overshadowed that of Communist governmental employees (Johnson, 2004: 31). In response, the State Department tightened its appointment practices, charging special personnel and investigators with uncovering homosexuality within the departmental workforce (Johnson, 2004: 73). Other governmental agencies also intensified efforts to remove homosexual employees (Johnson, 2004: 98). The 1950 report of the committee (chaired by Senator Clyde Hoey) charged with investigating homosexuality in the government added a further rationale for the dismissal of homosexual federal employees: whether or not they posed a security risk, their perversion undermined their moral and emotional balance, making them unsuited for government work (Johnson, 2004: 101). The report established a new bi-partisan orthodoxy, at least on the more narrow point that homosexual public employees were security risks (Johnson, 2004: 117). Between 1950 and 1952, the Department of State dismissed over 300 employees because of their homosexuality, nearly three times those dismissed 'for more straightforward security concerns' over the same period (Office of the Historian, 2011: 128–129).

This was the political climate in the United States when Burgess and Maclean's 1951 disappearance created a sensation in the press around the world (Vargo, 2003: 101). Two weeks after their disappearance, the *Sunday Dispatch* urged the UK government to follow the US example and dismiss 'sexual and political perverts' (Hodges, 2012: 501). The choice of words here is significant. 'Perversion' almost invariably means 'sexual perversion'; where it is used more broadly, it tends to connote a deviation from something regarded as the natural state of things or course of conduct. Thus, not only does the expression 'political perverts' construct certain political allegiances as unnatural, but it also subliminally sexualises them. The copula 'and' in 'sexual and political perverts' consolidates the link between homosexuality and Communism, suggesting that they (un)naturally go hand in hand. Conrad (2004: 35) argues that the idealistic and vocal socialism of some late nineteenth-century and early twentieth-century homosexual activists like Edward Carpenter and George Cecil Ives had contributed to a discursive association between homosexuality and forces aimed at destabilising the political status quo in Britain. The discursive connection between Communism and homosexuality following Burgess and Maclean's escape thus was probably enabled by a pre-existing association between homosexuality and political radicalism.

In 1952, the year after Burgess and Maclean's disappearance, the *Sunday Pictorial* (now the *Sunday Mirror*) published a three-part series wholly devoted to denouncing homosexuality (Higgins, 1996: 288). Among other things, it declared that homosexuals in the civil and diplomatic services posed a special danger due to their vulnerability to blackmail (Hodges, 2012: 502). Burgess and Maclean were not, in fact, victims of Soviet blackmail – they were willing Soviet spies – but the publicity given to their case no doubt encouraged a discourse on the interplay between Communism and homosexuality.

Indeed, while blackmail argument, as we have seen, had played an important role in the context of the US lavender scare, it too – like the association between homosexuality and political radicalism had a historical antecedent in Britain. In particular, Hyde (1970: 171) reports that, towards the end of World War I, a story had been taken seriously, according to which Germans were in possession of a list of British homosexuals who could be blackmailed into revealing state secrets.

After Burgess and Maclean's escape, the British Foreign Office informally consulted with the US State Department about homosexuality in the government; in 1952, the UK government introduced investigations into the 'character' of governmental employees (Johnson, 2013: 66). This was known as 'positive vetting' and involved proactive steps on the government's part to find out about the private lives of new personnel (Hodges, 2012: 502). In practice, however, the procedures fell short of their rather more exacting US counterpart (Higgins, 1996: 264–265).

In 1953, the incoming Eisenhower administration, whose slogan during the presidential campaign had been 'Let's Clean House', stepped up the security programme targeting homosexual federal employees, particularly in the State Department (Johnson, 2004: 119–125). Nothing comparable to the scale of the US lavender scare purges took place in Britain (Higgins, 1996: 265–266). Nonetheless, on 25 October of the same year the *Sydney Sunday Telegraph* reported that the United States had strongly urged the British government to remove from office homosexual men in important governmental positions 'as hopeless security risks' (Wildeblood, 1999: 45–46). It added that a top-ranking official from Scotland Yard had recently spent three months in the United States consulting with the FBI on the issue. According to the report, the 'special branch' (the political arm of Scotland Yard, with responsibilities for matters of national security and subversive activities) had blacklisted the names of 'known perverts in influential government jobs'; the idea was that they should be moved into less influential positions or put 'behind bars' (Wildeblood, 1999: 45–46). Two days later, London's *Daily Herald* provided a slightly different account – speaking of a three-week mission of two Home Office experts in the United States (LAG-26). In fact, the mission was led by a Home Office official accompanied by a Scotland Yard officer (Higgins, 1996: 258).[4] In any case, the *Daily Herald* reported that, following the mission, the Home Office had ordered the police to escalate the war on 'London vice', and the Home Secretary, Sir David Maxwell-Fyfe, had met London magistrates to discuss how they could assist in this effort (LAG-26).

The *Sydney Sunday Telegraph*'s report drew an explicit link between these developments in relation to a US-encouraged war on vice motivated by security concerns and the prosecution of Lord Montagu (Wildeblood, 1999: 45–46). Since then, Lord Montagu (2000: 98–99) himself and journalist Peter Wildeblood (1999: 45) have also drawn such a link. Wildeblood (1999: 56), co-defendant in the second Montagu trial, described Montagu as the 'real quarry':[5] unlike Montagu, neither Wildeblood nor the third co-defendant, Pitt-Rivers, had significant public functions. Lord Montagu (2000: 105), in his autobiography, echoed this view. He said that he felt responsible for Wildeblood and Pitt-Rivers: he thought they would probably have been left alone had his own prosecution not required their involvement. The trials, in fact, have passed down to history simply as the 'Montagu case'.

Higgins, however, has questioned the conventional historiographical wisdom according to which in the early 1950s an anti-homosexual witch-hunt was conducted in Britain in order to allay US anxieties about national and international security. He has also disputed that the Montagu trial had anything to do with such a witch-hunt. According to Higgins, the press was fed the witch-hunt line by Scotland Yard (eager to look like it was cracking down on vice) and was making too much of the idiosyncratic views of eccentric politicians whom no-one took seriously (Higgins, 1996: 258–259, 262, 266). Higgins is on firm ground where he argues that in the early to mid-1950s there was no generalised stepping up of the effort to clamp down on homosexuality. He shows that in previous decades the authorities – far from being soft on vice as the *Sydney Sunday Telegraph* reported – had been more than willing to persecute homosexuals (Higgins, 1996: 256). Higgins (1996: 256) also seems correct in arguing that the correspondent for the Australian newspaper ignored the existence of multiple independent police forces in Britain. This means that the London Police Commissioner had – unlike what the *Sydney Sunday Telegraph* suggested – no authority to drive a coordinated war on male vice beyond the capital. But Higgins's point here obscures the fact that different police authorities could take their cue from the Home Office rather than the London Police Commissioner. In any case, the Australian reporter's mistake is of little consequence if the main intended targets of the witch-hunt were homosexuals in political and governmental posts (rather than the general homosexual population). The capital being the centre of the country's political life, the most important targets would be largely moving precisely within the range for which the London Police Commissioner had jurisdiction.

Higgins also argues that the view that the Montagu trials were the result of a conspiracy (i.e. that they were staged to convey an image of the government being tough on homosexuality in order to appease the United States) commits one to some implausible assumptions. In particular, as we will see, the first trial involved allegations that Montagu and another man had sexual contact with two Boy Scouts at the peer's beach hut. However, Higgins (1996: 250) argues, we would then have to conclude that, incredibly, the Boy-Scouts too were parties to the conspiracy against Lord Montagu. It seems to me, however, that the point of reading the Montagu case in light of the hypothesis of an official witch-hunt is not to support the claim that the charges were manufactured by the authorities. Rather, it is to help explain the fact that, once the Boy Scouts made their report to the police, the authorities decided to go ahead with the prosecution regardless of the likelihood of obtaining a conviction in light of the available evidence. The witch-hunt theory also helps explain why the authorities tampered with the evidence and took care to secure great publicity for the trial.

Higgins (1996: 250) disputes a connection between the US lavender scare and the Montagu trial by arguing that if the trial was staged in response to Burgess and Maclean's 1951 disappearance, it was too late. He adds that the intention to appease the US authorities on the homosexuality issue was also short lived, coming as it did to an end in the spring of 1954 – with Cabinet's agreement to appoint what would be known as the Wolfenden committee (Higgins, 1996: 250). But the timeline of events is actually quite tight. As we have seen, at first the British government tried to conceal the spies' escape in 1951. When it could no longer do so, it consulted with the US government and introduced positive vetting in 1952. Then, with the Eisenhower administration's renewed emphasis on 'cleaning house' in 1953, a Home Office mission to the United States was organised. The high-profile prosecution of Montagu, a homosexual holder of political office, was secured as soon as practical thereafter, in 1953. This sequence of events and their timing, if anything, strongly confirms rather than undermines the conventional reading.

There are also reasons to reject the argument that Cabinet's agreement to appoint the Wolfenden committee signalled an abrupt change of policy and hence disproves that there ever was a US-inspired anti-homosexual drive. This argument oversimplifies both the motivations for the agreement to appoint the committee and, before then, the Home Office's initial proposal for an official body to investigate homosexuality. There is no inconsistency between the importation of the lavender scare and the appointment of the Wolfenden committee. After all, if homosexuality in the government was an issue, then studying the homosexual 'problem' and the best legal response to it would be likely to help solve that issue. Ironically, to the extent that the nature of homosexuality as a security risk was its potential for attracting blackmail, and that this was largely an artefact of homosexuality's illegality, the decriminalisation recommended by Wolfenden did implicitly point to a solution to the problem of homosexuality as a security risk. This, however, was undoubtedly not the solution that Maxwell-Fyfe was seeking or anticipating when he instituted the inquiry: the evidence shows that he was against liberalising the law and favoured incarceration of homosexual offenders (Bengry, 2012: 175–179).[6] Far from signalling an inversion of policy, the government's agreement to appoint the committee in response to calls for legal change may even have been motivated by the appreciation that setting up an inquiry was the best way to forestall actual reform (Jeffery-Poulter, 1991: 19–20). In sum, the appointment of the committee, as a sign of potential reform originating from within the government, may well be 'astonishing' when compared to what was happening at the same time in the United States (Engel, 2001: 70–71); but it is less than astonishing in its convergence with the UK government's view that homosexuality was a problem requiring containment.

Thus, Higgins's arguments – although they demonstrate that 1953–1954 did not see a steep rise in prosecutions and convictions for homosexual offences – do not disprove the narrower proposition that, after Burgess and Maclean's disappearance, concerns about homosexual public officials were taken seriously enough as to trigger specific actions intended to address these concerns. Britain had been aware that Maclean was a Soviet agent long before his escape with Burgess (probably since 1948); this intelligence was deliberately kept hidden from its American ally (Hamrick, 2004: 13). Thus, following the escape of the Soviet spies, Britain had strong reasons to want to appease Washington by importing a version of the lavender scare. Seen in this light, the label of 'witch-hunt' is as good as any to describe the measures taken after Burgess and Maclean's disappearance. As outlined above, these measures included: a consultation with US authorities about homosexuality in the government; the introduction of positive vetting; a mission to the United States to be briefed on homosexuality; the Home Secretary's urging magistrates to take homosexual crimes seriously; the high-profile conviction of a homosexual peer; and the careful management of the trial's publicity so as to ensure its exemplary character would not be missed. It strains credibility to look at these events as unrelated incidents.

As a member of the House of Lords, with no ministerial or other executive roles, Montagu was hardly likely to be in possession of the highly confidential information that could make him a 'security risk' in the technical sense of the word. But it does not follow that his sexuality was considered irrelevant to his public life. 'Although the 'lavender scare' was mainly centred around the notion that homosexuals were security risks, it also included, as we have seen, a more general idea of homosexuals' unsuitability for public office owing to their moral and emotional instability. It is worth noting that the latter idea implicitly references a quasi-medical understanding of homosexuality as a disordered condition. This suggests that the social science discourse on homosexuality, which was in its infancy during the Dublin and Cleveland Street scandals, could now be mustered in support of the proposition that homosexuality and public office were incompatible.[7]

In any case, there is some evidence that some did connect Montagu's prosecution to a perception of his posing a risk to national security – not in the sense of his being blackmailed into revealing confidential information, but in the sense of his homosexuality predisposing him to political disloyalty. When Montagu was in Paris to avoid the publicity of what was to be the first trial, he was approached by two men who suggested he might like to emulate Burgess and Maclean and escape to Russia. Montagu (2000: 102) was never able to discover whether this was a set up on the part of an entrepreneurial journalist or a genuine offer. If the former – or indeed if the men who propositioned him were members of the Security Agency or Special Branch – the incident is an indication that the notion that homosexuality inclined one to 'disloyalty' and Communism had acquired some purchase in Britain. Montagu's openness to cross-class intimacy, discussed below, may have made him a particularly likely target for speculations that, like Burgess and Maclean, he might be a crypto-Communist.

The first Montagu trial

Lord Montagu of Beaulieu – at 26 the youngest peer of the House of Lords – was initially charged with committing an unnatural offence with a 14-year-old Boy Scout (LAG-6). Some Scouts had acted as guides in Palace House, at Beaulieu, on the day of the 1953 August bank holiday. At one point Lord Montagu invited them and the adults present to go for a swim. Two Scouts agreed, as did Kenneth Hume, a film producer, whom Montagu had recently met and who had come to Beaulieu because he wanted to use the estate as a film location (LAG-30). The offences had allegedly been committed by Montagu and Hume each against one of the Scouts, in Montagu's beach hut, where they had gone to dry themselves after the swim (LAG-7).

After Montagu was committed for trial in Winchester Hall (LAG-33), Maxwell-Fyfe, the Home Secretary, declared in the Commons that homosexuals were 'exhibitionists and proselytisers and . . . a danger to others' and that he had 'a duty to protect people, especially the youth of this country' (LAG-12). He also went on to provide a taxonomy of homosexuals – an odd mix of pseudo-science and folk sociology – distinguishing between genuine inverts; opportunistic, as it were, homosexuals who sometimes have recourse to same-sex sexual activity instead of heterosexual intercourse; male prostitutes given to importuning; and 'sensationalists who will try any form of excitement' (LAG-12). Maxwell-Fyfe argued that imprisonment was particularly appropriate in the last three cases (LAG-12). Perhaps the Home Secretary's speech was calculated to recast the 'war on vice' within the government in the more neutral terms of a war on vice within society in general, so as to deflect or pre-empt accusations of McCarthyite persecutorial targeting of public employees (both McCarthyism and the lavender scare had not been without their critics in the United States).[8]

However, given evidence of Maxwell-Fyfe's unalloyed hostility to homosexuality (LAG-15; David, 1997: 163–164; Grey, 1992: 22; Bengry, 2012: 175–176), it seems his concerns about homosexual public officials were, in fact, genuinely part of a broader preoccupation with 'male perverts'. Conveniently, his ambiguous reference to an unspecified 'danger' posed by homosexuals is capable of being interpreted in terms of either gay men spreading sexual vice within society or their making British society vulnerable to the attacks of its political enemies (via blackmail or deliberate disloyalty). Even the one danger more specifically identified, that of corrupting 'the youth of this country', is stated in ambiguous terms. On its face, it seems to indicate a concern with young men's sexuality, but the word used to characterise homosexual men – 'proselytisers' – conjures up an imagery of political and ideological indoctrination rather than merely sexual initiation. This reinforces the conflation between homosexuality and subversion.

Montagu was indicted on the felony of committing an unnatural offence with the Scout, as well as of the misdemeanour of indecently assaulting him (LAG-7). The case of the prosecution was notable for resting on both shaky (LAG-21) and fabricated evidence (Wildeblood, 1999: 48–50; Montagu of Beaulieu, 2000: 105).[9] Many years later Montagu (2000: 104) declared he had felt both impotent and perplexed during this Kafkaesque trial in which the account of the prosecution 'bore no relation to reality'. In the end, he was found innocent of having committed the felony, but the jury could not agree on the misdemeanour, which would require a retrial (LAG-27).[10] The retrial, however, never took place. No sooner was Lord Montagu acquitted of the main charge in the Boy Scout trial than fresh charges were brought against him and two other men of having engaged in sexual activities with two airmen the year before. The three of them were found guilty in 1954 and the Crown elected not to pursue the charge of indecent assault against the Boy Scout. The justification proffered for this course of action was that offering new evidence on the charge would require subjecting the boys to dwelling on the incident once more (LAG-40).

The second Montagu trial

In the second trial, Lord Montagu, his friend the journalist Peter Wildeblood and his cousin Michael Pitt-Rivers were charged with conspiracy to incite air-craftman John Reynolds, 19, and corporal Edward McNally, 25, to commit gross indecency (LAG-28; LAG-8). In addition to the conspiracy offence, Lord Montagu was charged with attempting to commit an unnatural offence and gross indecency (with Reynolds). Wildeblood and Pitt-Rivers were charged with the actual commission (LAG-32). All defendants were found guilty of the conspiracy charge. Montagu was also found guilty of gross indecency, but the judge directed the jury to find him not guilty of attempting to commit serious offences. Pitt-Rivers and Wildeblood were found guilty of committing serious offences (LAG-45).

It was an investigation by the RAF security department into homosexual offences in the air forces that had led to the new charges. McNally had had sex with several men, but it was his relationship with Wildeblood and the lead it provided to Lord Montagu (Wildeblood having mentioned Beaulieu in one of his letters to the corporal) that got the authorities interested (Wildeblood, 1999: 61). Through Wildeblood, Montagu had happened to meet McNally, who had then introduced the young peer to Reynolds. On one occasion, Montagu had invited them to stay at his beach chalet at Beaulieu, where some of the offences were alleged to have occurred (LAG-44). Subsequently the party had moved to Pitt-Rivers's farm, with the exception of Montagu, whose need to leave Beaulieu on business had, in fact, prompted the change of scene for the other four men. McNally and Reynolds had been offered immunity from prosecution if they provided evidence against the three defendants (LAG-17).[11]

The case reveals the permeability of legal discourse to medico-scientific categories. Reynolds – 'a good-looking "queer"' who had elicited Lord Montagu's sexual interest, according to the prosecution (LAG-10) – apparently used the word 'homosexual' as a self-descriptor under cross-examination (LAG-44). The *Times* reported that McNally 'said he had never discussed homo-sexuality with Reynolds but had guessed that he (Reynolds) was a pervert' (LAG-9). The *Times* reporter's need to clarify that when McNally had said he suspected 'he' was a pervert McNally was speaking of Reynolds (and not himself) configures homosexuality not only as an object of knowledge, but also quasi-psychoanalytic sexual *self*-knowledge.

Alongside the pervert and homosexual, the 'invert' also made its appearance during the trial. During his cross-examination, Wildeblood was asked if he was an 'invert', i.e. someone who 'through no fault of [his] own' was subject 'to temptations and desires' from which 'a normal man' is immune (LAG-46). Wildeblood confirmed that he was. When asked why, considering this, he had invited McNally to his flat and risked giving in to those temptations, he replied that he thought he was safe as he 'had always managed to keep [his] desire under control' (LAG-46). In this exchange, Wildeblood emerges not only as an invert (a 'genuine' homosexual suffering from a condition for which he is not responsible) but an exemplary one – one who employs scientific knowledge in the service of successful self-management. The invert, it will be recalled, was the only 'type' of homosexual whom Maxwell-Fyfe contemplated might more appropriately be dealt with in some way other than imprisonment. The defence used Wildeblood's self-claimed invert identity to appeal not, in its own words, to the jury's 'pity' or 'sympathy', but to their sense of 'justice' – as Wildeblood suffered from a 'disease' for which he was not to blame (LAG-10).[12] In contrast to the characterisation of Wildeblood as a blameless invert, the defence stated that McNally was 'morally corrupt', a 'homosexual' who knew himself as such and had an interest in lying to avoid his own prosecution (LAG-10). A pervert, in the prosecution's words, was one 'who, from lust or wickedness, will get desire from either the natural function or the unnatural function' (LAG-29). The spurious distinction between 'inverts' and 'perverts' appears to have been taken as an established fact during the trial.

Pitt-Rivers, for example, said he did not know that Wildeblood was an 'invert' or Reynolds a 'pervert' (LAG-10).

If Wildeblood deliberately chose to characterise himself as an invert, Montagu's defence strategy was to deny the charges (LAG-31), apparently without admitting to same-sex attraction, let alone claiming membership of any particular homosexual typology. Montagu was clearly alive to the special damage that any imputation of same-sex desire could wreak upon his status as a peer, and was eager to distance his name as far as possible from any association with homosexuality in the public mind. Indeed, when protesting his innocence in the Scouts' affair, he had written to the chief constable of his awareness of the 'extreme danger' that the charge posed to his 'public position' (LAG-2). The same sentiment was voiced (albeit less than entirely prophetically, as we will see) by his counsel after Montagu was found guilty in the second trial and sentenced to twelve months in prison. He described Montagu as 'a useful member of the House of Lords and a kindly landowner' facing 'a bitter future' (LAG-45).

Before the jury issued the verdict, the prosecution warned that the 'high character' of the defendants was no bar to their guilt, adding: 'We are dealing with the dark and mysterious realms of sex . . . How little do we know, any of us, about the sex lives of our neighbours.' (LAG-10) In invoking a pseudo-Freudian picture of 'dark and mysterious' sexuality, this statement illustrates once again the colonisation of legal discourse by scientific knowledge – indeed, the deliberate deployment of the latter by the former. It also rhetorically performs anew the conflation between homosexuality and political disloyalty. The ominous reference, in particular, to our lack of knowledge about what goes in our neighbours' bedrooms implicitly references an imagery of political dissidents and Soviet sympathisers, plotting behind closed doors in the midst of 1950s picket-fenced, middle-class suburbia.

The implicit conflation of homosexuality with Communism was reinforced by the prosecution's construction of homosexuals as lacking in class-consciousness. Thus, the prosecution reasoned, Pitt-Rivers was a 'county councillor' and only sex could have been the link between him and Reynolds, an airman (LAG-10). Likewise, in the opening statement, the prosecution had made much of the fact that homosexuality led to a transgression of class boundaries. The prosecution argued that although Reynolds and McNally's evidence was tainted by the fact that they were 'perverts, men of the lowest possible moral character', corroboration was to be found in the singular fact that they kept company with their social superiors (LAG-32). Again, when in the witness box Wildeblood admitted he was an 'invert', the prosecution asked: 'It is a feature, is it not, that inverts or perverts seek their love associates in a different walk of life than their own?' The prosecution went on to say that McNally was 'infinitely' Wildeblood's 'social inferior' (Wildeblood, 1999: 77). Years later, Wildeblood would suggest that there was truth in the idea that homosexuals defy class barriers and that this is why they were resented and mistrusted by 'many of our political diehards' (Wildeblood, 1999: 26). Wildeblood (1999: 27) would add that if the experience of same-sex desire made one more aware of class injustice, then, in this sense, it was 'a force for good'.

The prosecution's obsessive insistence on the defendants' associating with their social inferiors echoes the proposition that homosexuality was a proxy for Communism. In so doing, it inflects with distinctly cold war connotations both Montagu's prosecution and, through it, the Home Office's mid-twentieth-century construction of the incompatibility between homosexual orientation and the exercise of public functions. The fact that the Special Branch was involved in the Montagu case – specifically, in Wildeblood's arrest (Wildeblood, 1999: 73) – lends further support to the theory that the case was not a routine prosecution for homosexual offences. Rather, it apparently involved concerns about the exercise of public functions by someone whose homosexuality made him politically suspect. This impression is reinforced if we consider that the involvement of the Special Branch was accompanied by abuses in the collection of evidence,[13] and if we look at it in the context of the 'extraordinary decision . . . to launch a second prosecution against Lord Montagu while similar charges . . . were still pending' (LAG-43).

Homosexuality in Parliament

In his autobiography, published many decades after the trials, Lord Montagu (2000: 108) declared that many suspected, and objected to, the government witch-hunting 'in high places' and conducting 'McCarthyite persecution'. The records of parliamentary debates from the period lend support to this view. Approximately one month after Montagu, Wildeblood and Pitt-Rivers were given prison sentences, the question of homosexuality in government jobs was discussed in the Commons in the context of a debate on the Atomic Energy Authority (AEA). David Eccles, then Minister of Works in the Conservative government, explained that, unlike an established civil servant who was made redundant, an AEA employee who was dismissed on the ground of being a security risk could not enjoy the benefit of being found alternative employment in the civil service (*Hansard*-2: 1862–1863). He then added that although an employee dismissed on suspicion of being a Communist would enjoy a right to have the dismissal examined by the Lord President, this safeguard would not apply to those who were 'bad' security risks for other reasons (*Hansard*-2: 1867). Eccles provided three paradigmatic examples – the incompetent worker, the alcoholic babbler or cases of 'moral turpitude' (*Hansard*-2: 1865) – which indicate the strong influence that the American doctrine of security risks (centred on the triad of the loquacious, the habitual drunk and the homosexual) had on British governmental thought on these issues. 'What, in short, [moral turpitude] includes', Eccles elaborated, 'is that if a man is a homosexual he is much more easily blackmailed, owing to the law being what it is at present, than almost anybody else'; as he clarified, '[t]here are cases in which the price which the blackmailer exacts is not money but secrets' (*Hansard*-2: 1865). At the height of the cold war, the notion that homosexuality posed such risks to security that it warranted homosexual men's dismissal from governmental jobs without the safeguards extended to suspected Communists may appear peculiar. It reveals, however, just to what extent the government had bought into the rhetoric of the US lavender scare.[14]

Some Labour MPs appeared less than convinced. Arthur Palmer sought further clarification about how the 'moral failing' described by Eccles affected national security (*Hansard-2*: 1866). After Eccles reiterated the blackmail argument, Frank Beswick asked:

> Is he saying that a homosexual is automatically now considered to be a security risk? . . . [I]t is a serious thing to say that in this country we now consider all those people to be security risks, and so ought to be discharged.
>
> (*Hansard-2*: 1866–1867)

Eccles's reply to my mind more or less puts to rest any doubts about whether the importation of the lavender scare into the UK was a fact or, as Higgins seems to claim, a fable made up by the Australian reporter for the *Sydney Sunday Telegraph* (whose article I discussed above). Eccles replied: 'I should like to take advice on that, but my impression is that the answer is "Yes." It certainly is in America.' (*Hansard-2*: 1867) Gilbert Mitchinson and Palmer ventured the opinion that it was 'a remarkable notion' (*Hansard-2*: 1868) and 'extraordinary' (1875) that homosexuality was considered *ipso facto* a security risk on the ground of potential blackmail. Mitchinson added that in any case the same rules should apply regardless of whether one's liability to blackmail was because of homosexuality or some other reason (*Hansard-2*: 1877). Beswick declared that we were getting into 'an extraordinary situation' if someone could be 'dismissed on security grounds because it is thought that they might conceivably have some moral practices with which society for the time being does not agree' (*Hansard-2*: 1870). George Strauss was even more eloquent:

> I must express my surprise and opposition to the policy announced this evening . . . that all homosexuals are considered a bad security risk and will not be employed at Harwell or other such places. I think that is as serious as it is wrong. I know it is general in the United States, but that does not make it any better.
>
> (*Hansard-2*: 1880)

Eventually Eccles changed his tune. One can almost picture, following the unanticipated backlash in the Commons, a note being slipped to the Minister of Works, instructing him to publicly back down. 'I may have made a mistake' he declared, 'in conveying to the House – though I do not think I did – that all homosexuals are necessarily suspect risks. If I conveyed that, I am sorry.' (*Hansard-2*: 1881)

Three weeks later the Lords were debating 'homosexual crime' and its putative increase. A few appealed once more to scientific discourse to promote a more progressive treatment of 'genuine' homosexuals (*Hansard*-5: 763–766; 752–753). Otherwise, the debate about this 'nauseating subject' (*Hansard*-5: 737) and 'filthy, disgusting, unnatural vice' (739) was dominated by ideas of 'moral declension' (739); of homosexuality being injurious to the nation's 'moral fibre' and 'physique' (744) and causing its loss of 'influence for good in the world' (745); of the homosexual world being rife with blackmail (745); of 'masses of male prostitutes upon the streets' posing a 'frightful risk' to the 'ordinary citizen' (748); of a large increase in homosexual offenders since the war (749); and of excessive contemporary 'laxity' (755) in dealing with the problem, leading to a 'downward slope' (757). While the debate made no particular references to the issue of the sexual orientation of those in government jobs or carrying out public functions, the treatment of the subject echoes the late Victorian rhetoric of exceptionality, representing homosexuality as a crime of the gravest moral character. As the debate reveals, several decades of rapid social change and two wars had not managed to displace this way of conceiving of homosexuality from the minds of a section of the British political class. As I argued in the last chapter, one of the effects of this rhetoric in the late nineteenth century had been to dispose of the need to articulate the reasons why homosexuality and public office should be considered incompatible. It seems plausible that the partial survival of this rhetoric in post-war Britain facilitated the reception of the lavender scare by Churchill's Conservative government – as had the sensation of Burgess and Maclean's disappearance in 1951.

In late 1955, the government having released a white paper on the Burgess and Maclean affair in September of that year, the Commons returned to the question of the fugitive spies. The issue of homosexuality in the government as a security risk reared its head once more. However, in contrast to the previous debate about the AEA, the issue remained in the background, with little effort – with one exception (*Hansard*-4: 1589–1590) – to make it an independent object of debate. The MPs showed themselves to be alive to the dangers and anti-Communist excesses of McCarthyism (*Hansard*-4: 1511, 1581–1582; 1594), which by this time had been discredited even in the United States. Nonetheless, while some Labour MPs the year before had vocally resisted the notion that homosexual public servants constituted a security risk, some of their colleagues now accepted that notion as a fact. Indeed, they seemed to accept even the broader point that homosexuality made one unfit for government work. Additionally, their contributions reveal a rhetorical association between homosexuality and drunkenness, which, as we have seen, was often at play in US debates about homosexuality as an index of bad character and a security risk. Marcus Lipton spoke of 'drunks, homosexuals, or people temperamentally unfitted by reason of their characters to occupy any position in any government Department' (*Hansard*-4: 1580, 1596). Alfred Robens asked how 'a couple of drunks, a couple of homosexuals' were allowed to 'occupy important posts in the Foreign Office' and declared that Maclean 'had homosexual tendencies when in drink' (*Hansard*-4: 1595–1597). Robens then resuscitated the class-based argument that there was one law for the privileged and another for the less privileged – an argument that, it will be recalled, had featured prominently in the Cleveland Street scandal:

> [W]hile these men were protected and excuses were made for their drunkenness and perversions, ordinary working men who had Communist affiliations were kicked out of their jobs almost at a moment's notice. Does this mean that there is one law for a Communist sympathiser from Bermondsey and another for a Communist sympathiser from Cambridge University?
>
> (*Hansard*-4: 1598–1599)

In the statement, the ordinariness of 'ordinary working men' appears to be not only a reference to their educational background, but also to their (presumed) heterosexuality. As in the late nineteenth century, homosexuality is portrayed as characteristic of the upper classes represented by the Conservative government. Robens rhetorically deploys homosexuality to make a case for the shortcomings of the Conservative government's practices and policies, which at one time imperil national security and offend against the principle of equality.

Debating the same matter of Burgess and Maclean's disappearance two weeks later, the Lords appeared rather more inclined than the Commons to dismiss concerns about McCarthyism (*Hansard*-1: 708–709, 717). When discussing homosexuality, the Lords raised it both in terms of it posing security risks (by virtue of making homosexual statesmen vulnerable to blackmail) (*Hansard*-1: 711) and in terms of it signalling poor character. Burgess's homosexuality (*Hansard*-1: 711), no less than his and Maclean's drunkenness, made him 'completely unreliable and unfitted to represent their country at home and abroad' (716–717, 731). For Viscount Astor, 'people, whether they are Members of Parliament or diplomats, who are in a capacity representative of their fellow citizens should have a higher standard of personal conduct . . . than those who engage in purely commercial and private pursuits' (*Hansard*-1: 710). He also deplored the fact (which he got wrong) that members in the House of Commons had failed to say that male perverts 'are not suitable for confidential positions in the public service or to go abroad in a representative capacity' (*Hansard*-1: 711). This argument is not as broad as the argument, which as we know surfaced in the US Hoey report, that homosexuality was a bar to *any* government job. But it does go beyond the more usual point that the problem with homosexuality is merely that it poses a security risk.

The Commons debate on Burgess and Maclean in late 1955 led to a report on security in the public services by a committee of privy councillors, discussed in the Commons in March 1956. The report stressed the potential of character defects for encouraging blackmail, but some MPs suggested that such defects matter in their own right (*Hansard*-7: 1265, 1292) and that they are relevant 'to the holding of all confidential posts' (1265). As illustrations of character defects, the report provided the customary twin examples of drunkenness and homosexuality, this time adding drug addiction (an extension of the former) and 'any loose living' (an extension of the latter) (*Hansard-7*: 1266). In contrast to the homophobic contributions of late 1955, some Labour MPs echoed the positions voiced by their colleagues in the April 1954 debates, disputing the link between homosexuality and security risks. Kenneth Younger pointed out that homosexuality had 'been given undue prominence in investigations in the United States, where it ha[d] been treated as something on quite a different plane in security from almost any other form of character defect' (*Hansard-7*: 1266). Younger argued that if it indeed was on such a different plane, this was merely an artefact of the criminalisation of homosexuality (*Hansard-7*: 1266–1267). Anthony Wedgwood-Benn went further, arguing that character defects should have no place in security programmes and challenging the new Home Secretary, Gwilym Lloyd-George, to provide examples of civil servants who had become spies as a result of being blackmailed (*Hansard-7*: 1297–1298). The homosexual Burgess and the straight-when-sober Maclean, after all, had been *willingly* working for the Soviets. On this basis, screening them for their political sympathies would have averted the damage they caused without any need, or reason, to screen them for homosexuality.

Lloyd-George was unable to meet the challenge, but reassured his audience 'that there is no danger in this country of witch-hunting for the sake of witch-hunting' (*Hansard-7*: 1314). The statement is paradoxical: witch-hunting is of course discreditable in its own right because it is about pursuing a manufactured enemy. It does not matter whether one carries the hunt out for the sake of witch-hunting (whatever that might mean) or, as is generally the case, because one is actuated by some higher motives. The Home Secretary's choice of words implies a belief in the desirability of some form of witch-hunting – one that is motivated, precisely, by those higher motives. It follows a utilitarian logic where, for the sake of society's greater good, sacrifices are imposed on putative security risks on the odd chance of catching out the occasional actual security risk.

The debates analysed in this section tend to treat homosexuality as a character flaw that results in security risks. The idea that homosexuality is a character defect that is in and of itself incompatible with the proper exercise of public offices (or certain public offices) appears less frequently. Nonetheless, there is little doubt that a number of MPs were committed to that idea. This is confirmed by some of the views that were expressed when the Commons debated the Wolfenden report in 1958. The proposition that homosexual statesmen, public officials or governmental employees would be undesirable quite regardless of security concerns appears as a logical implication of those views. For Labour backbencher Frederick Bellinger, homosexuals could be dangerously devious (*Hansard-6*: 420). For Conservative William Shepherd, homosexuals were 'bitter . . . twisted and distorted' in their mind because they resented their difference from other men (*Hansard-6*: 428). Shepherd added an argument to the effect that homosexual vice corrupted procedural fairness, including in political contexts: '[I]n many spheres of activity today the ability and the willingness to enter into homosexual acts is a means of promotion . . . even in business and maybe in politics.'

(*Hansard*-6: 429) The argument was echoed by Labour MP Jean Mann. Mann objected to the Wolfenden report's argument for reform to the effect that the current criminalisation of homosexuality encouraged blackmail. Thus, she turned the blackmail argument once again *against* homosexuals (a use not much different from that to which it had been put to only three years before, when the rhetoric of homosexuality as a security risk was at its height). According to Mann, powerful homosexual men were systematically blackmailing young deserving men into having sex with them upon threat of stopping their career prospects: 'Have none of us heard about fellows who are passed over, in favour of someone who is willing to render [same-sex sexual] service to someone up above? . . . This blackmail of the vilest type is running through our society like an evil thread.' (*Hansard*-6: 458–459).

It was left to people like Peter Rawlinson, who had been junior counsel in the second Montagu trial, to strike a note of sanity:

> I have seen at close hand some of the tremendous personal tragedies which arise from these cases, and if there are any hon. Members . . . who are prepared to pooh-pooh the extent of this human tragedy, then they are very wickedly wrong, because the penalty which society demands, which society obtains, arbitrary as it may be, for one single act to be paid perhaps after years of service with distinction, is such that to see it and witness it is something one can never forget.
>
> (*Hansard*-6: 472)

Ian Harvey's political exile

As it happened, one of those 'tragedies' had unfolded virtually at the same time as the Commons were debating the Wolfenden report. Ian Harvey, 44, Conservative MP and joint Parliamentary Under-Secretary of State for Foreign Affairs, had been caught having sex in St James's Park, London, with 19-year-old guardsman Anthony Walter Plant. They had been charged with gross indecency under the Sexual Offences Act 1956 and with behaving in a way 'reasonably likely to offend against public decency' contrary to the park regulations (LAG-19). They pleaded guilty to breaking the park regulations and the indecency charge was dropped (LAG-24).

Even before the outcome of the trial, Harvey gave up his seat in the Commons and tendered his resignation from his junior ministerial post. Before accepting it, the Prime Minister, Harold Macmillan – whose government, ironically, was later brought down, among other things, by a homosexual scandal involving yet another gay Soviet spy (Higgins, 1996: 306–321) – had given Harvey a chance to think it over during the weekend (LAG-38). Harvey's lawyer, Geoffrey Lawrence, spoke of 'personal disaster' (LAG-24). He mentioned Harvey's 'years of service', his 'ability and distinction in public life', the abrupt end of his political career, the loss of any prospect of resumption of public office, and his condemnation to 'the obscurity of private life' (LAG-24).[15]

Harvey declared he had fallen 'below the standards of people in public life' and would never return (LAG-18). Admittedly, he had broken the law. The circumstances under which he was apprehended had not been the most dignified (Harvey, 2011: 143–144). To make matters worse, he was married with two daughters (LAG-22). However, there is little doubt that the outcome of Harvey's predicament would have been the same had he been single and had his prosecution not involved his being caught *in flagrante delicto* in a public park. A Labour MP, William J Field, had incurred a similar fate five years before, when two policemen had observed him 'make frequent visits to pubs and public conveniences' and 'take an undue interest in young men, smiling at them' (LAG-35). Convicted of 'importuning men for an immoral purpose' (LAG-36), Field was forced to give up his seat (LAG-37).

The *Manchester Guardian* plausibly implied that anyone found guilty in 'judicial or quasi-judicial proceedings of whatever nature' (i.e. whether or not they related to a homosexual offence) would have to resign a ministerial post (LAG-39). But the same argument would not necessarily apply to a seat in Parliament. Nonetheless it is clear that Harvey felt he had no option but to give up his place in the Commons and there is no doubt that it was the homosexual 'nature of his offence' (LAG-20) that made Harvey feel he had to execute a complete exit from public life. Thirteen years after his resignation, Harvey published an autobiography in which he indicated that homosexuality was distinctive: while the Ten Commandments could be broken with relative impunity, he had broken 'the eleventh' (Harvey, 2011: 118). He clarified that even if some of his supporters encouraged him not to give up his seat, they inwardly disapproved of his conduct. It would have been inappropriate to exploit their 'loyalty to the Party' in order to stay (Harvey, 2011: 121), much more so that the general outlook of the Conservatives was uncompromisingly hostile to homosexuality (118, 126).

Harvey's autobiography was entitled, not altogether modestly, *To Fall like Lucifer* – an allusion to his forced plunge into the abyss of what a source called 'political deprivation' (LAG-14) at a time when the pinnacle of his ascending political career was in sight. In his book he stated that for him 'there were no longer any stars; only a dark night' (Harvey, 2011: 145). This set the tone for a spate of book reviews with titles playing up the theme of Harvey's irrecoverable loss, due to his homosexuality, of a life in the political limelight: 'Paradise Lost' (LAG-14); 'A Backward Look at Paradise' (LAG-23); 'A Career in Ruins' (LAG-4); 'A Shattered Career' (LAG-1); 'No Room at the Top' (LAG-34); 'Career Thrown Away' (LAG-5); 'Condemned by His Peers' (LAG-13). Well into the late seventies, the *Daily Express* was running an article pitching the bright universe of politics and glitter of public office against the twilight world of male homosexuality to which Harvey had been relegated (LAG-16).[16]

Harvey (2011: 144) characterised his conduct as a betrayal of 'his trust as a politician' and the institutions he believed in. He put the matter of his resignation in terms of 'the proper responsibilities' of holders of public office in a democracy (Harvey, 2011: 132). There are two elements to this argument, both of which I have foreshadowed above. One idea is that his party's outlook – which its own electoral base expected it to take – was hostile to homosexuality. The other is a more general theory of the citizenry's expectations about the public officials who are in charge of managing the state: society was generally antipathetic to homosexuality (Harvey, 2011: 156) and Harvey had, quite simply, fallen below the standards society expected of public officials (LAG-18). It did not matter whether or not those standards enjoyed a morally defensible justification: the fact that society held public officials to such standards disposed of the matter conclusively. The logic of this argument is 'conventionalist': Harvey determines the correct course of action for him to take – as well as the more general question of whether or not homosexuals should hold public office – by reference to the values conventionally accepted by society. Whether these values are morally sound is immaterial.

Only in one passage of his autobiography – one, unfortunately, not entirely easy to follow – does Harvey reflect on the relationship between public offices and homosexuality in a way that, initially at least, appears to depart from this conventionalist logic. Harvey starts by referring to the sexual bond between Edward II and Piers Gaveston and compares it to that between Charles II and his mistress Nell Gwyn. Harvey (2011: 169) then states that the problem with these statesmen was 'the influence of the inferior element on the public conduct and authority of the superior', rather than the sexual activities themselves. One might expect Harvey to make a point, at this juncture, about the lack of a rational basis for penalising homosexual statesmen when, to the extent that a statesman's sexual relationships may adversely affect the quality of his work, this may happen regardless of whether those relationships are homosexual or heterosexual. Surprisingly, however, Harvey (2011: 169) argues instead that consequently 'similar associations between men' who do not have public roles are of less social significance. While this is an implicit plea for acceptance of homosexuals who do not exercise public functions, it comes at the cost of conceding that there are reasonable grounds for excluding same-sex attracted men from public office by virtue of their homosexuality. This seems incongruous in light of Harvey's claim throughout his book that had it been possible for him to stay, he would have made a successful public man.

There are two possible explanations for Harvey taking this line of argument. The first is that his analogy between heterosexual and homosexual relationships imperilling the performance of public tasks does not involve a comparison between homosexuality and heterosexuality in themselves, but between homosexuality on the one hand and pathological instances of heterosexuality on the other. Harvey's (2011: 169) use of the expression 'various conditions of heterosexuality' seems significant in this connection – although it is anyone's guess which specific heterosexual 'conditions' he had in mind. This analogy between homosexuality and *pathological* expressions of heterosexuality is consistent with Harvey's (2011: 187–188) own identification not as a homosexual, but as a bisexual, by which he means an otherwise regular male member of mainstream society who happens to have sex with males. This disavowal of homosexuality, coupled with the analogy between homosexuality and pathological manifestations of heterosexual desire, would explain Harvey's stance to the effect that heterosexual (and presumably bisexual) men can generally be presumed to carry out public functions competently (the presumption being rebuttable if one's heterosexuality is of the pathological variety). Those genuinely suffering from the 'condition' (Harvey, 2011: 169) of homosexuality, however, are more or less routinely exposed to the sort of dangerous relationship dynamics that befell the likes of Edward II. Hence excluding them from public office is reasonable (although it is unreasonable to penalise homosexuals who have no public functions). It is worth noting that this argument turns on its head the pervert/invert dichotomy that, as we have seen, tended to stigmatise the former and excuse the latter in the context of the Montagu trials. The pervert is now a normal member of society, while the invert is the potentially dangerous outsider (or at least an outsider to public and political life).

The second way of making sense of Harvey's argument about Edward II is that it is only on its surface that the argument was departing from the conventionalist view that homosexual statesmen need to bow to society's belief that they should not manage public affairs. Under this interpretation, both homosexuals (like Edward II) and heterosexuals (like Charles II) are equally liable to let the interpersonal dynamics of their sexual relationships have an adverse effect on their public functions. But it is only with respect to homosexuality that society tends to see this as a problem; consequently, only homosexual statesmen are expected to bow to society's prejudice. This interpretation reintroduces a conventionalist logic into Harvey's argument. It enables us to make sense of Harvey's (2011: 169) conclusion that homosexual public officials should pay the penalty exacted by society when they choose to disregard the fact that same-sex relationships à la Edward and Piers may be problematic for those in 'positions of authority'.

It is perhaps striking that neither in the press coverage of Harvey's resignation nor in his book is there any mention of national security concerns. The reasoning that had been so prominent only three years before to justify excluding homosexuals from government jobs has all but disappeared. Instead, we are returned to a more vague and amorphous assumption about the general incompatibility between homosexuality and public office. In this book I have paid close attention to the discourses of historians, judges, politicians, journalists and others in order to uncover the reasons that have been variously used to rationalise the view that same-sex desire and public office are mutually exclusive. The search for such reasons is not futile. But Harvey's conventionalist outlook, with its focus on the surface fact of society's belief that homosexual men should not hold public office, reminds us of the solidity of that very fact – quite apart from the rationalisations that were (or, just as often, were not) offered in support of this belief.

One of the commentators who reviewed Harvey's book argued that it was not entirely inconceivable for the former junior minister to have retained his seat in the Commons and, after a suitable period of penance, eventually return to his former position in government (LAG-5). Harvey (2011: 133), however, declared that those who expressed similar views were 'misguided', and he rated the idea that the public world of politics would take him back into its fold as 'completely untrue'. The closest Harvey came to holding public office again was nearly three decades after his resignation, when, one year before his death in 1987, 'he was chosen as conservative candidate for the Westminster North division of the . . . Inner London Education Authority' (LAG-41).

Montagu's comeback

Lord Montagu, however, staged a successful comeback to public office. I use the word 'staged' not because his return was accompanied in the least by any fanfare, but because it was carefully planned, in the sense I will clarify below. Lord Montagu (2000: 126) recalls that after the guilty verdict, he had to endure a prison governor telling him how, having 'disgraced [his] class', he could expect to be forever ostracised. The peer would prove him wrong. After his ordeal, Montagu (2000: 95) immediately decided he would go back to Beaulieu, public life and, eventually, the House of Lords. He was also clear about how this could be successfully accomplished: he would do his utmost to disassociate his name in the public mind from the trials and homosexuality. It would be easy enough to dismiss this as caving in to society's prejudice, but contemporary scholarship recognises the protective function of the closet and its importance to lesbian and gay survival strategies in homophobic societies (Eskridge, 2002: 58; El Menyawi, 2006).

Montagu (2000: 138) describes the strategy he had for restoring his life and his 'blueprint for the future'. First of all, he committed to a 'vow of silence' on the whole matter. He refused to write about it until the publication of his autobiography nearly half a century later. The first thing he (2000: 96) did after his release was put all the material relating to the trials – transcripts, newspaper cuttings and correspondence – in a trunk, which he deposited in a bank vault and never accessed until he chose to write his own account of the events in his autobiography. The imagery of trunks and vaults doubles the symbolic impact of his act of secreting away the reminders of the association between his name and a homosexual scandal, and graphically enacts the logic of the closet. Montagu's vow of silence, however, was not enough; a more proactive strategy was required. His training in public relations had taught him that he could use the fact that people have a short memory to his advantage. Thus, Montagu (2000: 138) would obliterate the association between his name and acts of indecency with young men by managing publicity in a way that would make other connections come to the fore. The peer (2000: 96) says that a mention of his name today would probably call to mind Beaulieu, English Heritage and cars, not homosexual scandals.

Significantly, Montagu (2000: 139) portrays his resumption of political office – his reappearance in the House of Lords in early 1958 and his active participation in the debates – as the final and crowning step in his return to public life and the restoration of his reputation. The significance of this achievement can hardly be overstated – Montagu (2000: 207) declares that the formal announcement of his conviction to the House had been like 'an expulsion order'. It is possible that the fact that his seat in Parliament was associated with a hereditary title, rather than resulting from popular election, contributed to a sense of entitlement that assisted him in resuming his public functions. In this sense Harvey may have been, to some extent, the victim of accountability to his Conservative constituency. However, another factor may account for the different outcomes of Lord Montagu's and Harvey's trials. It is true that three decades and vast changes in the moral and cultural climate separate the publication of Harvey's autobiography from that of Lord Montagu. Nonetheless, after reading them, one is left with the distinct impression that Lord Montagu had always been reconciled with his same-sex desire in a way that Harvey was not – for all of Harvey's protestations to the contrary and all of Montagu's efforts to disassociate his name from same-sex desire in the public mind. This may have helped Lord Montagu (2000: 213) face a return to public office less than four years after his conviction, providing him with the inner resources that enabled him to hold his head high before Maxwell-Fyfe and the other Conservative 'bigots . . . who had connived at [his] downfall'.

Conclusions

Harvey's exile from public office and Montagu's return to it are contrasting outcomes of the trials they endured because of their sexuality. Montagu's re-entry into the House of Lords, however, required a deliberate re-branding effort directed at neutralising any association between his name and same-sex desire. Consequently, these two cases tell very similar stories about prevailing constructions of the relationship between same-sex desire and public office in 1950s' Britain. A notable difference, however, is the absence in the case of Harvey's trial and its coverage of even indirect references to the security risks posed by homosexuals in public office. A major concern for the government and Parliament at the time coinciding with the arrest and trial of Lord Montagu, the largely US-derived idea that homosexuality in the government was a security risk seems already a distant echo by the time of Harvey's resignation. Much had happened in the four intervening years – the main development, of course, being the Wolfenden report. It seems difficult to exaggerate the influence the 1957 Report of the Committee on Homosexual Offences and Prostitution had on re-framing the terms of the debate about homosexuality in both intra- and extra-institutional contexts. The report – whose first print of 5,000 copies sold out within a matter of hours (BBC, 1957) – captured the public imagination and realigned the debate on male homosexuality on a wholly new trajectory, at least for a time.

The discourse of homosexuality in the government as a security risk was complex – it sometimes went hand in hand, and sometimes parted ways, with the representation of homosexuals as being inclined to disloyalty, as temperamentally unsuited for public office and as alcoholic babblers. The most recognisable, stable core of that discourse in Britain was blackmail: a public officer would be prepared to divulge sensitive information to the enemy if they were threatened with being outed. The discursive intertwining of blackmail and sodomy in England dates to the eighteenth century. At that time, the meaning of extortion was extended to cover threats to damage the victim's reputation precisely out of a concern with deterring blackmailers from making accusations of sodomy against their well-to-do victims (Mclaren, 2002: 10–13). In the early to mid-1950s, the vulnerability of homosexuals to blackmail had been recast as a security problem requiring a punitive response targeting homosexuals themselves. The Wolfenden report successfully re-conceptualised, at least temporarily, the issue of blackmail as a problem for the homosexual victim rather than for the government: the law, and the government that supported it, was creating, through the criminalisation of homosexuality, the very conditions that allowed blackmailers to victimise homosexuals. As the re-conceptualisation of the blackmail question indicates, by the time of Harvey's trial institutional debates about homosexuality were no longer foregrounding national security but justice. Ironically, the negative publicity attracted by the Montagu case – initiated in the context of the Home Office's drive to target homosexual holders of public office – acted as one of the catalysts, via the Wolfenden report, for the realignment in public discourse on homosexuality from questions of national security to questions of justice.

In any case, the shift, for which the Wolfenden report was largely responsible, towards discussing homosexuality as a problem of justice rather than security in the late 1950s did not prevent the re-emergence of the issue of homosexuality in the government as a security risk in the early 1960s. After all, until the report's recommendations were acted upon, the illegality of sexual activities between males made the proposition that homosexual civil servants could be blackmailed into disclosing sensitive information a real possibility. While Burgess and Maclean's espionage had been due to their political convictions, the blackmail script was followed more closely in the case of John Vassall. A homosexual clerk at the British embassy in Moscow, Vassall gave in to (and later even, as it were, courted) Soviet blackmail and was tried for espionage in 1962 (Higgins, 1996: 306–321). Predictably, both the Labour opposition and the press made much of the Vassall case in order to attack the Tory administration. They portrayed the government as too lenient on homosexuality and – in a move reminiscent of the rhetoric utilised in the Cleveland Street scandal – they depicted homosexuality itself as a vice of social elites (Higgins, 1996: 318–319).

Furthermore, the temporary realignment in public discourse on homosexuality from questions of national security to questions of justice in the late 1950s does not mean that the government accepted that the legal treatment of homosexuality was unjust. It merely means that the terms of the debate on homosexuality shifted to foreground the question of whether homosexuality's criminalisation was just. But the liberal neutralist way in which the report, even as it recommended the decriminalisation of sex between males,[17] dealt with that question of justice did not do much to encourage a re-thinking of the question of the desirability of homosexuality in government posts. The report did reject the view that homosexuality was a disease, but incongruously it still recommended psychiatric treatment for homosexual offenders under 21 (Committee on Homosexual Offences and Prostitution, 1957: 15, 65). More importantly, its main recommendation that adult same-sex sexual acts in private be decriminalised – based as it was on the Millian ground that participants harmed no-one without their consent (Weeks, 2007: 53–54) – left it very much open for anyone to think that homosexuality might be harmful to those practising it or might be a disorder of some description or another. Indeed, pleas for law reform in the 1950s, making the case for the injustice of criminalising same-sex sexual activity, frequently hinged on representing homosexuals as blameless victims of an involuntary condition as much as of blackmail. The report's failure to successfully displace the view that homosexuality was harmful to those who practised it and that it was an unfortunate condition are perfectly illustrated in a *Guardian* article from 1957. After clarifying, and apparently endorsing, the report's position that two consenting male adults who have sex in private harm no-one but themselves, the article noted that this left two problems unanswered. First, a homosexual couple could limit its sexual activities to the private sphere but 'flaunt' their homosexuality in public in a way that was 'offensive or demoralising' to others. Secondly, if homosexuals were free to do as they pleased in private, they lost an incentive to seek treatment for their condition (LAG-11). These points about the injuriousness and pathological quality of homosexuality sit entirely comfortably with – indeed, they carry as their logical implication – the proposition that homosexuality is an undesirable trait in those who hold public office. No wonder then that in the early 1970s, a review of Harvey's book, describing him as 'a might-have-been', stated that the belated decriminalisation of sex between males four years before had not 'removed the stigma, at least for would-be participants in public life' (LAG-42).

That stigma has since been expressed mainly in the form of 'media trials' rather than judicial ones. Smith (2012) has recently published a study of gay politicians in the British press – which, because its assumed audience is largely heterosexual, she describes as a heterosexual public space (36). Smith (2012: 196, 201) argues that a politician's homosexuality remained clearly scandalous well into the 1980s (although this seems truer of national rather than local political figures).[18] Unlike the approach I have taken in this book, Smith's analysis is more structural than interpretive, systematically tracking the recurrence of patterns in media representations of gay politicians rather than interrogating their *raison d'être*. Nonetheless, Smith's analysis is of much relevance to this project, particularly as – spanning as it does the period from the 1950s to the present day – it picks up the thread just where this book will leave it. Smith finds that since New Labour's election in 1997, and the legal reforms it introduced directed at achieving legal equality for lesbians and gay men, the representation of gay politicians has markedly improved. Nonetheless, Smith (2012: 201) demonstrates that an implicit asymmetry persists in the way heterosexuality and homosexuality, as attributes of holders of public office, are valued in newspapers. Through a series of case studies, Smith argues that the tabloid press remains 'powerfully heteronormative' in its treatment of gay politicians: the press reserves a kinder treatment to those who are out, apparently relaxed about their homosexuality and partnered, and who pose less of a challenge to the heteronormative order (Smith, 2012: 201).

Smith also points out that the homosexuality of politicians tends to trump their other identity attributes, so that gay MPs often respond – in a move, I will add, reminiscent of what I called Montagu's 're-branding' strategy – by emphasising that they are not 'single issue' politicians. Smith (2012: 201) argues, plausibly, that this is indicative of the fact that a politician's homosexuality is still potentially perceived as problematic. Indeed, a politician's homosexuality has tended to remain newsworthy and to some extent controversial even in the twenty-first century. Finally – and this may be, for this book, Smith's most interesting finding – newspapers place on contemporary gay politicians an expectation of wholesale disclosure of their sexual orientation. Failing this, gay politicians will be outed and treated less sympathetically (Smith, 2012: 202).

From the point of view of democratic political processes, it is self-evident that an uncompromisingly homophobic public would want to know if their elected representatives are gay. Yet this cannot explain the press's urge to know about the sexuality of gay politicians – unless it massively misjudges the proportion of the British population that is homophobic in just that way.[19] Several factors may be at play. First, in representative democracies, people are regarded as the source of political power, which links them, via the construct of representation, to public authorities, who exercise political power in the form of public powers. More broadly, the European tradition tends to link constitutionalism (albeit in complex ways) to the idea that the people, through their consent, are the source of political legitimacy. The circulation of political power (or political legitimacy) from the people to the public authorities via the medium of representation (or consent) creates a contingent identity between the government and the governed. These forms of identity in political systems characterised by constitutionalism inevitably make the question of politicians' sexual desire politically charged. In particular, the blurring of the distinction between the rulers and the ruled can be expected to result in intense investment on the part of the people in policing the boundaries of their leaders' sexuality.

Secondly, Calhoun (2000) has argued that much of contemporary lesbian and gay subordination occurs via the displacement of lesbian and gay identity from the public sphere. While Calhoun's point has explanatory power in a number of contexts, it seems clear that something quite different accounts for the injunction to *disclose*, rather than *displace*, one's sexuality that Smith has identified in the contemporary media treatment of gay politicians. I think that this injunction must be put in the context of what Foucault (1998) describes as confessional technologies of the self and the 'will to know'. For Foucault, since the late nineteenth century, and mainly through the discourse of the human sciences, sex has become loaded with a meaning out of all proportion to that which sexual acts held previously. Our sexuality – or, more accurately, knowledge about it – has been assumed to hold the key to the truth about ourselves, to be able to account for who we are and why we are the way we are. Foucault puts this into the context of what he calls the disciplinary society – one where power operates and societal regulation is managed less through coercive legal processes, than through bodies of knowledge that facilitate both normalisation and self-discipline. The imperative to confess our innermost sexual secrets to an expert holds the promise that the truth about us will be revealed and of possible reform of any unwanted deviancy (Foucault, 1998). When I invoke Foucault's framework to interpret Smith's findings, my point is not that curing homosexuals of their homosexuality is part of mainstream contemporary discourse about homosexuality in Britain. Nor do I want to imply that the injunction that gay politicians come out can be explained in terms of a need to normalise them in the sense of curing them of their homosexuality. Rather, I want to clarify the origins of the urge to know about someone's sexuality and the injunction to confess placed on contemporary gay politicians. The urge persists because, as far as we may have come from the idea that homosexuality requires therapy, we are, like our early twentieth-century counterparts, still under the spell of sexual aetiology – the idea that sex may be the root cause of everything (Foucault, 1998). We still assume that the truth about our sexuality reveals something about our subjectivity – that it is especially capable of accounting for the particular kind of human beings that we are. The phenomenon described by Smith is indicative of the existence of, as it were, a collective hunch – however ill-defined it may be – that the homosexuality of holders of public office, because it is definitional of their subjectivity, cannot but be relevant to the question of their use of public powers. Consequently, the more momentous those powers are, the more crucial a disclosure of homosexuality is. The last point perhaps explains why the expectation that politicians disclose their homosexuality may be less urgent when applied to local, rather than national, politicians. Analogous reasons seem to account for the discrepancy, noted above, between the media's treating national politicians' homosexuality as problematic in the 1980s relative to their less aggressive treatment of local gay politicians.

Perhaps the most powerful illustration of the persistence of a collective hunch that the homosexuality of holders of public office matters to their use of public powers is the *Sun*'s treatment of the case of Liberal Democrat MP David Laws. In 2010, Laws resigned his post as Chief Secretary to the Treasury after only about two weeks in office when it was revealed that he had claimed expenses for a flat he was renting from a landlord who was, in fact, secretly his same-sex partner. As Smith (2012: 194) explains, most newspapers focused on the obvious question of the conflict of interests and Laws's unlawful conduct (it contravened the parliamentary rules). *The Sun*, however, also ran a survey of its readers in which it asked, among other things, whether gay people should be Cabinet ministers (Smith, 2012: 194). I have shown that over the last 2,300 years, the proposition that the same-sex desire of holders of public office is a problem for the good exercise of public powers has been rationalised on a variety of grounds. In an age of full legal equality and undeniably increased tolerance in mainstream society for lesbians and gay men, it must be difficult to articulate *any* plausible reasons to defend that proposition. But in the context of a centuries-old tradition by and large committed to that proposition (albeit on changing grounds), and in light of a more recent emphasis on confessing the truth of one's sexuality as the explanation for everything, it is not surprising that the belief that same-sex desire matters to good government is hard to let go of – even if it may now be floating free of its original moorings. *The Sun*'s posing the question of the acceptability of a Cabinet minister's homosexuality was widely criticised in other newspapers (Smith, 2012: 194). But in the context of a press still riveted on the question of gay politicians' sexuality, the *Sun* was acting no differently than the proverbial child commenting on the emperor's new clothes.

References

BBC, 'Homosexuality "should not be a crime"' (1957) *On This Day: 1950–2005*, 4 September, retrieved 14 September 2014: news.bbc.co.uk/onthisday/hi/dates/stories/september/4/newsid_3007000/3007686.stm.

Bengry, J (2012) 'Queer Profits: Homosexual Scandal and the Origins of Legal Reform in Britain' in Bauer, H and Cook, M (eds), *Queer 1950s: Rethinking Sexuality in Postwar Years* (Houndmills: Palgrave-Macmillan) 167–182.

Calhoun, C (2000) *Feminism, the Family, and the Politics of the Closet* (New York: Oxford University Press).

Carlston, E (2013) *Double Agents: Espionage, Literature, and Liminal Citizens* (New York: Columbia University Press).

Committee on Homosexual Offences and Prostitution (1957) 'Wolfenden Report', Command Paper 247 (London: Her Majesty's Stationery Office).

Conrad, KA (2004) *Locked in the Family: Gender, Sexuality and Agency in Irish National Discourse* (Madison: The University of Wisconsin Press).

Cooper, D (1994) *Sexing the City: Lesbian and Gay Politics within the Activist State* (London: Rivers Oram Press).

Croft-Cooke, R (1955) *The Verdict of You All* (London: Secker and Warburg).

David, H (1997) *On Queer Street: A Social History of British Homosexuality, 1895–1995* (London: HarperCollins).

Driberg, T (1956) *Guy Burgess: A Portrait with Background* (London: Weidenfeld and Nicolson).

El Menyawi, H (2006) 'Activism from the Closet: Gay Rights Strategising in Egypt' *Melbourne Journal of International Law*, vol 7, 28–51.

Engel, SM (2001) *The Unfinished Revolution: Social Movement Theory and the Gay and Lesbian Movement* (Cambridge: Cambridge University Press).

Eskridge, WN, Jr (2002) *Gaylaw: Challenging the Apartheid of the Closet* (Cambridge: Harvard University Press).

Foucault, M (1998) *The History of Sexuality, vol 1: The Will to Knowledge* (London: Penguin).

General Council of the Bar (1955–1956) 'Law Reform Committee: Matters Arising from the Trial of Lord Montagu and Others', from *Criminal Procedure and Powers of the Police (re Lord Montagu). Memorandum by the Bar Council's Law Reform Committee* (LCO.2/5107), held at the National Archives (Kew, London).

Gleeson, K (2007) 'Discipline, Punishment and the Homosexual in Law' *Liverpool Law Review*, vol 28, 327–347.

Grey, H (1992) *Quest for Justice: Towards Homosexual Emancipation* (London: Sinclair-Stevenson).

Hamrick, SJ (2004) *Deceiving the Deceivers: Kim Philby, Donald Maclean and Guy Burgess* (New Haven: Yale University Press).

[*Hansard*-1] Disappearance of Burgess and Maclean. *HL Deb 22 November 1955 vol 194 cc708–731.*

[*Hansard*-2] First Schedule. – (Provisions as to the United Kingdom Atomic Energy Authority). *HC Deb 29 April 1954 vol 526 cc1862–1886.*

[*Hansard*-3] Foreign Service (Missing Officials). *HC Deb 11 June 1951 vol 488 cc1668–1675.*

[*Hansard*-4] Former Foreign Office Officials (Disappearance). *HC Deb 07 November 1955 vol 545 cc1483–1611.*

[*Hansard*-5] Homosexual Crime. *HL Deb 19 May 1954 vol 187 cc737–767.*

[*Hansard*-6] Homosexual Offences and Prostitution (Report). *HC Deb 26 November 1958 vol 596 cc365–508.*

[*Hansard*-7] Public Services (Security). *HC Deb 21 March 1956 vol 550 cc1255–1314.*

Harvey, I (2011) *To Fall like Lucifer: The Lost Story of a Very British Sex Scandal* (London: Biteback Publishing).

Higgins, P (1996) *Heterosexual Dictatorship: Male Homosexuality in Post-War Britain* (London: Fourth Estate).

Hodges, A (2012) *Alan Turing: The Enigma* (Princeton: Princeton University Press).

Houlbrook, M (2005) *Queer London: Perils and Pleasures in the Sexual Metropolis, 1918–1957* (Chicago: The University of Chicago Press).

Hyde, HM (1970) *The Other Love* (London: Heinemann).

Jeffery-Poulter, S (1991) *Peers, Queers and Commons: The Struggle for Gay Law Reform from 1950 to the Present* (London: Routledge).

Johnson, DK (2004) *The Lavender Scare: The Cold War Persecution of Gays and Lesbians in the Federal Government* (Chicago: The University of Chicago Press).

Johnson, DK (2013) 'America's Cold War Empire: Exporting the Lavender Scare' in Weiss, ML and Bosia, MJ (eds), *Global Homophobia: States, Movements, and the Politics of Oppression* (Champaign: University of Illinois Press) 55–74.

Lafitte, F (1958–1959) 'Homosexuality and the Law: The Wolfenden Report in Historical Perspective' *British Journal of Delinquency*, vol 9, 8–19.

'Lord Montagu on the Court Case Which Ended the Legal Persecution of Homosexuals' (2007) *London Evening Standard*, 14 July, retrieved 14 September: www.standard.co.uk/news/lord-montagu-on-the-court-case-which-ended-the-legal-persecution-of-homosexuals-6597923.html.

Lovell, CR (1949) 'The Trial of Peers in Great Britain', *The American Historical Review*, vol 55, 69–81.

McLaren, A (2002) *Sexual Blackmail: A Modern History* (Cambridge: Harvard University Press).

Montagu of Beaulieu (2000) *Wheels within Wheels: An Unconventional Life* (London: Weidenfeld & Nicolson).

Office of the Historian, US Department of State (2011) *History of the Bureau of Diplomatic Security of the United States Department of State* (Washington, DC).

Power, J (2011) *Movement, Knowledge, Emotion: Gay Activism and HIV/AIDS in Australia* (Canberra: ANU E Press).

Smith, D (2012) *Sex, Lies and Politics: Gay Politicians in the Press* (Eastbourne: Sussex Academic Press).

Vargo, ME (2003) *Scandal: Infamous Gay Controversies of the Twentieth Century* (New York: Harrington Park Press).

Wald, AM (2012) *American Night: The Literary Left in the Era of the Cold War* (Chapel Hill: University of North Carolina Press).

Weeks, J (2007) *The World We Have Won* (London: Routledge).

Wildeblood, P (1999) *Against the Law* (London: Weidenfeld & Nicolson).

Whisnant, CJ (2012) *Male Homosexuality in West Germany: Between Persecution and Freedom, 1945-69* (Houndmills: Palgrave-Macmillan).

Press Cuttings held at LAGNA (Lesbian and Gay Newsmedia Archive) [LAG] (Bishopgate, London):

[LAG-1] 'A Shattered Career' (1971) *Catholic Herald*, 3 September.

[LAG-2] 'Allegation against Lord Montagu' (1953) *The Times*, 16 November.

[LAG-3] 'A Social Problem' (1953) *The Sunday Times*, 1 November.

[LAG-4] Barber, D (1971) 'A Career in Ruins' *Tribune*, 25 June.

[LAG-5] Boyne, HB (1971) 'Career Thrown Away' *Daily Telegraph*, 3 June.

[LAG-6] 'Charge against Lord Montagu' (1953) *The Times*, 17 October.

[LAG-7] 'Charges against Lord Montagu' (1953) *The Times*, 15 December.

[LAG-8] 'Charges against Lord Montagu' (1954) *The Times*, 25 January.

[LAG-9] 'Charges against Three Men' (1954) *The Times*, 17 March.

[LAG-10] 'Charges against Three Men' (1954) *The Times*, 23 March.

[LAG-11] 'Crime and Sin' (1957) *The Guardian*, 5 September.

[LAG-12] 'Fyfe: My Duty to Guard Youth' (1953) *Daily Mail*, 4 December.

[LAG-13] Gritten, J (1971) 'Condemned by His Peers' *Morning Star*, 17 June.

[LAG-14] Hardcastle, W (1971) 'Paradise Lost', 3 June.

[LAG-15] Harvey, I (1971) 'The Homosexual's Plight' *New Statesman*, 9 April.

[LAG-16] Hickey, W (1978) 'Downtown Job for 50s Golden Boy' *Daily Express*, 26 April.

[LAG-17] 'House of Commons' (1954) *The Times*, 1 April.

[LAG-18] 'Ian Harvey (and the Guardsman) fined £5' (1958) *The Star*, 10 December.

[LAG-19] 'Indecency Charge' (1958) *The Times*, 21 November.

[LAG-20] 'John Gordon Column' (1958) *Sunday Express*, 14 December.

[LAG-21] 'Judge Questions Boy in Montagu Trial' (1953) *News Chronicle*, 19 December.

[LAG-22] 'Junior Minister Accused of Offence in the Park' (1958) *Evening Standard*, 20 November.

[LAG-23] Kiley, B (1971) 'A Backward Look at Paradise' *Dublin Sunday Independent*, 13 June.

[LAG-24] '£5 Fine on Ian Harvey' (1958) *The Times*, 11 December.

[LAG-25] 'Law and Hypocrisy' (1954) *The Sunday Times*, 28 March.

[LAG-26] 'London Vice War to Be Stepped Up' (1953) *Daily Herald*, 27 October.

[LAG-27] 'Lord Montagu' (1953) *The Times*, 17 December.

[LAG-28] 'Lord Montagu and Two Others Charged' (1954) *The Times*, 11 January.

[LAG-29] 'Lord Montagu Case: The Three Accused in the Witness Box' (1954) *News of the World*, 21 March.

[LAG-30] 'Lord Montagu in Box' (1953) *The Times*, 16 December.

[LAG-31] 'Lord Montagu in the Box' (1954) *The Times*, 20 March.

[LAG-32] 'Lord Montagu on Trial' (1954) *The Times*, 16 March.

[LAG-33] 'Lord Montagu Sent for Trial' (1953) *The Times*, 17 November.

[LAG-34] Midforth, P (1971) 'No Room at the Top' *The Birmingham Post*, 5 June.

[LAG-35] 'MP Dismissed' (1953) *News of the World*, 22 February.

[LAG-36] 'MP's Appeal Dismissed' (1953) *News of the World*, 22 February.

[LAG-37] 'MP to Resign' (1953) *News Chronicle*, 14 October.

[LAG-38] 'Mr Ian Harvey, MP Resigns' (1958) *The Times*, 25 November.

[LAG-39] 'Mr Ian Harvey Resigns' (1958) *Manchester Guardian*, 25 November.

[LAG-40] '"Not Guilty"' (1954) *The Times*, 7 April.

[LAG-41] 'Obituaries: Ian Harvey' (1987) *Daily Telegraph*, 13 January.

[LAG-42] Pickard, W (1971) 'Man Who Fell like Lucifer' *Scotsman*, 27 May.

[LAG-43] 'The Police and the Montagu Case' (1954) *The New Statesman and Nation*, 10 April.

[LAG-44] 'Three Men Sent for Trial' (1954) *The Times*, 1 February.

[LAG-45] 'Three Men Sent to Prison' (1954) *The Times*, 25 March.

[LAG-46] 'Wildeblood in the Box' (1954) *The Times*, 19 March.

Notes

1 Only thirty-four peer trials have taken place since Tudor times in the House of Lords. The last of these were in 1935 and 1901 (Lovell, 1949: 78, 80). Considering this timescale, five years – the time elapsing between the repeal of the privilege to be tried in the House of Lords and Montagu's prosecution – is a relatively short time. This lends credibility to the claim that Montagu's was the first prosecution of a peer before an ordinary judge and jury since the repeal.

2 Higgins (1996: 250) states that there is no evidence that the decision to hold an inquiry into homosexuality was prompted by the 'bungled prosecution' in the first Montagu trial. However, the fact that, as Higgins (1996: 20) himself reports, one of the questions addressed by the Wolfenden committee was the criticism levelled at the conduct of the police in the Montagu case suggests otherwise. This is not to say that the Montagu trial was the only determinant – as opposed to an important catalyst – of the decision to appoint the committee. In particular, concerns (pre-dating the Montagu trial) with the popular press's sensationalistic coverage of homosexual scandals and with its possible unwitting contribution to an increase in the incidence of homosexual offences were a major reason for instituting the inquiry (Bengry, 2012: 167–182).

3 Ironically, the American Communist Party was itself, at the time, far from welcoming homosexuals within its ranks (Wald, 2012: 118–119).

4 In support of his argument denying that a witch-hunt against homosexuals ever took place in Britain in the early 1950s, Higgins (1996: 258) has taken issue with the *Sydney Sunday Telegraph*'s report, arguing that according to newspaper reports the mission was only for the purpose of studying prostitution, not homosexuality. But the *Daily Herald* (LAG-26) report corroborates the *Sydney Sunday Telegraph* on the point that addressing homosexuality was one of the reasons for the mission.

5 To support the claim that the authorities were interested in targeting specifically Montagu, Wildeblood (1999: 69) reports that he had produced evidence that one of the Crown's main witnesses in the second Montagu trial – Wildeblood's lover – had a sexual relationship with another man; but this man was never charged.

6 The committee did give Maxwell-Fyfe what he wanted at least where it recommended an increase in maximum penalties for some same-sex offences involving people under 21.

7 Anecdotal evidence of contemporary official belief in this incompatibility comes from an autobiographical novel by Rupert Croft-Cooke, imprisoned for same-sex offences at about the same time as Montagu. Croft-Cooke (1955: 149) pointed out that in the microcosm that is a jail, prison officers considered an inmate's homosexuality – unlike convictions for crimes involving dishonesty or fraud – a total bar to being put in positions of authority or trust within the prisoner community.

8 This is not to say that, in declaring a war on homosexual vice within society generally, Maxwell-Fyfe was on wholly safe ground, for there is evidence that British public opinion was divided on the issue of homosexuality (LAG-3).

9 The police had apparently tampered with Montagu's passport to make his movements abroad in the aftermath of the incident look suspicious and cast him in a bad light.

10 The case of the defence rested, among other things, on portraying Montagu (2000), who later in life identified as bisexual, as a paragon of heterosexual romanticism. Counsel for the defence pointed out that 'the trial was taking place at a time when public attention had been focused upon this type of vice'. He then asked how Lord Montagu could possibly commit such a 'filthy crime', when he had been planning to present a ring – in a spot of the Beaulieu gardens especially meaningful to him – to his fiancée, with whom he had recently become engaged (LAG-30).

11 Reynolds denied giving evidence out of self-interest but, interestingly, he also denied having done so in the interest of society, apparently refusing to concede that homosexuality was dangerous to the community. He simply stated that the investigation had thrown him into a state of panic and anxiety and he had agreed unthinkingly (LAG-43).

12 After the guilty verdict, the defence called a consultant physician in psychological medicine to testify to the fact that Wildeblood was not a 'typical type of homosexual'. Because of his intelligence and willingness to be treated, treatment could probably succeed if he was not imprisoned (LAG-44).This last-ditch attempt to save Wildeblood from prison bore no fruit.

13 The police failed to secure search warrants, questioned the defendants incommunicado and, possibly, put pressure on the main witnesses (General Council of the Bar, 1955–1956; Montagu of Beaulieu, 2000: 133; LAG-43).

14 At this time, homosexual public servants were looked upon with suspicion in other countries too. Sometimes this suspicion took the form of specific governmental action – as in Australia (Power, 2011: 7) – and sometimes it did not – as was the

case, apparently, in West Germany (Whisnant, 2012: 61–63). I found no instances of countries other than the US being held up, either directly or indirectly, as examples for the British government to emulate in its treatment of homosexual holders of public office. But any influence (either unilateral or reciprocal) between these countries and Britain may have simply gone unacknowledged.

15 Lawrence's words echo those of his counterpart in the 1941 case involving Conservative MP Sir Paul Latham (court-martialled for sexual activity with military and civilian men), who had declared his client's life 'pretty well damned' (Hyde, 1970: 212).

16 Harvey was 'a man who nearly made it to the top of Tory Politics', one of Prime Minister Harold Macmillan's 'golden boys', until his 'career crashed' and he ended up 'in a rather sleazy Camden Town Office', 'producing a publication full of male pin-ups' (LAG-16).

17 Others have drawn attention to some problematic aspects of the report, particularly the way in which its recommendations benefited some more than others and inaugurated more subtle forms of discipline: Gleeson (2007); Houlbrook (2005; 241–263).

18 During the 1980s, openly gay councillors in some British Labour-led local authorities played a key role in developing equal opportunities policies for lesbians and gay men (Cooper, 1994: 27, 33, 46, 66, 83). In her detailed analysis of the tabloid press's hostile treatment of these developments, Cooper (1994: 126–145), significantly, does not report that the homosexuality of local politicians was one of the strategies specifically used to discredit these policies.

19 Smith (2012: 34) reports that 'only' 36 per cent of people, according to the British Social Attitudes data, think that adult same-sex sexual relationships are always wrong.

Conclusions

In the introduction I hypothesised that the discursive relationship between political authority and male same-sex desire is a particularly fertile site for the generation of social meaning. The case studies I analysed are consistent with this hypothesis, testifying to the construction of rulers', statesmen's and public officials' same-sex desire as, almost invariably, a problem for the good exercise of public powers. The implication of this construction is that political authority requires a disavowal of same-sex desire: this is because legitimacy lies at the core of the idea of political authority and legitimacy is inseparable from (albeit not reducible to) the idea of good government.

The case studies I examined reveal the remarkable plasticity of concrete invocations of the proposition that statesmen's or public officials' same-sex desire is a problem for good government. Thus, whereas some cases brought sexual activity to the fore, others left it in the background. Some of the trials expressly articulated, while others only assumed, the relevance of same-sex desire to the question of the good exercise of public powers. Some of the trials were enacted in the courtroom, others textually. Same-sex desire was sometimes invoked in itself as a problem for good government; in other cases it was taken to be such a problem only when it took particular forms (e.g. sexual passivity or if accompanied by infatuation). Furthermore, critics of a statesman's same-sex desire occasionally deployed their critiques in the service of progressive goals, but more often in order to advance reactionary ones.

Perhaps the most striking feature of the trials analysed is the sheer variety – the imaginativeness – of the grounds and strategies used to indict statesmen's same-sex desire as a problem for good government. Desire between males was variously represented as making them incapable of self-control (Alexander, Elagabalus, Timarchus); leading them to betray the interests of the state (Timarchus); encouraging them to subvert time-honoured institutional traditions (Elagabalus); making them uninterested in public affairs (Hadrian, Edward, James); making them vulnerable to bad counsel (Edward); distancing them from the governed and an appropriate appreciation of their needs (Edward, James); making them draw arbitrary distinctions while allocating advantages and disabilities (Edward, James); making them willing to let others govern instead of them or alongside them (Edward, James); inclining them to pursue the wrong kind of policies (James); turning them into poor examples for the people (James); contaminating their public work (the Dublin scandal); converting them into security risks, or predisposing them to political radicalism and disloyalty (Montagu); and causing them to fail to live up to the standards of public life (Harvey). In some cases, desire between males was not argued to be incompatible with public office on any of the above grounds; that incompatibility was simply taken for granted as a matter of unreflexive common sense (the Dublin and Cleveland Street scandals). Classical Athens was anomalous in balancing the proposition that same-sex desire, in its discreditable forms, was incompatible with public office, against the idea that same-sex desire, in its pederastic incarnation, was foundational to democratic life. This balancing move, however, reinforced the status of women as political outsiders.

As in the case of Marie Antoinette's trial on incest charges in France's revolutionary tribunal, in many of the cases I analysed, a statesman's same-sex desire was targeted opportunistically. Curtius attacked Alexander's love for Bagoas to make a point about Caligula's excesses. Aeschines accused Timarchus of selling his body to prevent Timarchus and Demosthenes's prosecution against him for mishandling the peace negotiations with King Philip. James's opponents made his same-sex desire the butt of satirical work during his lifetime to discredit peaceful foreign policy. O'Brien and Labouchere put legal and social homophobia in the service of, respectively, nationalist and egalitarian politics. The publicity of Montagu's trial was managed, apparently, to prove that the UK took the problem of homosexuals in the government seriously. This opportunism means that, conceivably, the instigators of the trials may not always have shared the belief that the same-sex desire of the accused *actually* was a problem for their good exercise of public powers. The important point, however, is that, in the pursuit of their contingent political goals, the instigators of the trials felt that they could leverage on the social belief that same-sex desire is a problem for good government. In exploiting that belief, the trials performatively re-enacted or consolidated the discursive sexualisation of political authority in ways that specifically disavow same-sex desire, or some of its forms.

Because it is the physical manifestations of same-sex desire that tend to attract formal law's punitive responses, all of the judicial trials I have discussed (the oration against Timarchus, the Cleveland Street and Dublin Castle scandals, and Lord Montagu's and Ian Harvey's cases) brought same-sex sexual activity to the fore. This is the case also for some of the textual trials (notably that of Elagabalus). Other trials, however, were more ambiguous, stressing emotional bonds over physical ones. In the case of Alexander's relationship with Hephaistion, for example, what attracted the historians' rebuke was the Macedonian king's loss of control grounded in his love for his deceased companion. In the case of Edward, it was his extravagant love for Piers that was considered the root cause of the king's willingness to let his favourite govern instead of him. However, a common subtext to these textual trials is the categorical instability of ostensibly sexless intense same-sex attachments. By categorical instability of sexless relationships I mean either their potential for escalating to sodomitical passion, in the case of Edward, or *philia* threatening to revert to *eros*, in the case of Alexander. Alexander's reaction to Hephaistion's death may not have been symptomatic of the loss of self-control that the ancients associated with male sexual passivity, but it did come dangerously close to the excesses that *erastai* inflamed by erotic passion *may* display when courting their *eromenoi*. Edward's pliability to his favourites' desires sat unstably between a minority view tying it to the subordination of the sexually passive male and a majority discourse imputing this pliability to romantic intoxication.

I analysed the purported incompatibility between same-sex desire and public office in order to shed light on the ways in which political authority has been discursively constructed in relation to male same-sex desire. One effect of this discursive construction is the way in which it may have precluded same-sex attracted men from accessing public office or excluded them from such office when they had managed to access it. Openly gay politicians, however, are a fact of life in twenty-first century Britain. Does it follow that the sexual constitution of political authority no longer requires a disavowal of same-sex desire? Smith (2012) argues, as indicated in the last chapter, that politicians' homosexuality remains newsworthy, and that the 'indulgence' of the British press towards gay politicians is contingent on their being out of the closet as well as their failure to openly challenge the heteronormative order. I suggested that this inquisitiveness about, and merely conditional toleration of gay politicians' sexuality can be accounted for by invoking two factors: first, the distinctly modern ways in which we treat sexual knowledge as profoundly meaningful (Foucault, 1998); and secondly, the adage that old habits (namely, a centuries-old tradition constructing same-sex desire as a problem for good government) are hard to break.

The *Sun*'s 2010 survey mentioned at the end of the last chapter is not the only piece of evidence supporting the view that the British mainstream has not yet fully consigned to the dustbin of history the proposition that same-sex desire is a problem for good government. Consider the scandal, recently erupted at the time of writing the conclusions to this book, about Tory cabinet members 'abusing underage boys at drug-fuelled conference parties' in the 1980s (Moss and Drake, 2014). Ostensibly, the scandal is about child abuse; indeed, the *Mirror*'s article from which I have just quoted does not even mention the gender of the victims in its title. Reading on, however, the article goes on to talk about the Thatcher government's emphasis on 'family values' and how it spawned Section 28 of the 1988 Local Government Act – which famously barred councils from promoting 'the acceptability of homosexuality as a pretended family relationship'. 'Ironically', the article states, the introduction of Section 28 took place approximately at the same time as Thatcher's parliamentary private secretary was 'indulging his sexual appetite for boys as young as 15'.

The irony to which the passage alludes could be interpreted merely as a function of the failure of Tory sexual practice – involving as it did underage sex – to match its theory of family values. But the passage goes to the trouble of specifically mentioning the anti-*homosexual* Section 28 as the paradigmatic example of Thatcherite family values; and it does not speak generically of the private secretary engaging in underage sex, but uses *gender-specific* terms. In swinging back and forth between homosexuality and underage sex, the text seems to mean something more specific when it speaks of irony: namely, that the Tories were guilty of the very thing they were publicly denouncing (namely, homosexuality) through the enactment of Section 28. Thus, while the weakness of Tory *individuals* involved in this scandal is a function of their engaging in *underage sex*, in their quality as *statesmen* the weakness of these Tory politicians is a function of their voting for the wrong (*homophobic*) kind of policies. But it is a weakness – the article implies – made ironic (and worse) by their hypocrisy; this hypocrisy, in turn, is dependent on the circumstance of their *homosexuality*. Indeed, was their homophobia motivated by the fact that they had something to hide? Were they protesting too much? The text, then, while declaring itself committed to a non-homophobic sexual morality, appears internally torn between this commitment and a residual hunch that same-sex desire is a problem for the good exercise of public powers – a hunch that unwittingly animates its rhetorical moves.

Reflection about the ways in which the ruler/ruled relationship is symbolically sexualised strengthens the conclusion that the presence of openly gay politicians in contemporary Britain has not displaced the disavowal of same-sex desire from the sexual constitution of political authority. I discussed the sexualisation of the ruler/ruled relationship at several junctures in this book. Thus, the way in which the dynamics of pederastic relationships mapped onto the mechanisms of Athenian direct democracy made the *eromenos/erastes* relationship a strikingly fitting metaphor for the relationship between public officials and the citizen body in the *polis*. An *eromenos* in a consensual pederastic relationship was acceptably subordinated to the *erastes*, but once he became an adult he would himself become an (active) *erastes*. Likewise, an Athenian male citizen was temporarily subordinated to the public officials appointed by lot, but he himself was eligible for public office and may well become a magistrate in the next term. As we have seen, it is also entirely fitting for heterosexual marriage – with its expectation of permanence and subordination of the female party – to have done the metaphorical work when it came to conceptualising the relationship between the ruler and the ruled in early modern monarchies. But (how) is the relationship between the government and the governed metaphorically sexualised in contemporary society?

In the introduction I endorsed Cooper's (1993: 271) argument to the effect that that relationship is metaphorically a heterosexual one between a masculine state and a feminised community.[1] In keeping with twenty-first century Britain's commitment to formal equality on the ground of sexual orientation, I want to reformulate Cooper's argument, in a way that, while maintaining Cooper's insight about the asymmetrical nature of that relationship, does not construct that relationship in specifically heterosexual terms. Let me start with a popular contemporary conception of authority (applicable to political authorities), which centres it on the idea of service. The service authorities perform consists in issuing directives that, if followed by the governed, are more likely to result in the governed acting in accordance with right reason than their self-determined conduct would be. This does not mean that the governed should slavishly obey the authority; they should comply with the authority's directives only to the extent that doing so is more likely than self-determined conduct to comply with right reason (Raz, 2006: 1014). The attraction of the service conception is that, in some areas of life at least, one can choose to plan on the authority's service. But this temporary abdication of responsibility sounds rather like the appeal of being a bottom. I want to suggest, then, that according to this understanding of political authority in contemporary liberal democracies, the relationship between the ruler and the ruled mirrors sexual role-play between tops and bottoms.[2] Bottoms may be *ultimately* in charge, because they retain the power to end the game (by failing to follow directives that do not comply with right reason, and by ousting poorly performing tops); nonetheless, the game requires a credible top – the authority – to do the service.

If, as I argued in this book, social understandings of political authority are sexually charged, then politicians who socially register as sexual bottoms may not be perceived as credible vessels of state authority. The fact that an uncompromisingly effeminate gender presentation triggers a more-or-less conclusive societal presumption of sexual-passivity-as-penetrability-as-subordination partly accounts, I think, for the paucity of male politicians who have just that kind of gender presentation. Analogous reasons may partly account for why, as Sissa (2009: 117) argues, even high-profile involvement of women in politics has not displaced the 'trains of thought that associate manliness with credible leadership and reliable command'. Finally, the top-bottom metaphor for the relationship between the ruler and the ruled provides an answer to the question I raised about the place of same-sex desire in the contemporary sexual constitution of political authority. It suggests that the acceptability of (gender-normative) gay politicians in present-day Britain may be partially contingent on their failure – which Smith (2012) has documented – to disclose the *details* of their sexual lives. This vagueness about matters of detail opens up the opportunity, I suggest, to presume them to be tops more frequently than they are likely to be.

This analysis is predicated on Bersani's (1987: 212–218) claim that because being penetrated tends to be phenomenologically associated with the loss of the sense of self, it is being penetrated that is discursively constructed to signify passivity and subordination and penetrating that signifies activity, agency and control. To be sure, the construction of male same-sex desire as a problem for good government cannot be reduced to the symbolic meanings associated with being penetrated. As I have shown in the case studies, the various reasons for considering same-sex desire to be incompatible with good government are often independent of sexual role; furthermore, as I have argued above, to the extent that penetrability undermines one's credibility as a political leader, it affects all those who are socially legible as penetrable, including women. The symbolic association of penetrability with a failure of the agentic self (and thus with the loss of self-control) *was*, however, at the root of the belief in the incompatibility, in antiquity, between male sexual passivity and the good exercise of public powers. For much of the history of the Graeco-Roman world, same-sex desire was not considered morally problematic per se (including in terms of its implications for good government). Sexual passivity, however, was considered legally and morally incongruent with 'civic authority' (Bersani, 1987: 212). Likewise, mainstream discourses in present-day Britain refuse the moral indictment of same-sex desire in and of itself, making redundant many of the grounds on which, until recently, a statesman's same-sex desire was constructed as a problem for the good exercise of public powers. But the resiliency and pervasiveness of the belief that 'to be penetrated is to abdicate power' (Bersani, 1987: 212) makes one's social intelligibility as available for phallic penetration an extra hurdle for would-be holders of political office.

Further democratisation of access to political office along gender and sexuality lines, then, may be partly contingent on a shift in sexual consciousness, through a proliferation of what Butler (1997: xxxi) calls practices of 'subversive resignification'. These might neutralise the power that being penetrated has to signify passivity, subordination and loss of subjecthood and the power that penetrating has to signify agency and control; alternatively, or additionally, they might involve a de-gendering of sexual roles, as in some gay subcultures' 'masculinisation of bottoming' (Dean, 2009: 56); more radically, they might involve a transvaluation of the failure of agentic selfhood embodied in the sexually penetrated subject, celebrating it as an ethically preferable positioning to that of the dominant, phallic self (Bersani, 1987: 222); finally, they might aim at de-centring penetration as the paradigm of sex.

A reflective shift either away from penetration, or so as to celebrate the dissolution of the self that penetration precipitates, may also aid radical re-conceptualisations of the meaning and practices of government. I argued that an affinity between discourses on political authority and those about sexual desire follows from the difficulty (not necessarily the impossibility) in disentangling, phenomenologically and discursively, penetrative sex from power/powerlessness (Bersani, 1987). Consider now sexual desire between women. Lesbian sex may or may not involve one part of a body (usually not a penis, though this ultimately depends on the bodily make-up of those claiming a lesbian identity) entering another. To this extent Bersani's arguments are less relevant to lesbian sex. If political authority is, as I think, practically inseparable from ideas of hierarchy, but lesbian sex is not – either phenomenologically or in terms of its social intelligibility – mainly a matter of hierarchy, then the discursive relationship between political authority and lesbian desire is probably not so productive as that between political authority and penetrative sex. Reflection on lesbian desire, however, may assist *re*-imaginings of government *without authority* – by which I mean government without a body making any (phallic) claims (whether justified or unjustified) to legitimate authority. Alternatively, those re-imaginings may be facilitated by taking up Bersani's (1987: 222) invitation to intellectually and emotionally invest in penetration's potential for the dissolution of the self: for if state authority is predicated on the state's intelligibility as a subject, then government without authority may require 'fucking with' the state to precipitate its de-personalisation.

If the idea of government without authority sounds like a contradiction in terms, the oxymoron merely draws attention to the utopian quality (not the same, of course, as political pointlessness) of re-imaginings that centre that idea. Flipping the telescope, however, we can look at authority-based government as the fantasy that is never fully realisable, requiring constant papering over the tensions and contestations that threaten the unitary state from within. Public officials, in carrying out their functions, do not always act as faceless bureaucratic bodies mechanically implementing directives coming from above. When the focus shifts from the political-philosophical interrogation of state power to an analysis of the operational field in which government policies are (or fail to be) delivered, the point of focusing on the logic of lesbian desire or the penetration-induced loss of subjecthood is not to inspire future re-configurations of government without authority. Rather, it is to shed light on what already happens when the task of government is carried out in ways that challenge state claims to authority. Consider, for example, the argument that doing government work in a way that defies state authority requires practices of 'active citizenship' (Cooper, 2013: 121). Active citizenship, in this sense, requires state actors not only to 'challenge, by-pass or overplay role-contingent modes of appropriate political conduct', but also to 'align their actions with membership of a community, polity or constituency, so they are active as citizens rather than as bureaucratic agents' (Cooper, 2013: 121). 'Screwing' (in Bersani's sense of de-subjectifying) the state, may be as revealing a metaphor to describe the former aspect of practices of active citizenship as the notion of a lesbian feminist erotic praxis may be for the latter. Reflection on lesbian desire and the penetration-induced annihilation of the self, then, may well illuminate the conditions of possibility, sustainability, replicability and ethical validity of these practices.

References

Bersani, L (1987) 'Is the Rectum a Grave?' *October*, vol 43, 197–222.

Butler, JP (1997) *Gender Trouble: Feminism and the Subversion of Identity* (London: Routledge).

Cooper, D (1993) 'An Engaged State: Sexuality, Governance and the Potential for Change' *Journal of Law and Society*, vol 20, 257–275.

Cooper, D (2013) 'Public Bodies: Conceptualising Active Citizenship and the Embodied State' in Roseneil, S (ed.), *Beyond Citizenship? Feminism and the Transformation of Belonging* (Houdmills: Palgrave-Macmillan) 112–137.

Crain, E (2011) 'Woman on Top: The Sexiest Mattress Move of All' *Cosmopolitan*, 1 April.

Dean, T (2009) *Unlimited Intimacy: Reflections on the Subculture of Barebacking* (Chicago: University of Chicago Press).

Foucault, M (1998) *The History of Sexuality, vol 1: The Will to Knowledge* (London: Penguin).

Moss, V and Drake, M (2014) 'Tory Child Abuse Whistleblower: "Margaret Thatcher knew all about underage sex ring among ministers"', *Mirror*, 13 July, retrieved 14 September 2014: www.mirror.co.uk/news/uk-news/tory-child-abuse-whistleblower-margaret-3849172.

Raz, J (2006) 'The Problem of Authority: Revisiting the Service Conception' *Minnesota Law Review*, vol 90, 1003–1040.

Sissa, G (2009) 'Gendered Politics, or the Self-Praise of *Andres Agathoi*' in Balot, RK (ed.), *A Companion to Greek and Roman Political Thought* (Chichester: Blackwell) 100–117.

Smith, D (2012) *Sex, Lies and Politics: Gay Politicians in the Press* (Eastbourne: Sussex Academic Press).

Notes

1 More recently, Cooper's (2013: 130) emphasis has shifted towards the sexual qualities of *intra*-state relationships and processes. Specifically, she suggests that it may be analytically and politically useful to interrogate the desire- and pleasure-driven ways in which state actors engage and renegotiate state corporeality when, in the pursuit of radical policies, they use state power to reach beyond, and temporarily shatter, the will of the state as a unitary, coherent, intending body.

2 Contemporary gay men frequently use 'tops' to refer to sexual partners who prefer to penetrate and 'bottoms' for those who prefer to be penetrated ('versatile' is one term applied to those who are happy to switch from one role to the other). In S&M sex, bottoms are those who submit; tops those who dominate. In some other sexual contexts, top and bottom may refer to the actual bodily position of lying over or under a sexual partner. In each of these cases the underlying idea is that tops *play the role* of being in control. This is more evident in S&M role-play, but it is also the connotation carried by the terms in the context of (non-S&M) gay male sex. A gay man can of course describe himself, or be described, as an 'aggressive' or 'dominant' bottom; but one does so precisely to displace the 'standard' connotations of submission and passivity that attend the bottom's role (it is hardly necessary to add that, phenomenologically, bottoming or topping may be experienced in varied ways). Even where top and bottom are used (as they may be outside the context of S&M or gay male sex) to refer to one's physical position relative to a sexual partner, the connotations are often the same (see Bersani, 1987: 216). Consider the following extract from a popular women's magazine: 'Woman on Top . . . the carnal configuration that flips missionary sex on its head and puts you in total control' (Crain, 2011). The language here is conveniently ambiguous between being in control of one's sexual pleasure and being in control within the sexual encounter.

Index

n refers to note numbers

For Product Safety Concerns and Information please contact our EU
representative GPSR@taylorandfrancis.com
Taylor & Francis Verlag GmbH, Kaufingerstraße 24, 80331 München, Germany

www.ingramcontent.com/pod-product-compliance
Lightning Source LLC
Chambersburg PA
CBHW070419270326
41926CB00014B/2847

9 781138 241695